Food *for* Life

Food *for* Life

Preventing Cancer Through Healthy Diet

Based on the groundbreaking findings of
the World Cancer Research Fund

Oliver Gillie

Hodder & Stoughton

First published in 1998 by Hodder & Stoughton
A division of Hodder Headline PLC

10 9 8 7 6 5 4 3 2 1

A CIP catalogue record for this book is available from the British Library

ISBN: 0 340 71230 9

Printed and bound in Great Britain by
Butler & Tanner Ltd

Hodder and Stoughton
A division of Hodder Headline PLC
338 Euston Road
London NW1 3BH

Contents

Preface

THIS BOOK is good news. It tells you that cancer is a preventable disease.

We all know that smoking is the chief cause of lung cancer, now the most common cancer in Britain and in the world: bad news, of course, not only for smokers but also for people in regular contact with cigarette smoke. However, scientists now also know that diets and associated lifestyles are the most important factors affecting cancer risk. So this book is good news, because it shows you how you can reduce your risk of cancer by enjoying healthy food and by maintaining a healthy lifestyle. Indeed, by changing to a healthy diet and lifestyle the risk of all cancers can be reduced by at least one-third. And 60–70 per cent of all cancers can be prevented by healthy diets and by not smoking.

In countries like Britain, which have been industrialised and economically developed for generations, the most common serious diseases are not infections. Everybody knows that tooth decay and gut disorders such as constipation are mostly caused by unhealthy diets – that is, diets poor in nourishing food like vegetables and fruits, that include too much fatty food, too much sugar, and not enough fibre – and that overweight and obesity are mainly caused by such diets plus inactivity.

In the 1980s, British scientists and policy makers finally agreed that unhealthy diets are an important cause of coronary heart disease.

The good news from this revelation is that we can all reduce our risk of heart disease by eating well and living well. Now, a decade later, we know that cancer is preventable too. This of course does not mean that cancer could become extinct, like smallpox. Some people are born at very high risk, and cancer is also a disease that is inevitably more likely later in life. However, the risk of cancer can be substantially reduced if we each choose to follow the recommendations in this book.

Perhaps the best news of all is that the most effective ways to prevent cancer are also the most effective ways to prevent heart disease and other common disagreeable and disabling, as well as deadly, chronic diseases.

Those of us who live in Britain and other privileged countries, where food supplies are secure and where infectious diseases are relatively uncommon, now have the opportunity to enjoy an active life well into old age.

This is an exciting prospect. The tragedy of cancer and heart disease is that more often than not, people suffer from these diseases and are disabled by them for a long time, sometimes many years, before death. This book really does give you the opportunity to maximise your chance of enjoying life into your seventies and eighties.

In recent decades a vast mass of evidence linking diet with cancer has been published in scientific journals. Much of this evidence comes from studies of human populations carefully carried out by epidemiologists. For example, it has been known for many years that when people migrate from one part of the world to another, their risk of cancer changes even within one generation, and that the types of cancers migrants are most likely to suffer are similar to those of the host country within one or two generations. Studies of migrants are just one of the many lines of evidence that have encouraged scientists to believe that the chief causes of cancer are environmental.

The question then, of course is: what are the key environmental factors modifying cancer risk? There is no doubt that smoking is the main cause of lung cancer. Other studies show that viruses are a significant cause of a number of cancers. Excessive exposure to strong sunlight certainly increases risk of skin cancer. And, in addition, what literally thousands of studies now show is that the risk of most common cancers is determined by our diets – the foods and drinks we consume every day.

People often tend to believe that diet is relevant to cancer risk because traces of chemicals identified as carcinogenic – causing cancer – are contained in the food we eat. In particular, it is often thought that residues of agricultural and industrial chemicals such as pesticides and food additives are an important cause of human cancer. But this is not what the human evidence shows. The overwhelming weight of scientific evidence, accumulated especially in the last 20 years, shows first that the key factor is food, drink and diets as a whole; and that appropriate diets *protect* against cancer.

The World Cancer Research Fund, in common with research scientists in the field, has been well aware of messages such as these for many years. But the story told in any individual piece of published research is rather like a single piece of a jigsaw puzzle. To see the entire picture you have to assemble all the pieces. In 1992, the World Cancer Research Fund decided therefore to assemble 'this big picture'. Together with our colleagues at the American Institute for Cancer Research, we commissioned a panel of fifteen scientists from all over the world, and asked them to take responsibility for reviewing and assessing all the evidence linking diet and cancer, particularly that published in the 1980s and 1990s.

Panel members from the UK were Professor Philip James, currently best known in Britain as the architect of the new Food Standards Agency, and Professor Tony McMichael of the London School of Hygiene and Tropical Medicine. The panel was chaired by Professor John Potter, born in the UK, raised in Australia, and now working in the USA. Distinguished panel members from the USA and Europe such as Professor Walter Willett and Professor Anna Ferro-Luzzi were joined by colleagues from Africa, Latin America, India, China and Japan. The panel was supported in its work by expert observers from three agencies of the United Nations: the World Health Organization, the Food and Agriculture Organization, and the International Agency for Research on Cancer. More than 100 contributors, advisers and reviewers also helped the panel in its task.

The report of the panel, *Food, Nutrition and the Prevention of Cancer: a global perspective*, was published in late 1997. The findings of the report, and the recommendations the panel made for the diets we are best advised to eat to have the best chance of reducing our risk of cancer, are the basis of this book.

A total of 30,000 copies of the report have been distributed to policy makers and scientists all over the world, and in 1997 the first English language edition was launched in the UK, the USA, Europe, Africa, Latin America and Asia. We at WCRF would like to thank our 700,000 supporters in the UK and our 8 million supporters in the USA whose contributions have made this massive partnership of science and education possible.

At this point, readers may be eager to know the good news in this book! You can of course now turn to Chapters 3 and 4, where the recommendations of the WCRF report are outlined.

What you will find in *Food for Life* are the report's recommendations in detail, how they apply to us in Britain and other economically developed countries, and how we can put them into practice in our everyday lives so that we and our families can protect ourselves against cancer. The special value of this book is that it tells you and your family, in clear, plain, practical language, what you can do right now to reduce your cancer risk. It includes current, reliable, science-based advice, all integrated into a practical plan for healthy living. It includes suggestions for delicious healthy meals, and tips on how to make your everyday life more active. *Food for Life* is designed to empower you.

You may also be interested in the issue of cancer not just as an individual person, but also as a member of society – a citizen. You may have thought that on the whole, cancer is a dreadful disease which you 'catch' as if it is an infection, and that the most relevant approaches to cancer are screening, medical or surgical treatment, and care to reduce the pain and suffering of the disease. Medical research and treatment of cancer continue to advance; and some cancers, particularly those most common in childhood, can often be cured. But treatment of cancer is usually a long drawn-out, expensive and frightening process, which we would all like to avoid.

We at the World Cancer Research Fund believe in 'stopping cancer before it starts'. Backed by the most reliable science now available, you can be sure that cancer is mostly a preventable disease, and that above all the messages are: enjoy the healthy food and drink recommended in this book, and do not smoke.

Begin today to enjoy the foods and drinks that will lead to a healthy life for years to come. Good health! Long life!

Marilyn Gentry
President, World Cancer Research Fund
Geoffrey Cannon
Director of Science, World Cancer Research Fund

Introduction

IN BRITAIN, cancer is now the biggest single killer disease. In 1998, the number of people in Britain dying from all cancers taken together is more than the number of people dying from coronary heart disease.

To some extent this awful statistic reflects the success of national campaigns to prevent heart disease. People in Britain now generally smoke less than they did in the 1970s and 1980s; and many people now eat healthier foods. But the rates of most cancers are increasing, not only in Britain but world-wide.

In most parts of the world now, populations are ageing and also increasing. There is also compelling evidence that as people move from the countryside into cities in Africa, Latin America and Asia, and as their diets and lifestyles therefore change, they are much more likely to suffer types of cancer historically uncommon in those parts of the world, but now very common in economically developed countries like Britain. This book is dedicated to reversing this trend.

World-wide, rates of cancer are increasing fast. In 1996, according to World Health Organization estimates, there were over 10 million new cases of cancer throughout the world. In Britain, the most recent figures show over 280,000 new cases of cancer each year.

Statistics like these are frightening because we tend to think of cancer as largely unavoidable. Everybody knows now that smoking is the chief cause of lung cancer, and that the risk of skin cancer is increased by long exposure to sunlight. These factors aside, we tend to fear cancer, rather like a plague that might descend at any time, and against which we are largely defenceless.

This book, reflecting the findings of a major expert report, *Food, Nutrition and the Prevention of Cancer: a global perspective*, published by the World Cancer Research Fund in 1997, shows that, just like heart disease, cancer is largely preventable, and that you and your family can reduce your risk of cancer, starting today. Scientists now estimate that 30–40 per cent of all cases of cancer can be prevented by healthy diets and associated lifestyles, notably physical activity. Globally, this means that between 3 and 4 million cases of cancer a year are preventable. In Britain, healthy diets together with physical activity could at current rates prevent around 100,000 cases of cancer each year.

You may be surprised to learn that the food and drink we consume is so important in cancer. Perhaps you have heard that many processed foods contain chemicals that cause cancer. This is not true: the evidence from human studies does not suggest that food additives and contaminants have a significant carcinogenic (cancer-causing) role. And if you have heard that coffee and artificial sweeteners are carcinogenic, there is more good news: the best evidence indicates that these do not increase cancer risk.

The most impressive findings from what now amount to thousands of human studies, as reviewed in the WCRF report and as reflected in this book, in many cases prove beyond reasonable doubt that healthy diets protect against most common cancers. What is more, diets that prevent cancer also prevent heart disease, help stop you becoming overweight or obese, and may well also prevent diabetes, and digestive and bone diseases.

How can scientists be sure of judgements such as these? How can you rely on the recommendations made in this book? Early evidence that cancer is largely preventable, and that food, among other environmental factors, is important as a way to prevent cancer, came from studying groups of people who have migrated from one part of the world to another. For example, when Japanese people migrate to Hawaii and then later to California, their patterns of cancer change dramatically, within one or two generations. This alone is strong evidence that, generally, cancer is not genetically predetermined. Stimulated by studies such as these, epidemiologists, the scientists who investigate patterns of disease among populations, have, especially in the last 20 years, conducted increasingly ambitious and complex studies designed to discover which environmental factors have the most effect on our risk of getting cancer.

In some cases, we now know that certain cancers are caused at least in part by microbes such as viruses and bacteria. We also know that carcinogens (cancer-causing chemicals) created by industrial processes can increase cancer risk: asbestos is one striking example. And it is certain that smoking and chewing tobacco is an important cause of cancers of the mouth, throat and oesophagus (gullet) as well as of the lung.

At the same time, the most remarkable and consistent evidence emerging from careful studies of human populations, often strengthened by studies of animals, shows that diets play a vital role in cancer. We know for certain that diets with plenty of a variety of vegetables and fruits, especially when eaten all year round, protect against most common cancers. Scientists have concluded that, overall, the diets that protect us against cancer are based on foods of plant origin. This does not mean that people are best advised to be vegetarian: modest amounts of meat and other foods of animal origin are nourishing and are unlikely to increase risk of any disease significantly.

Remarkably though, the diets that protect against cancer and hence decrease rates of cancer, have much in common with traditional diets eaten in Mediterranean countries, and also in Latin America and Asian countries such as India and China, when people enjoy a varied and plentiful diet all year round. Correspondingly, rates of cancer are now increasing rapidly throughout the world as people adopt diets and lifestyles similar to those of economically developed countries like Britain and the USA.

This of course does not mean that we are best advised to live like Indian peasants! Nor does it mean that we should go back to the kind of monotonous and stodgy diets that older people remember having to suffer in the 1940s and 1950s.

Food for Life shows you how, beginning today, you and your family can enjoy, every day, foods and drinks that are most likely to reduce your risk of cancer, and how you can have a healthy life now and in years to come.

How to use this book

This book will help you reduce your risk of developing cancer and other diseases. It provides recommendations for choosing predominantly plant-based diets containing a variety of vegetables and fruits, pulses and minimally processed starchy staple foods such as bread, potatoes, rice or pasta. These are diets which will also help those who are overweight to reduce their weight, especially if they increase their physical activity as well. The recommendations in Chapters 3 and 4 also explain how to start working out a new approach to food. First you might wish to read in Chapter 2 about how cancer develops and how food can influence this process in a number of ways. Or you may prefer to jump straight to the recommendations in Chapter 3.

If you are overweight or feel you need to be more physically active turn first to Chapter 4.

You may have heard that the number of calories you use up in exercise is too little to make any difference. This isn't true. The value of daily physical activity adds up and makes a big difference. And if you adopt a diet containing many more plant-based foods, which have a high bulk and high water content, you may find yourself losing weight without too much effort.

If a particular type of food is of interest to you or you want to check out how a particular food contributes to a healthy diet then look it up in Chapter 7 – The A-Z of foods.

If you look up fruits you will see, explained in detail, why fruit is so important to health. You can also read under fertilisers and other agricultural chemicals why pesticides are probably not a risk to health for the general public, or, if you enjoy coffee, you can read about the reassuring findings that it is not linked to cancer or heart disease. Browsing through the A-Z you can read more, for example, about the healthy virtues of green leafy vegetables or the health risks of salt.

If you are worried about a particular type of cancer, perhaps because a close relative has developed it or died of it, then look it up in Chapter 8 – An anatomy of cancers.

The entry will give you an appraisal of what we know about the causes of that particular cancer. It will also tell you which particular foods or aspects of diet will increase your risk of getting that cancer, and, more importantly, what foods to eat to reduce the risk.

A person who has a relative with cancer has a greater than average risk of developing the same type of cancer. This is partly because there may be a hereditary predisposition to certain types of cancer, but there is another reason. Families develop a taste for particular types of food and for particular styles of eating. Each individual within a family has their own special preferences, but they tend to eat similar food. So if one person in a family has developed cancer the risk of another developing the disease is likely to be greater than average. Anybody with a relative who has cancer or has died of cancer would be especially wise to adopt a healthy diet and lifestyle and so reduce their own risk of getting the disease.

If you want to begin right away with some new ideas for eating healthy food, turn to Section 2 – The best of all foods and Recipes for health.

You can begin by planning tomorrow's healthy breakfast and once breakfast is sorted out you can start on the other meals. Chapter 6 contains dozens of recipes which will help you get started. Within a short time you will be enjoying a healthy diet and lifestyle that will decrease your cancer risk.

SECTION 1
1 A longer and healthier life

By EATING the right food, we can prevent much of the illness and disease that plagues modern life. Cancer, heart disease and stroke account for two-thirds of all deaths in Britain, and a similar proportion in other industrialised countries. There are strong links between diseases and the diets that many people eat today, and with our increasing inactivity and other lifestyle factors, notably smoking. Now, after decades of scientific investigation, we have a very good idea of what food we need to eat for optimum health and to reduce our risk of these diseases.

Most readers who care about their health will know these facts by now. The good news in this book is that healthy diets are just as important in the prevention of cancer as in the prevention of heart disease. The best food for health is based on relatively unprocessed plant products and includes generous portions of cereals, vegetables and fruits. But why do we need to eat more vegetables and fruits? And why do diets containing many fatty, sugary and salty foods increase the risk of serious diseases like cancer?

In the last 150 years our diets have changed rapidly. They now contain more industrially processed foods than ever before. Many of the foods which pack the shelves of our supermarkets and food shops did not exist 30 years ago. Most of these new foods are highly processed and our bodies are not adapted to them. And most people in Britain, and other industrialised countries, consume diets that lack fresh vegetables and fruits and are short of nutrients essential for good health.

The health problems arising from our present diets are increasing rapidly. For example, the number of people in Britain suffering from diabetes is increasing, and it occurs mainly in older people who are overweight and who have inadequate diets. The future increase in adult-onset diabetes, as it is called, is likely to be accompanied by increases in a number of cancers and of other diseases linked to being overweight and with diets containing too much fat and insufficient fruit and vegetables. The life expectancy of the average person in Britain has been increasing steadily for 200 years or more. But we are now reaching a point where the effects of poor diets could, for the first time, begin to put that trend into reverse.

Understanding of how and why modern diets promote these diseases has grown steadily in the last 30 years. Nutritionists used to think that it made little difference whether the body obtained its energy from fat, starch or sugar. Now, an excess of fat and sugar, combined with a lack of fibre and starchy foods, is recognised as the cause of major imbalances in our diets that lead to obesity, cancer and heart disease.

Nutritionists used to think that they knew about all the vitamins, about which diseases were caused by lack of vitamins, and about how to treat them. But now the existence of other nutrients, which, like vitamins, are vital for long-term health, has been recognised. We know how some of these micronutrients, as they are called, work in the body; for others we only have a general idea. These micronutrients are plentiful in vegetables and fruits and we know they are immensely important to health.

We now also know that micronutrients work together in groups. To act effectively, it seems they must be consumed in foods, perhaps because they need to be present in the body with others of their group. Research has shown that taking vitamins and other micronutrients in the form of pills is probably not good for health. It is humbling for scientists and doctors, who have been successful in understanding deficiency diseases caused by vitamins, to have to acknowledge this additional level of complexity.

We now understand that healthy diets must be based on changing the types of food we eat, not simply swallowing pills. For this reason the recommendations for healthy diets given in this book are based primarily on foods, and not on nutrient or vitamin requirements.

We also understand the essentials of healthy diets. We know not only what we must eat for everyday health but what we must eat to preserve our health long term from cancer, heart disease and other diseases. The importance of vegetables and fruits and of wholegrain foods in healthy diets will come as no surprise to those who have long believed in the special value of whole foods. A rationale for healthy eating can now be derived from well-established scientific evidence, and this rationale provides individuals and families with guidance which will reduce the risk of various cancers and of other chronic diseases. Healthy diets will greatly improve our general health and will prolong the lives of many people.

The diets recommended by the World Cancer Research Fund for prevention of cancer are based on foods of plant origin – vegetables, fruits, pulses (such as peas and beans), roots and tubers, and cereal products. Meat is not a necessary part of a healthy diet and most people eat more than enough of it. Fish and poultry should be preferred to red meat (beef, pork and lamb) for good health. The recommendations emphasise the importance of eating a larger proportion of starchy foods such as bread, potatoes, rice and pasta, and eating less fat, sugar and salt. Eating the right foods, drinking less alcohol, avoiding becoming overweight or obese and taking more exercise, will reduce the risk of cancer.

Scientists now estimate that 30–40 per cent of all cancers can be prevented if we eat healthy diets. World-wide this would reduce the number of cancers by 3–4 million cases each year. Diets and associated lifestyles are probably even more important in the prevention of cancer than not smoking tobacco. Even more positively, these recommendations designed to reduce cancer risk are practically the same as recommendations for preventing heart disease, obesity and other chronic diseases, and so will protect health and prevent diseases generally.

Our changing diets

To understand why people today in the industrial, economically developed world are suffering from such high rates of heart disease and cancers we must go back to the origins of the human race.

The story begins $2\frac{1}{2}$ million years ago, when early hominids, pre-human species from whom we have evolved, survived and flourished by gathering seeds, fruits and roots in the woods and grasslands of Africa. These hominids probably ate meat as well when they could find it, often scavenged from kills left by large predators such as lions and tigers. Early humans evolved around 400,000 years ago and continued to eat similar diets. The diet of early humans was probably not very different from the diet of gorillas and chimpanzees today – mainly leaves and fruits. Human genes are only 2–3 per cent different from those of gorillas and chimpanzees, showing that our metabolism has not evolved far from that of apes.

The idea that early humans lived mainly on roast meat is now known to be wrong. Certainly, early humans discovered fire, using it to roast food and to cook in vessels of wood and clay. This first step in food processing was beneficial. It made the food safer and easiest to digest. There were times when food was scarce and diets were often monotonous, but the simple processing done by early humans caused no significant loss of nutrients.

Human beings have a craving for sweet food, for salty foods and for concentrated-energy foods high in fat. These cravings were helpful to early humans and continue to be helpful to peoples who live traditionally, close to the land, without modern manufactured food. A sweet taste tells us when vegetables and fruits are at their ripest and are easiest to digest. For gatherer-hunter peoples who live on wild vegetables and fruits, often far from the sea, salt is a scarce commodity. The human body is highly adapted to prevent the loss of salt and our taste buds are designed to seek it out – so we still crave it today.

Before the development of farming, people often experienced periods of hunger. To survive these periods it was helpful to eat diets rich in fatty foods, to put on body fat, and so to increase the chances of surviving through the time when food was scarce. Today, when food in Britain is plentiful and much of it has been heavily refined in the manufacturing process, our cravings for sweet, fat and salty food, together with our instincts for survival, encourage us to eat more than our bodies need, and so we put on weight.

The value of these cravings for salt, sugar and fat became less important for survival with the development of farming around 10,000 years ago. People in the Middle East discovered that grains such as wheat could be cultivated. In other parts of the world maize and rice were developed as crops. Humans obtained a degree of control over nature which enabled a more regular supply of food to be provided. Cereal crops such as wheat, barley, rice and oats provided concentrated sources of energy which could easily be stored and transported. It became possible for cities to develop. Vegetables and fruits were less easy to transport and people in cities then ate less of these than their predecessors. But for centuries the cities remained relatively small and the links with the countryside were strong because the majority of the population lived there. Most people continued to eat food which was relatively unrefined, rich in micronutrients.

Industrialisation of the food supply brought radical change. In the late nineteenth century food supplies in Europe and North America were transformed by agricultural and industrial developments which led to the mass production of food. Foods which previously had only been eaten by the rich became available to everyone. Steel roller mills powered by steam, first developed in the 1870s, sifted and separated the component parts of wheat grains on an industrial scale, producing uniform white flour from which the bran and germ had been removed. White bread, which replaced brown or wholemeal bread for the vast majority of the population, contained lower levels of fibre, essential oils, vitamins and minerals than wholegrain products.

Consumption of sugar also increased spectacularly during the late nineteenth century when the sugar tax was lifted and sugar grown in the colonies was plentiful and cheap. Industries developed to mass-produce sugary biscuits, cakes, chocolate, confection-ery and soft drinks. The mid-afternoon tea became more common. At this meal, biscuits, cakes and other baked produce made with white flour, sugar and flavourings were served with measured ritual in British drawing rooms at home and abroad. The English steamed pudding, until then a rare dish reserved for the rich or for special occasions, was made with refined flour and a lot of sugar and promoted as a regular dish for all classes of society. This taste for sugared foods has since been exported to many countries round the world. Large new cities developed, and more and more people turned to fatty sweetened diets based on refined white flour.

At the same time, a naive belief in the importance of animal protein for human health developed from the discovery in the mid-nineteenth century that animal protein promotes growth. Meat and dairy products, not previously plentiful in the diets of ordinary people, came to be seen as staple foods. Artificial foodstuffs were increasingly used to fatten livestock which until then had been left to browse on fallow or marginal land, and meat became plentiful. The English breakfast with sausages, bacon and fried bread, became a national institution. Such cooked breakfasts had hitherto been eaten primarily by the rich.

In the twentieth century, people in Europe and North America came to perceive meat as the centrepiece of main meals, despite shortages during two world wars. The increased consumption of meat and also of full-fat milk, cheese and butter greatly increased the proportion of fat in the diet. And an entirely new source of fat, margarine, became generally available in the early years of the twentieth century as a result of a new process, hydrogenation. This is a way of making oils into a solid fat which provides a cheap alternative to butter. At the same time hydrogenation preserves oils so they can be kept for long periods without going rancid.

These developments mean that people in Britain, and other industrialised countries, have moved away from traditional diets based on wholemeal bread, potatoes, dried peas and beans, and vegetables, often flavoured with a little bacon, cheese or milk. Traditional diets tended to be repetitive and boring and required more effort to prepare. People began to eat fewer cereal products, potatoes and starchy roots, and more sugar, fat, meat and dairy products. They drank more alcohol. These changes have been more dramatic in northern Europe than in southern Europe.

In Scotland, for example, where the traditional diet was closely defined by short northern summers, oats, dried peas, potatoes, neeps (swede) and other roots were major items of the everyday diet in the eighteenth and nineteenth centuries. Oats, which were used to make porridge, once Scotland's national dish, have almost disappeared from the diet of the ordinary person north of the border. As societies become industrialised the starchy staples such as oats and potatoes decline from providing about 50 per cent of the total energy in the diet to around 25 per cent.

Everyday diets in northern Europe were always much more monotonous, limited as they were by a short growing season, than diets of southern Europe. Even so, the trend towards more refined diets has occurred all over the developed world and is now happening in urban areas of the developing world. The epidemic of cancer, heart disease and diabetes that has resulted from refined twentieth-century diets has left few communities untouched. As people in Asia, Africa and Latin America move away from their traditional diets these diseases have all become more common.

Today, when so much food is manufactured

using cheap ingredients such as fats and sugar, the cravings evolved by early humans work against us. These cravings encourage us to overload the body with refined foods: we eat diets that are completely out of balance. These highly refined foods trick the palate. Food manufacturers exploit our inborn cravings for sweet and salt foods: many highly processed foods such as savoury snacks tend to be heavily salted, and biscuits and breakfast cereals are often very sweet. These highly processed foods have another disadvantage: they are not very satisfying – we feel hungry again very soon after eating them. Unrefined foods, on the other hand, take longer to eat, are more filling and release sugar more slowly into the blood. As a result they remain satisfying for longer. If we return to everyday diets that have a high content of unrefined foods with more bulk, then our appetites will work in a more natural way and not mislead us so easily.

People in industrialised northern countries with relatively cold climates, like Britain, now tend to eat fatty, sugary, salty diets, with a lot of meat and meat products and other foods of animal origin, and relatively small amounts of vegetables and fruits. Diets like these lack nourishment, and increase the risk of many diseases.

Foods from the Mediterranean

What can we do to improve our diets and thus our health? Help is close at hand. Nowadays, supermarkets offer a wide range of healthy foods and drinks.

For northern Europeans, the most attractive healthy diets are from the Mediterranean region – southern France, southern Italy, Greece, the Lebanon, Turkey and northern African countries such as Tunisia, Morocco and Egypt – as celebrated in many popular cookbooks.

The high fruit and vegetable content of Mediterranean diets make them protective against cancer and generally healthy. Traditionally, diets of the Mediterranean countries are rich in vegetables, fruits, and the local starchy staple foods, which may be pasta, rice or bread. Pulses such as beans and chickpeas are also popular, and many herbs are used to flavour foods.

Meat is used in traditional Mediterranean diets in a modest way as a garnish and flavouring, although on special occasions it may provide the central dish and be eaten in larger quantities. Fish and seafood form a substantial part of Mediterranean diets where they are readily available. Olive oil is used in most Mediterranean countries.

The diets of northern and southern Italians differ in certain crucial respects which illustrate the healthy benefits that derive from living in the south where there is a long growing season for vegetables and fruits. Poverty binds the peasants of southern Italy to the land and gives them little alternative but to grow their own food. They make ingenious use of the vegetables and fruits which grow prolifically. Naples has given its name to the southern Italian dishes that are now eaten everywhere in Britain. Pizza Napolitana, for example, is the pizza with a lot of tomato, a few olives, a little cheese, and a couple of anchovies. It is an economical dish which is also very healthy because a high proportion of its energy content comes from the starchy staple (the bread base of the pizza). It provides some vegetable in the form of tomato and only a modest amount of cheese which adds flavour without overloading the body with animal fat. Eaten with a good salad, the pizza Napolitana is an excellent food. In Britain many people prefer to eat a pizza which is loaded with extra cheese or sausage.

Piled up like this with fatty extras the pizza ceases to be a healthy Mediterranean food.

Spaghetti Bolognese, a dish which takes its name from the northern Italian town of Bologna, is popular in Britain because of its rich beef sauce made with butter. Spaghetti Napolitana, on the other hand, depends on a simple tomato sauce which is delicious when made from fresh tomatoes, olive oil, garlic and herbs. The contrast between these dishes tells the story of the difference between the cuisine of northern and southern Italy. The northern Italians eat more meat, fewer vegetables and fruits and less olive oil, and they have a higher incidence of heart disease and breast cancer.

Secrets of the East

The other great cuisines of the world in their traditional form make full use of vegetables and fruits and relatively unprocessed grains such as rice or cracked wheat, and pulses.

The low incidence of heart disease and breast cancer in China and Japan commends their food to us. The traditional Chinese and Japanese cuisines use vegetables, beans and rice in imaginative ways, often employing meat as a garnish, a flavouring or in sauces to enhance dishes. However salt is used excessively in Japanese cookery and sodium glutamate, frequently used in Chinese cooking, may add further to the sodium burden of the body. Increased consumption of sodium in food increases the risk of blood pressure and stroke. A high intake of salt also increases the risk of stomach cancer. Nevertheless, Chinese and Japanese foods have much to recommend them as part of a healthy diet because they provide a large proportion of calories as a starchy staple (rice), and they are also relatively low in fat and meat.

Indian diets vary greatly in different parts of the sub-continent. Some Indian food uses large quantities of ghee, a heavy fat consisting of clarified butter, or coconut oil, or a mixture of these with other oils. Ghee contains a large proportion of saturated fat which, when eaten regularly in large amounts, increases the risk of heart disease. People from the Indian sub-continent living in Britain have a considerably higher risk of heart disease than British people who, in turn, have a much higher incidence of heart disease than Japanese, Chinese or southern Italians. For this reason, Indian food, when cooked traditionally with ghee, cannot be recommended. However, Indian restaurants usually also serve a good selection of vegetarian curries and it is not difficult to choose dishes which are well balanced in the quantities of vegetables and rice or chapatis (an unleavened wheat bread).

The problem with restaurant food in general is that it tends to be feast food, the kind of food that is eaten at celebratory meals on special occasions, and that is richer than the traditional everyday cuisine of the country of origin. It is higher in meat and fat and often also sugar, than everyday practical food. This is true for all restaurants, not only those serving Indian food. Restaurants serving foods from other countries usually adapt their menus in the UK to make the food fattier and more sugary. Try plainer, simple, dishes. These are often the most delicious.

Good food and good health

The good news in this book is that we now know what to eat to reduce the risks of cancer and heart disease and to provide the best chance of good health. The recommendations of the WCRF report for healthy eating and lifestyle are given in Chapters 3 and 4, and in Section 2 we show how we can all put these into practice to produce good food and construct healthy diets.

Healthy diets are easier than ever to achieve. Improvements in agriculture and transport, together with membership of the European Community, mean that it is now easier and less expensive in Britain to eat diets containing more fresh vegetables and fruits. We are no longer limited by winter shortages, and the supermarkets are full of fresh food the year round. Supermarkets also stock a wide range of ingredients for making dishes based on foods from around the world. Although it is tempting to live on fast foods and snacks like burgers, sandwiches made from white bread, and other fatty or sweetened products, we can all take positive steps to change what we eat.

The advice given in this book was developed with the help of hundreds of scientists and nutrition experts from around the world. It is firm and authoritative. It is itself based on thousands of scientific studies undertaken in many countries. The experts involved with the World Cancer Research Fund report have defined the state of the art.

With the help of this advice we can each revise our own food choices and move towards healthier diets and lifestyle. The advice may be used to adapt familiar British recipes or we can draw on dishes from around the world. Some people may decide to explore the healthy delights of traditional Mediterranean, Asian and Latin American cuisines to provide varied and delicious dishes and meals. In the chapters that follow the advice is explained in detail and suggestions made about ingredients and recipes.

2 The causes of cancer

WE KNOW ENOUGH about how foods and drink affect our risk of cancer to be able to make dietary recommendations designed to reduce cancer risk. How? And how does diet affect what happens in our bodies, in ways that modify cancer risk?

This chapter describes how we study the relationships between food and cancer, how we assess the evidence produced by large numbers of studies of human populations, and what we now know about the causes of cancer.

Evidence on food, nutrition and cancer

The expert report published by WCRF in 1997 reviewed over 4,000 scientific papers, most published in the last 20 years. The scientists responsible for the report looked at the results of these individual studies, assessed them as a whole to come to judgements about the causes of cancer, and then agreed recommendations for the diets we should eat.

Developments in molecular biology are now enabling scientists to understand the processes in the body involved in cancer, and to understand that these in turn involve DNA, the genetic material in our cells. Scientists also know how the constituents of the foods we eat interact within cells and the cellular processes that can either cause cancer or help protect us against it.

Epidemiological studies are a tool used by scientists to investigate disease. These studies describe, and seek to explain, the distribution of health and illness in human populations. They compare groups of people in order to show what factors affect who develops a disease and who does not. Epidemiological studies are widely used in formulating public health policy.

How the assessments were made

Assessment of epidemiological studies of diet and disease can be particularly complicated. Often the studies rely on people answering questionnaires on what they have eaten, both recently and at some time in the past – this can be prone to error. And we do not yet know how long some cancers take to develop, nor when diets may be most relevant in the cancer process. However, epidemiological studies have greatly widened our understanding of diet and cancer, from a view that was largely based on studies of nutrients to one that covers all aspects of food and nutrition.

Epidemiological studies on diets and cancer look at what people consume, both foods and drinks and the constituents of foods and drinks, and at other related factors such as energy intake, physical activity or how food is cooked and processed. The numbers of people who have cancer, or who die from cancer, are then compared with those who don't.

A comparison between two groups of people might appear to show, for example, that people who eat a lot of salted foods more often develop stomach cancer. Careful investigation is then needed to find out if the difference in incidence of cancer between the two groups is really a result of the amount of salt they eat or if it may be accounted for by something else such as a difference in the average age of the two groups, a difference in social class, a difference in the numbers who smoke, or other possible relevant factors. The possible effect of such factors has to be allowed for. If a difference remains after these effects have been removed from the data, statistical tests are then done to find out if the remaining difference is significant or if it might simply be a result of chance.

As well as epidemiological studies, scientists can carry out experiments on laboratory animals (controlling what they eat in a way not usually possible in humans) and investigate possible biological pathways, to increase our understanding of what is happening in the body. All this information is relevant, and judgements on causal links between diet and cancer (and other diseases too) usually draw on human evidence, animal and other experimental evidence, and also identification of plausible biological pathways.

Types of study

Correlation studies

Epidemiological studies of different groups of people are made in several different ways, and each way has advantages and disadvantages. When different types of comparison suggest the same link, a confident judgement may be made that the cause of a particular type of cancer is likely to be related to a particular type of food.

Correlation studies are conceptually simple. They look at different rates of cancer in different populations and relate them to the diets in those populations. For example, on a population basis, people who eat a lot of meat also have a high rate of colon cancer. This is an example of a strong correlation in purely statistical terms. However, it cannot immediately be concluded that high meat consumption increases the risk of colon cancer.

People who eat a lot of meat also tend to eat diets high in fat and sugar, and may well drink a lot of alcohol. In addition, people who eat a diet high in meat tend to have high incomes, live in urban areas and are generally physically inactive. So, without more careful study it is not possible to be sure that meat is the key factor that leads to an increase in cancer of the colon. For similar reasons, a genuine relationship may not be observed by simple correlation studies because it may be obscured by overlying factors.

Despite the difficulties in interpreting correlation studies, they may provide important clues to the cause of disease because of the wide differences in the types and amounts of food consumed by different groups of people.

The incidence of heart disease and breast cancer, for example, is greater in countries which have a greater average consumption of fat. Yet within countries it is difficult to find a difference in the incidence of these diseases associated with fat consumption, because differences in fat consumption between individuals within a country tend to be relatively small. In addition, changes in incidence of disease in a country over the years may also provide important clues. For example, there has been a dramatic increase in colon cancer in Japan since 1950, and at the same time average consumption of meat and fat has increased.

Unusual diet studies

It is generally not possible to experiment with what people eat, so we can get useful information from groups of people whose diets are very different from those in the rest of their population. An example is the Seventh-day Adventists.

In the United States, the mortality of Seventh-day Adventists from colon cancer is about half that of the population as a whole. Seventh-day Adventists are often vegetarian and so this finding supports the suggestion that meat may cause colon cancer. However, they also drink less alcohol, smoke less, and eat more vegetables. Studies of other special groups such as vegetarians or vegans have provided further clues.

Migrant studies

People migrating from one country to another with a different incidence of cancer will, within one or two generations, have much the same risk of cancer as people in the new country in which they have settled. For example, Japanese women living in Japan have a low incidence of breast cancer, but after they migrate to California they or their daughters develop a high incidence of the disease similar to that of other women in America.

Such findings were some of the first to suggest that environmental factors, including diet, not genetic factors, are responsible for the large differences in cancer rates in different regions and countries.

The major differences between the incidences of cancers of the stomach, colon, and rectum in different countries, with evidence showing that the incidence of these diseases changes on migration, and other epidemiological and experimental evidence, shows that these cancers are mostly avoidable by maintenance of healthy diets and associated lifestyles.

Case-control studies

In case-control studies patients with a particular type of cancer (cases) are compared with a group of people who don't have cancer (controls) who are similar in age and other ways. The diets and lifestyles of the two groups may then be compared and any differences found can be related to the cause of the cancer. For example, the group without cancer may eat more vegetables and fruits than the cancer patients.

If a particular dietary factor, for example drinking alcohol, is almost always linked with another lifestyle factor, for example smoking tobacco, this is called a confounding factor. An analysis of smokers and non-smokers, and other possible confounding factors, would be needed to throw further light on the differences found. It is usual in many case-control studies to make allowance for the effects of age, gender, and smoking habits.

Large case-control studies can sort out a number of confounding factors and produce valuable results. However, in analysing the data, epidemiologists also have to take into account the difficulty of obtaining accurate information from people about their diets, particularly about their past diets. And if the overall nutrient content of the diets of cases and controls do not vary greatly it may be difficult to get a clear answer.

Cohort studies

Cohort studies follow a large group of people over a period of perhaps five or ten years, during which time a number of people in the study will develop cancer. Information about the diets of individuals is collected during the course of the study and specimens of tissue may be taken. At the end of the study all the information is analysed in order to find differences that may explain why some individuals develop cancer and some do not.

Cohort studies avoid many of the problems

of other types of study, but, because many thousands of people need to be enrolled on the study to make them statistically valid, they are expensive, and practical only for investigating common diseases. In some of the largest cohort studies, 50,000–100,000 people have been studied.

Controlled trials

In some circumstances it *is* possible to 'experiment' with people's diets. In controlled trials two groups of people are observed: one group is given a standard diet with the test food and the other group is given the standard diet with a comparison food. For example, a vitamin pill might be compared with a dummy pill.

There are many variations of this type of trial. In the best trials the subjects are put in the different groups at random and neither they nor the investigators know who is being given the test food and who is being given the dummy food. This method is successful for comparison of vitamins or other micronutrients that may be given in the form of a pill, but is difficult or impossible to organise for most other foods. These trials may have to continue for a long period of time before a result is obtained. Furthermore a negative result is not conclusive because it can always be argued that a positive result might have been obtained if the trial had continued for longer.

Meta-analysis

Unless an epidemiological study is large enough, some important links between diet and cancer may be missed. Meta-analysis is a technique for using the results from a number of studies to investigate these links, by pooling the results.

Because each of these different types of epidemiological study has different strengths and weaknesses, they need to be given different weight when the evidence as a whole is reviewed. In general the scientists responsible for the WCRF report decided that case control, cohort and controlled trials provide the best evidence for causal links between food and nutrition and cancer. The strongest evidence is when different types of study in different populations give consistent findings.

Biological observations

Analysis of blood, the chemistry or pathology of body tissues, and other biological markers are now widely used in human studies and play an important part in identifying likely factors that increase or decrease cancer risk. For example, the amount of sodium in the urine may be measured as an indication of the amount of salt (sodium chloride) in the diet. Observation of certain pre-cancerous states such as polyps in the intestine may provide important clues about the dietary causes of colon cancer.

Tests in animals, or on cells or micro-organisms in the test tube, may show that a particular food or chemical causes mutations or cancer. However, a substance that causes mutations in micro-organisms will not necessarily cause mutations or cancer in animals or humans. Valuable clues may be obtained from such studies, but the scientists responsible for the report concluded that they do not provide strong evidence unless they are supported by evidence from studies of humans. Animal research may suggest a biological pathway which leads to protection against cancer or to the development of cancer. Knowledge of the pathway may suggest ways in which the chain of causation may be interrupted and cancer prevented. For example, salt is known to irritate and damage the lining of the stomach. This observation strengthens independent evidence showing that a high intake of salt and salted foods is associated with stomach cancer. Similarly, evidence that alcohol affects the metabolism of the hormone oestrogen strengthens the likelihood that the relationship between high alcohol intake and an increased risk of breast cancer is indeed a causal link.

Each of these categories of biological observation may contribute some valuable evidence to support the evidence from epidemiological studies. Investigations of pre-cancerous lesions, and identifying biologically plausible pathways, are the most important.

Making evidence-based judgements

Dietary recommendations, as given in Chapter 3, are made on the basis that there is enough evidence of a causal relationship between cancer and that particular food. Causation is always an inference. It is not observed directly. Scientists are likely to decide that the associations between a particular food and cancer, found from all the various studies, is causal when these associations are consistent, unbiased, strong, graded, coherent, repeated, predictive and plausible. This set of criteria was first set out in 1965, and is now a standard for establishing causality.

For example, there is a variety of epidemiological evidence from correlation, case-control and cohort studies that aflatoxin (produced by a mould in certain foods stored in warm damp conditions) is linked with primary liver cancer in humans. Aflatoxin is a potent carcinogen in some experimental animals. Mechanisms whereby aflatoxin binds to the DNA in cells and is associated with the mutation of a gene to a state in which it no longer suppresses cancer have been identified. All these studies point to the same conclusion that aflatoxin is a cause of liver cancer.

As another example, many case-control and cohort studies have found that people who eat larger amounts of vegetables and fruits have a lower risk of lung cancer than those who eat less of these foods. This is true both for non-smokers and smokers. Generally, evidence on foods and drinks is stronger and clearer than evidence on constituents of food. For example, people who have less of the vitamin beta-carotene (which comes mostly from vegetables and fruits) in their blood have a higher risk of developing lung cancer, suggesting that beta-carotene protects against lung cancer. However, controlled trials in which beta-carotene was given to one group and a dummy pill to a control group have found that beta-carotene does not reduce the risk of lung cancer and may in fact increase the risk. Is this because some other substance or substances in vegetables and fruits protect against lung cancer? Or is it because the type or amount of beta-carotene used in the studies was inappropriate? So far nobody knows for sure. Meanwhile it is safe to recommend diets high in a variety of vegetables and fruits.

As already stated, the scientists responsible for the WCRF report reviewed and assessed the evidence from more than 4,000 studies of diet and cancer in order to establish the strength of the evidence between particular food, nutrition and cancer, and to make dietary recommendations. Evidence from human studies was agreed to be strongest. Experimental and other evidence was agreed to be suggestive, and also provided important backing for human evidence.

The scientists also defined what they meant by 'convincing' evidence, or evidence of 'probable' or 'possible' causal relationships between diet and cancer risk, and where there was 'insufficient' evidence. In general, the scientists agreed that judgements that causal links were convincing or probable

The strength of evidence

The criteria used by the scientists responsible for the WCRF report in making judgements of convincing, probable or possible causal links between food, nutrition and cancer risk are as follows:

Convincing

20 or more good epidemiological studies are consistent; there is little or no evidence to the contrary. The association is biologically plausible. Laboratory evidence is usually supportive or strongly supportive.

Probable

Epidemiological studies are not so consistent, some may not support the association, or else the number of studies or type of studies not extensive enough to make a more definite judgement. Laboratory and other evidence, as above.

Possible

Epidemiological studies are generally supportive but are limited in quantity, quality or consistency. There may be no supportive laboratory data and no suggested biological pathway. Alternatively there may be few or no epidemiological data, but strongly supportive evidence from other disciplines.

should generate a dietary recommendation. Their reviews and assessments were made for a complete range of foods and drinks, for many dietary constituents and methods of food processing, and for cancers at eighteen sites of the body.

It is not enough to know that the risk of cancer is affected by diet. The key question is: 'By how much?' This is important both to individuals and to policy makers who are involved with public health planning. For example, if diets high in vegetables decrease the risk of a number of cancers, what's the limit? If alcohol increases the risk of breast cancer, how much alcohol? Whether recommendations are made for populations, or for families and individuals, it is vital to quantify them. Only then is it possible for policy makers, and for us as consumers, to know what to do.

So, wherever possible, the scientists responsible for the WCRF report drew conclusions not only about causation and about the degree of risk to the public, but also about what quantity of particular foods and drinks should be consumed to decrease the risk of cancer.

When the scientists had completed their work of reviewing and assessing the evidence, they discovered that clear patterns emerged. Foods, drinks, dietary constituents or methods of food processing that evidently protect against one cancer or a group of cancers, do not increase the risk of other cancers. Likewise, aspects of diet that evidently increase the risk of some cancers are not protective against other cancers. Even better news is that dietary recommendations designed to protect against cancer are almost always practically the same as those already known to protect against heart disease and other major chronic diseases.

For example, the evidence that diets high in vegetables and/or fruits decrease the risk of cancers of the mouth and pharynx, oesophagus, lung, stomach, colon and rectum, and bladder, is convincing; and such diets probably or possibly decrease the risk of cancers of the larynx, pancreas, liver, breast, ovary, endometrium, cervix, prostate, thyroid and kidney. Equally important, there is no evidence that such diets increase the risk of any cancer. Thus, in this case, recommendations can be made with confidence for cancers as a whole; and these recommendations are practically the same as those designed to prevent heart disease.

How food and nutrition affect cancer risk

Cancer is primarily a disease of cells. It occurs when the genetic information of a cell causes it to multiply out of control and form a tumour. The tumour may then grow and spread and invade other neighbouring organs.

As it grows, a tumour usually destroys surrounding tissue, becomes supplied with more blood vessels that nourish it, and may spread to other organs or tissues in the body. Tumours may also spread throughout the body when some of the cells of an existing tumour break off and, through the bloodstream or the lymph circulation, reach and colonise other organs of the body, where they grow into secondary tumours.

Normal cells go through a number of stages before changing into a cancer cell. The various stages of cancer may be accelerated in various ways by inappropriate diets. The good news though, is that appropriate, healthy diets, rich in protective constituents, may slow down, halt or even possibly reverse cancer at most if not all stages of its development.

There are about 10^{13} (ten million million) cells in our bodies, and the development of cancer needs only one cell to start behaving abnormally – so cancer is a very rare disease at the cellular level. Many mechanisms exist to protect cells and help limit any damage that does occur.

Cancers occur only in cells that are dividing and reproducing themselves. Once a cell is damaged and behaving abnormally, that abnormality can be passed on to later generations of cells. The fact that DNA is liable to both change and damage is central to its ability to evolve and adapt. If DNA did not change in response to environmental pressures, there would be no potential for natural selection. Cancer is, in a real sense, the price we pay for the adaptability of the human species.

The change from a normal cell into a cancer cell begins with a change in the DNA of a cell called a mutation. Such mutation may occur as a result of radiation or a chemical damaging DNA, or as a result of a virus altering DNA, or as the result of a random mistake in the copying of DNA which occurs when cells multiply. Chemicals which cause mutations are called mutagens, and chemicals which cause cancer are called carcinogens.

Most but not all mutagens are carcinogens. A substance may be shown to be a mutagen in tests on cells in the laboratory, yet additional tests on animals may show that the substance does not cause cancer. The reason for this is that some mutagens are destroyed and eliminated from the body before they can do any damage to cells.

In addition to mutation, other changes in DNA may cause cancer in a different way. General changes in the activity of DNA can cause the wrong genes to be switched on or off and so make cells produce the wrong products. This may occur as a result of a normal process of cell metabolism known as methylation going wrong. When DNA is insufficiently methylated it may be more vulnerable to mutation. Methylation is kept at healthy levels by a number of substances in food, including the B vitamin known as folic acid or folate, found in leafy vegetables and other foods of plant origin.

The risk of carcinogenesis is increased by exposure to human carcinogens, but many substances in foods are also anti-carcinogenic in humans. Carcinogens and anti-carcinogens are more or less common in different diets and foods and drinks depending in part on the general composition of diets and on how food is prepared. Cells have ways of correcting mutations, to repair the damage to the DNA, but once a cell with a mutation has divided, the mutation becomes fixed and it can no longer be corrected. The greater the load of mutagenic chemicals in the body, the greater the chance that a mistake will go uncorrected and develop into a cancer. One important cause of mutations is believed to be oxygen, which, under certain circumstances, develops into highly reactive oxygen radicals. This is why the substances in foods of plant origin known as antioxidants are believed to be effective anti-carcinogens: they protect cells against damage from oxygen radicals.

Generally, a cell must mutate several times and multiply before it becomes established as a small tumour. Conditions in the environment and the body must favour multiplication of cells for this process to occur. If conditions do not favour cell multiplication, then the mutated cell will take much longer to develop into a cancer cell. Some chemical substances found in food speed up the development of cancer by increasing cell multiplication and in other ways. These substances are called promoters. Alcohol is an example. And diets that are high in protein, fat or calories have been found to act as cancer promoters in animal experiments. On the other hand, the mineral selenium and vitamin D are protective against tumour promotion.

The final stage in the development of cancer is known as progression. At this stage the small bunch of cancer cells which has grown from a single mutated cell expands into an invasive tumour mass. At this late stage further damage and changes occur to DNA which favour aggressive growth of the cells. These changes may occur as a result of further exposure of the DNA to damage by oxygen radicals or carcinogens. It is not yet clear whether carcinogens in food may speed up this process and whether protective agents in food may slow the process down or stop it, but there is growing evidence that these processes may well affect cancer even at this late stage of its development.

What about when cancer is established in the body? Will people with cancer benefit from the diets recommended in this book? Scientists do not yet know the answer to this vital question. It is possible that healthy diets may delay the progression of cancer if the disease has been identified at a relatively early stage, for example a small unattached breast lump with no evidence of spread. This suggestion is based on the fact that progression of a tumour involves additional damage to DNA that may be halted by healthy diets.

Our dietary advice might also delay or perhaps even prevent a second independent tumour from arising. For example, once a woman has developed a tumour in one breast she is more likely to develop another different tumour in the other breast. This is because cancer may develop independently in different places in the body when conditions favour it. The promotion and progression of a second independent tumour might be delayed, or even possibly prevented, by diets that minimise the risk of cancer developing in the first place. What is known is that following the advice in this book will improve general health and so bring benefits which alone will make the change worthwhile.

3 Eating for health

THE RISK of serious chronic diseases, such as coronary heart disease, stroke, diabetes and common cancers, is affected by the foods and drinks we consume regularly. Evidence that proves the links between diets and health has been accumulating in the scientific literature for 40 years and more. Moreover, committees of scientific experts who have reviewed and judged the evidence of these links between diets and health virtually all come to the same broad conclusions.

The first expert reports identifying links between diet and cancer were published in the early 1980s. *The Causes of Cancer*, by the British epidemiologists Professor Sir Richard Doll and Professor Richard Peto, was published in 1981; and *Diet, Nutrition and Cancer*, a report prepared by a committee of experts for the US National Academy of Sciences, was published in 1982. Since then, over 20 major reports on diet and cancer have been published. The World Cancer Research Fund's report, *Food, Nutrition and the Prevention of Cancer: a global perspective* is, as its title suggests, the first to take a world-wide view, and it is also the first to use the key word 'prevention' in its title.

The World Cancer Research Fund's report also tackles issues not attempted in other reports. Do diets that protect against cancer also protect against other diseases? What are the best diets as a whole to eat to reduce your cancer risk? How does being physically active affect cancer risk?

The World Cancer Research Fund's report makes 14 dietary recommendations on what sorts of foods and drinks we are best advised to consume to protect ourselves against cancer. This chapter and Chapter 4 spell out these recommendations.

Re-shape your diet

Taken together, the WCRF recommendations are for whole diets. By following the recommendations we can decide what kinds of foods to eat to make up all our daily meals. This 'whole diet' approach has not been attempted before in the context of cancer prevention. This chapter specifies how much of each type of food and drink will reduce the risk not only of cancer, but also of other serious chronic diseases.

> *Plant-based diets*
> **Choose predominantly plant-based diets rich in a variety of vegetables and fruits, pulses, and minimally processed starchy staple foods**

The first and most important recommendation is that our diets should contain mostly foods of plant origin. Our diets are most likely to protect us against cancer in general when they are rich in a year-round variety of vegetables and fruits, together with pulses (beans, lentils, and other such plant foods that are rich in protein), cereals (such as wheat eaten in the form of bread or pasta, and rice, oats, and other grains, preferably wholegrain) and in roots and tubers (such as potatoes).

Strong and consistent evidence shows that diets with plenty of vegetables and fruits reduce the risk of many types of cancer, and also reduce the risk of heart disease. Minimally processed starchy staple foods may protect against cancer and are a better choice than fatty or sugary foods or meat-based diets. Plant-based diets high in starch also help prevent us from becoming overweight or obese. Plant foods are relatively bulky and so more satisfying. Energy is released more slowly from foods that are eaten whole or minimally processed. As a result blood sugar levels remain more constant and so it takes longer for a feeling of hunger to return.

A plant-based diet doesn't necessarily mean a vegetarian diet. Diets that contain modest amounts of red meat can be as healthy, but moving to a plant-based diet is quite a change from 'meat and two veg'. The healthy choice is meals that are usually dominated by foods of plant origin – our plates will then look very different.

A substantial meat meal is fine once in a while, but red meat is best eaten only in small quantities and occasionally. Think of meat as a flavouring or a garnish in dishes that include generous quantities of vegetables and starchy staples such as pasta, rice, or potatoes.

Foods and drinks

Vegetables and fruits
Eat 400–800 grams (15–30 ounces) or five or more portions a day of a variety of vegetables and fruits, all year round

The phrase 'vegetables and fruits' is deliberate. We tend to down-grade vegetables by referring to 'fruit and vegetables' or, worse, 'fruit'n'veg'. Phrases like this reflect the fact

---

Principles of cancer prevention
The dietary recommendations follow a number of principles:

The recommendations are devised both as goals for populations aimed at policy makers, and also as advice for individuals. Generally, this book gives the advice to individuals.

The recommendations are based on foods and drinks rather than dietary constituents. For example, the recommendations focus on vegetables and fruits, rather than on fibre or vitamin C.

The recommendations are quantified, and give the ranges of intake most likely to protect against cancer. Thus, the recommendation on vegetables and fruits is for five or more portions of 80 grams (3 ounces) a day.

The recommendations are designed for everybody, not just people at higher risk of cancer, and together amount to realistic and enjoyable diets most likely to reduce the risk of cancer and other chronic diseases.

---

that most people in Britain eat only half or even less of the amounts of vegetables that are best for good health and protection against diseases such as cancer. Our definition of vegetables and fruits excludes starchy roots and tubers (like potatoes), and bananas. However, non-starchy roots such as parsnips and carrots are classed as vegetables. 'Vegetables' also exclude pulses (such as beans, peas, lentils) that are high in protein. These foods are covered in the advice on 'other plant foods', below.

Quantifying the advice to enjoy a diet that is rich in a variety of vegetables and fruits makes the recommendations meaningful. Thus, we should all eat at least five portions of vegetables and fruits, every day. A 'portion' is defined as weighing 80 grams (or 3 ounces) on average. This is roughly the weight of an orange or an apple, and also roughly the weight of a serving of vegetables. A daily minimum of 400 grams (15 ounces) of vegetables and fruits amounts to about 7 per cent of our total calorie intake.

Over 200 studies in the scientific literature show that diets high in vegetables, and often fruits as well, protect against cancer. Diets high in vegetables and fruits possibly, probably or certainly reduce the risk of sixteen different cancers which together account for nearly 80 per cent of all cases of cancer world-wide. These include the cancers most common in Britain: those of the colon and rectum, the breast, the prostate, the stomach, the mouth and throat, and also the lung.

If we all included at least five portions or 400 grams (just under 1 pound) of a variety of vegetables and fruits in our diets all year round, our risk of any cancer would be reduced by 20 per cent, compared with people who eat only 250 grams (9 ounces) or so daily, which is about the British average. The 'five a day' message has also been recommended by the UK report on diet and cancer produced by the Committee on Medical Aspects of Food Policy (COMA) for the UK government and published in 1998. And 'five a day' is also a vital message to protect against heart disease and other chronic diseases.

Much of the research on the vegetables and fruits and cancer risk has focused on specific dietary constituents in these foods, or else on specific groups of vegetables and fruits. Vegetables and fruits are rich in vitamins, minerals and other bioactive compounds compared to other foods. They are generally good sources of fibre, vitamin C, carotenoids, folate and potassium – different vegetables and fruits have different amounts of these various vitamins and minerals. Some groups are good sources of the B vitamins, of calcium and of iron.

When we look at the evidence on these various dietary constituents of vegetables and fruits we find that fibre, found in cereals as well as in vegetables and fruits, may reduce the risk of cancers of the pancreas, colon and rectum, and breast. Carotenoids and vitamin C may reduce the risk of a number of cancers and the evidence on lung cancer in the case of carotenoids, and on stomach cancer in the case of vitamin C, is strong enough to judge that they probably reduce cancer risk.

Because the scientific studies relate to the foods we eat, it is always hard to be sure that the evidence relating to any one specific dietary constituent applies just to that constituent, rather than others in the same food. For this reason, the panel responsible for these recommendations emphatically stated that the only judgement that can be made with complete confidence is that diets with plenty of a variety of vegetables and fruits prevent cancer.

Calculating recommended quantities of food

Recommendations for the quantities of food we should eat are given in two ways: either in terms of portions per day, or else as weight per day. The recommendation on vegetables and fruits is for five or more portions (average 80 grams/3 ounces per serving) or else for 400 or more grams (15 ounces or more) a day.

These recommendations are calculated for a person who requires 2,000 calories from food a day. This is more than many smaller or inactive people need. In Britain, most women with sedentary occupations, who are not physically active in other ways, may need only 1,600 calories a day from food. On the other hand, many bigger or active people will require more: an energetic man needs 2,500 or more calories a day. And of course younger children require less food.

How to enjoy 5+ a day helpings of vegetables and fruits

Once you know that an apple or an orange counts as one portion of fruit, and that an onion, a couple of tomatoes and two or three carrots, any of which will weigh around 80 grams (3 ounces), also counts as a portion, eating at least five portions a day of vegetables and fruits may not seem a lot. Nor is it, for many people. In sunny countries where people enjoy fresh food, such as the Mediterranean region, Latin America, and the richer countries in Asia, it's usual to see people eating lots of green vegetables, salads and fruits.

In Britain, people usually eat far less vegetables and fruit, on average only two to three portions a day, and that includes fruit juices, and the bits and pieces of vegetables and fruits found in processed and prepared foods such as flans, pizzas and pies, that also include lots of fat or sugar. Until recently, people in many parts of Scotland ate hardly any fresh vegetables or fruits – and the rates of colorectal cancer, breast cancer and coronary heart disease in Scotland are almost the highest in the world.

When you think of vegetables and fruits you may well first think of fresh varieties such as salads and whole fruit. Good! Enjoy a big salad with your main meals, and keep a bowl full of fruits in the main rooms in your home and in your office, for you and everybody else to eat as ideal snacks. If you eat an orange and an apple in one day, this is two portions. Salad vegetables such as lettuce, cucumber, tomato and sweet peppers are full of nourishment: a large helping can easily amount to a couple of portions.

You may also think of the cooked vegetables you eat with meals. Good! Serve up twice or three times the usual amount of your favourite vegetables with meals, and order double portions in restaurants. Half a pound (about 225 grams) of spinach, leeks or courgettes may look a lot raw and unprepared, but once cooked by your favourite method, they are filling, very nourishing, and can amount to two portions a day by themselves.

What about juice? Because prepared fruit and vegetable juices come with little or no fibre, and lose some of their nutrients in processing, count any juice you drink as only one of your daily portions. Make your own drinks from whole fruits and vegetables for delicious alternatives. Mix any combination of fruit you like in a blender. Experiment! You can try vegetables as well. Try banana and mango, perhaps also with pineapple or papaya, as an exotic favourite; mix apple and carrot for maximum taste and colour. Citrus fruits are fine too, of course. Add some water, or milk, as you like, and ice in the summer. You can also add wheatgerm and nuts, for a juice absolutely full of nourishment. Do not add sugar! There is no need, as fruits contain plenty of natural sugar. This is a much better breakfast than ready-to-eat breakfast cereals or bacon sandwiches, and sets you up for the whole day.

These home-made juices are useful for mothers too. You can make up delicious vegetable drinks of different consistencies, and smuggle in those nourishing vegetables that kids may not like to eat by themselves.

Making 5+ vegetables and fruits part of your everyday life can be done in countless ways. All good supermarkets now stock a wide range of fresh vegetables and fruits all year round. Experiment, and suit your own nature. Some people will prefer to build up to five portions a day, or a bit more, by gradually increasing consumption of vegetables and fruits throughout the day; just as some people will build up their physical activity by walking everywhere. Other people (rather like going to the gym or an aerobics class to achieve much of their daily physical activity in one go) will prefer to eat several portions of vegetables all together in one meal. It's up to you!

Yes, the vegetables and fruits contained in processed and prepared products also count towards the 5+ a day, but at a price: these mostly come with a lot of fat or sugar or salt. Frozen vegetables and fruits are fine of course, if sometimes a bit costly. If you buy canned products, avoid those with added sugar or salt.

Most foods of plant origin are now known to contain a vast number of bioactive compounds (sometimes called phytochemicals) which, like vitamins and minerals, may well have some role in protection of human health. But many of these compounds were unknown to nutritional scientists until the 1980s and 1990s. In time to come it may be possible to make confident judgements about some of these compounds. Meanwhile, keep eating lots of vegetables and fruits!

Studies that have been made on some specific vegetables and fruits, or 'families' of vegetables and fruits, show they are important in reducing the risk of particular cancers. There is convincing evidence that diets high in vegetables of the onion or allium family (onions, shallots, chives, leeks and garlic) protect against stomach cancer. Likewise, the evidence that eating lots of citrus fruit (such as oranges, grapefruit, lemons and limes) protects against stomach cancer is convincing, as is the evidence that diets high in a variety of green vegetables protect against stomach and also lung cancer. Even some individual vegetables are strongly protective: carrots and tomatoes, for example. But, to a large extent, strong evidence on families of vegetables and fruits reflects waves of interest in specific compounds found in such foods (such as allium compounds, and antioxidants); and in future years we may know more about the roles of other compounds, and other groups of vegetables and fruits.

Other plant foods
Eat 600–800 grams (20–30 ounces) or more than seven portions a day of a variety of cereals, pulses, roots, tubers and plantains. Prefer minimally processed foods. Limit consumption of refined sugar

In a plant-based diet, what plant foods should we be eating, as well as vegetables and fruits? 'Other plant foods' (not a memorable name!) includes cereals (such as wheat, rice, corn, oats, rye and barley) and cereal products (bread and pasta are obvious examples), pulses, also known as legumes (which include beans, peas, lentils and their products), and starchy roots and tubers (potatoes, for example). Starchy roots and tubers such as sweet potatoes and cassava are important in other parts of the world, as are plantains. The only plantain we eat regularly in Britain is the banana. And nuts and seeds are also, of course, plant foods.

What most starchy foods have in common is that they contain little fat. Cereals contain on average 70 per cent starch, and varying amounts of fibre, protein, B vitamins, vitamin E, iron and other trace elements. Roots and tubers by contrast have between 12 and 50 per cent starch, but are good sources of fibre, and of carotenoids, vitamin C, potassium, and other vitamins and minerals. Pulses and nuts and seeds are the richest plant source of protein. They are high in fibre and bioactive compounds. However, while pulses are low in fat, nuts and seeds may have up to 70–90 per cent fat – mostly unsaturated oils.

The evidence on the relationship between cereals, pulses and other plant foods, and cancer risk, is rather limited and confused. So, unlike the other recommendations, this one is not based on evidence of probable or certain causal links with cancer.

The advice on other plant foods is made for a number of reasons. First, the recommendations are designed so that, when taken together, they amount to advice on whole diets; and there are many reasons to believe that starchy foods are better for health than fatty and sugary foods and meat-based diets. Second, diets high in starchy foods protect against other important chronic diseases and so are advisable on general health grounds.

How to make 7+ a day of cereals, pulses and other starchy plant foods the staples of your diet

A minimum of seven portions a day of cereals, pulses and other plant foods, may sound like a lot. Remember first, though, that a portion is not the same as a meal! We define one portion as 80 grams or 3 ounces of food when cooked or ready to eat. Sometimes the difference between the whole food and the food as eaten is not significant. For example, a raw potato (an average-sized potato weighs around 80 grams/3 ounces) and a boiled potato weigh much the same. Cereals, however, become heavier with cooking, because they absorb water: cooked rice is about two and a half times heavier than raw rice. Likewise, dried beans and other pulses become a lot heavier once cooked in water.

There are plenty of simple strategies you can use to reach your 7+ portions a day. The first mental breakthrough is to stop thinking that a main meal needs meat as its centrepiece, or indeed needs meat at all. This does not mean this book recommends vegetarianism. There is nothing whatever wrong with mixed, varied vegetarian diets. But diets that include small amounts of meat and other animal foods are also nourishing, of course.

Make pasta and pizza the centre of some of your meals. Be careful with the ready-made varieties; these are usually swamped with fatty ingredients and fillings. Make your own, accompanied and covered with delicious vegetables, using a little meat if you like as a relish. Italians use very strong-tasting salami or anchovy very sparingly on pizzas. And when you eat pasta or pizza, serve a big helping of salad or vegetables – or both! Learn to make main-meal dishes based on rice or other cereals – see the recipes in Section 2 for ideas. A main meal based on pizza, pasta or rice can count as two or three of your daily portions.

Potatoes are the tuber everybody in Britain knows. Nowadays there are many varieties of spud on sale in markets and supermarkets. Try a different variety every week or month. Try different ways of cooking potatoes. Baked potatoes in their jackets are super fast food for adults and for children, and a big potato weighing in at half a pound (about 225 grams), counts as more than two portions. Try less familiar roots and tubers. Many city markets now stock sweet potatoes and yams, which are delicious and very nourishing!

Bananas are not strictly fruit, strangely enough, but plantains, and more like these other plant foods than fruit in their composition. Eat one as a snack to add another portion to your daily total.

Think about what accompaniments you serve with meals. Eat bread and become a bread enthusiast. Do what people do in many European countries: enjoy the wonderful variety of wholegrain breads on display in many supermarkets and bakers' shops. Try the heavier breads, like wholewheat, corn, and rye, and the breads eaten in the Middle East, Latin America and Asia. Have a big plate of breads on the table with main meals. Ask for bread in restaurants and cafés. Good bread is delicious eaten by itself and therefore even more delicious with your favourite filling. Make it the basis of a lunchtime sandwich or eat it with a salad for a light meal.

Going back to the beginning of the day, make your own muesli (see page 71). Many breakfast cereals are very sugary; the sweetest brands are really a type of confectionery. Surprisingly perhaps, some brands are very salty. (Granola and cereal bars are also a type of confectionery too; the idea that such sticky fatty foods have health benefits is absurd.)

Starchy foods may sound dull, but cooked in interesting ways they are not. Discover new and exciting ways to cook and eat them. Leave behind boring boiled rice and the rather unimaginative ways in which we prepare potatoes.

Since Latin American food is rather neglected in Britain, why not try an extremely delicious, basic, everyday Brazilian dish, which, in Portuguese, is called 'arroz com feijão' meaning, rice Brazilian-style with beans – and it has garlic in it too.

Third, when the evidence is reviewed carefully, the issue with starchy foods may well be not just their starch content but the extent to which they are processed. Most of the non-starch nutrients are concentrated in the outer parts of the cereal grain, and these are removed during processing.

Diets high in processed cereals and cereal products such as white bread and pasta may possibly increase cancer risk, whereas other evidence consistently suggests that diets high in wholegrain cereals protect against cancer. The less processed cereals are, the more fibre, vitamins and minerals they contain; and some of these constituents may protect against cancer as well as other diseases.

Taking the evidence all together, it is safe and prudent to recommend diets that are high in relatively unprocessed starchy foods, and in pulses.

Diets high in sugar are unhealthy. Most of the sugar we eat is refined from sugar cane or sugar beet. It is added to processed foods, to cakes, biscuits and confectionery and soft drinks, and we add it when we cook and at table. There is a fairly impressive body of evidence suggesting that diets high in sugar may increase the risk of colon cancer.

You may be thinking that 600–800 grams (20–30 ounces) of plant foods, which amount to 45–60 per cent of the total calories consumed by somebody who needs 2,000 calories a day, is a lot of food. First, remember that these are the weights of processed or cooked food. Rice and beans weigh a lot more once cooked in water than in a raw or dried state. But, yes, these diets, in common with the diets recommended by many other expert groups, are much bulkier than diets now typically eaten in Britain.

Do people eat such bulky, starchy diets anywhere in the world? Of course! Traditional diets now eaten in Africa, Latin America and Asia are mostly made up of starchy foods, balanced between cereals (such as rice, wheat, corn) and pulses (such as lentils and beans). In such parts of the world meat, fish, dairy products, and other foods of animal origin are usually also eaten, but sparingly. The same was generally true in Britain until around 200 years ago; historically, only rich people ate 'the roast beef of Olde England' and other such foods on a daily basis. And the idea that we need meat for its protein, is untrue. We do indeed need protein for growth and maintenance of body functions, but we can get the right balance of amino acids, the building blocks of protein, from the cereals and pulses in our diets.

Does this mean that we should eat a monotonous peasant diet that is likely to starve us? Of course not! Thanks to popular cookbook writers and the rapid growth of restaurants and cafés from other parts of the world, everybody knows that the traditional cuisines of countries in Asia such as India and China, and from the Mediterranean region such as Italy, Greece, Turkey and Egypt, are wonderfully delicious. The same is true of other parts of the world such as Latin America whose cuisines are not yet as well known in Europe.

Give meat a lower priority

> *Meat*
> **If eaten at all, limit intake of red meat to less than 80 grams (3 ounces) daily. It is preferable to choose fish, poultry or meat from non-domesticated animals in place of red meat**

Everybody who reads newspapers will have heard in late 1997 and early 1998 that meat causes cancer – or does it? This is because a report on diet and cancer produced by the official British government advisory Committee on Medical Aspects of Food Policy

(COMA) for the Department of Health, was leaked to a leading national daily paper in September 1997, and heralded by headlines like 'Big Meat Eaters Cancer Warning', 'Beef Industry Counters Red Meat Scare' and 'Row Over Report on Meat and Cancer'.

The scientific evidence tells a less sensational story. Meat is not the main issue in relation to cancer risk: it is only part of a much bigger story. What is true, as was found by the experts responsible for the WCRF report, the separate COMA panel, and also by panels of scientists who have assessed the evidence from studies published over the last 20 years or so, is that red meat – beef, lamb and pork – when eaten regularly in substantial quantities, is an issue. The WCRF report judges that diets high in red meat probably increase the risk of cancers of the colon and rectum, and may increase the risk of cancers

of the pancreas, breast, prostate and kidney. The COMA panel came to similar conclusions.

Meat is a good source of protein and of the B vitamins, and of minerals including iron, zinc and selenium. So, what is the matter with red meat? The problem may be that meat from intensively reared animals is fatty; diets high in animal fat possibly increase the risk of cancers of the lung, colon and rectum, breast, endometrium and prostate. Alternatively, or additionally, the problem may be to do with how we cook the meat; eating a lot of grilled or barbecued meat may increase the risk of cancers of the stomach, the colon and the rectum. (See page 28 for the recommendation on cooking.) Some of the meat we eat has been cured and/or smoked, and this may also affect our cancer risk (see page 28).

Most people in Britain would be well advised to reduce how much beef, lamb and pork (and

But I like meat, why should I cut down?

Many readers of this book may be thinking 'But I like meat'. What then? First, this book gives you the best advice on reducing your cancer risk that is currently available; advice based on a very large number of scientific studies. You can choose if you want to follow the advice.

Second, of course it is not true that if you eat more than 80 grams (3 ounces) of red meat a day, you are doomed to die from colon cancer. The more red meat you eat, the greater your risk of colon cancer and perhaps other cancers too.

There is quite a lot of evidence that the risk of cancer among meat eaters increases further if their diets are unhealthy in other respects. It is reasonable to assume that for people who eat lots of vegetables and fruits, the amount of red meat they eat is less of an issue. (Similarly, smokers who eat lots of vegetables have a high risk of lung cancer, but the risk is higher still among smokers who don't eat many vegetables.)

Another helpful point for lovers of red meat is that the problem with red meat may be either its high fat content, or else the way it is cooked. It is reasonable to suppose that lean cuts, and meat cooked by stewing or roasting, are less of a risk than fatty meat and meat products like burgers, and meat that is grilled, barbecued or fried.

The advice is only about red meat – beef, lamb and pork. Many people who like meat like poultry and fish as well; switch to these, and game animals and birds too. There's a wide variety of fish on the market now in Britain and the number of recipes for delicious fish cooked by steaming, boiling and baking is endless.

But do you really want to eat a lot of red meat? Many of us have been brought up to believe that main meals should have meat as a centrepiece, and also have been told that protein from meat and other animal foods, is essential. This is not true. Perhaps the best policy for readers who love the taste of red meat is to enjoy a substantial portion of really good-quality meat on special days as feast food, and otherwise eat it as a relish with simpler plant-based meals.

products made from these meats such as burgers, pies, pasties and sausages) they eat, and instead choose poultry, fish, and game animals and birds.

The WCRF advice is a maximum of 80 grams (3 ounces) a day of cooked meat – no more than 10 per cent of daily calories for somebody needing 2,000 calories a day. The COMA report eventually published a rather higher maximum figure as part of its advice, but the general principle is the same: it's advisable, if you want to reduce your risk of colon and maybe other cancers, to go easy on red meat and its products. In Britain our average consumption is only slightly higher than the recommendation, but many people eat over 200 grams (7 ounces) a day.

This recommendation is not another way of saying 'vegetarianism is best'. Vegetarians have a lower incidence of cancer compared with people who eat meat, but this may be because they eat more vegetables and other plant foods and are generally more health-conscious. However, benefits to health provided by vegetarian diets are probably also obtained from diets that include some meat also.

The fat factor

Total fats and oils
Limit consumption of fatty foods, particularly those of animal origin. Choose modest amounts of appropriate vegetable oils

It used to be thought that the main issue in relation to diet and cancer was fat and, until fairly recently, advice on reducing cancer risk tended to emphasise the risks of high-fat diets.

However, as scientific knowledge has grown in the last fifteen years or so, the story has changed somewhat. First, the good news on reducing cancer risk is: eat more vegetables

and fruits. Second, the strongest scientific evidence is now usually about foods rather than dietary constituents. For example, evidence that diets high in red meat (which is typically fatty) increase cancer risk is rather stronger than evidence on the direct effects of fat.

But the story on fat and cancer can still be told. Diets high in fat, as typically eaten in Britain, may increase the risk of cancers of the lung, colon and rectum, breast and prostate, and diets high in animal fats or other saturated fats may increase the risk of cancers of the lung, breast, colon, rectum, womb and prostate. Experts also agree that such diets increase the risk of heart disease.

Scientists generally agree that fatty diets increase the likelihood of becoming overweight and obese. And evidence that obesity increases the risk of cancers of the breast (after menopause) and the womb, and also of the kidney, is strong. Obesity may also increase the risk of colon cancer. If you are overweight in early or middle life, you are more likely to become obese later in life, so, in the context of cancer, it is advisable not to be overweight at any time in your life.

Hence the advice that fats and oils together should contribute less than 30 per cent of the calories in our diets. This is quite a big drop from the amount typically consumed in Britain; for most of us fat contributes nearly 40 per cent of the calories. The fat in our diets comes not only from meat and dairy products, but also from baked goods, cakes and confectionery, from the fats and oils we use in cooking, and from the spreads we use at table on bread. You are unlikely to achieve a diet with only 15–30 per cent of calories from fats if all you do is switch to low- or no-fat milk and other products. It's more effective to cut some fats, like spreads, almost completely out of your diet. (What, no butter? Enjoy it only as an occasional treat.)

When you cook, use oils sparingly. Choose unsaturated oils: corn oil is a cheap choice; olive oil is more tasty although some people don't like it. Many recipes can be cooked without adding oil at all: meat can be cooked in its own fat and plant foods cooked in their own juices. What about fatty fast foods and snacks like burgers, cakes, biscuits, chocolates, crisps? If you like foods like these, think of them as a special treat. Eaten every day they are bad news. Sorry, but there it is.

Alcohol – is it really worth the risk?

Alcoholic drinks
Alcohol consumption is not recommended. If consumed at all, limit alcoholic drinks to less than two drinks a day for men and one for women

You are likely to have read that moderate drinking of alcohol is good for you. This is not true. What is true, is that *small* amounts of alcohol – one, or at the most two, drinks a day – almost certainly give some protection against heart attacks. But that is the end of the good news about alcohol for drinkers.

The story on alcohol and cancer is different. Alcoholic drinks increase the risk of cancers of the mouth, throat (pharynx and larynx) and oesophagus (gullet), and the risk increases greatly for those who also smoke. Similarly, alcohol increases the risk of colon cancer, and heavy and persistent drinking of alcohol is a cause of liver cancer, as a result of liver cirrhosis. Any type of alcohol – beer, wine and spirits – has the same effect: the significant factor is the alcohol itself.

As well as all this, relatively recent evidence from a large number of studies shows that drinking alcohol probably increases the risk of

Babies and young children
The recommendations in this book are for everyone except babies and children up to two years old.

The best food for infants is of course breast milk. Babies who are breast-fed are protected against many diseases and disorders of infancy and childhood, and breast-feeding to three or six months – or even older, as is customary in some parts of the world – is best. And there is some evidence that women who are breast-fed as babies are less likely to suffer from breast cancer later in life.

Weaning diets, and the diets of children under two years, should follow the recommendations, except these diets should contain a higher level of fat: around 30–40 per cent of calories, in the form of relatively unsaturated fat (similar to breast milk itself). It is important to sustain a baby's energy intake during weaning, when the capacity of the stomach is modest in relation to the child's high energy demand.

breast cancer; and this risk is increased however little is drunk – even an average of a few drinks a week. Women who drink small amounts of alcohol need not panic: the increased risk of breast cancer among women who drink at most one or two drinks a day on average, is small. But, across the whole population, this small increased risk adds up to a lot of cases and a lot of deaths, because breast cancer is the most common cancer in women.

Women who are concerned solely to minimise their risk of breast cancer should not drink alcohol. However, one alcoholic drink a day provides protection against heart disease and only increases the risk of breast cancer by a relatively small amount. Women with close relatives who have had breast cancer have a higher risk of developing the disease and may be advised to avoid alcohol altogether. On the other hand women with close relatives who have had heart disease may opt for the one drink a day. Pregnant women should not drink alcohol because consumption of alcohol in pregnancy can be a cause of birth defects and low birth weight.

The recommendation balances what we know about how alcohol increases the risk of some cancers, and its role in offering some protection against heart disease. If you drink alcohol at all, limit it to one drink a day if you are a woman, two drinks a day if you are a man.

Measurement of alcoholic drinks

There is no international standard for measuring alcoholic drinks. In the UK a standard measure of spirits is 25 millilitres or 1 fluid ounce (which contains 8 grams/about $1/4$ ounce of alcohol), while in the US a standard measure is 45 millilitres (containing 14 grams of alcohol). We define a drink as 8 grams of alcohol: roughly equivalent to 300 millilitres ($1/2$ pint) of beer or lager, one glass of wine (at eight glasses to the bottle) or one UK measure of spirits.

Food processing

A lot of evidence indicates that what influences cancer risk is not only foods themselves, but what is done to foods before we eat them. This is another reason why a food-based approach to prevention of cancer is sensible. Food processing, using that term in its widest sense, includes methods of agriculture, manufacture, storage and preservation, food additives and contaminants, and also food preparation in the home.

As mentioned above, one reason why the relationship between starchy staple foods and cancer risk is not yet clear may be because, so far, researchers have not paid enough attention to the differences between relatively unprocessed cereal foods (such as wholegrain bread) and relatively highly processed versions of these foods (such as white bread), which are known to contain less nourishment.

Other reasons to look at food processing and cancer risk are the common misconception that additives and contaminants present in manufactured foods and drinks are an important cause of cancer; and the complex story about food cooked at high temperatures and cancer risk.

Taken without a pinch of salt

Salt and salting
Limit consumption of salted foods and use of cooking and table salt. Use herbs and spices to season foods

Preservation
Use refrigeration and other appropriate methods to preserve perishable food as purchased and at home

In a British context these two recommendations basically say the same thing: consume a lot less salt, and take advantage of the fact that the use of refrigeration throughout the food chain keeps perishable food fresh and is an alternative to preserving foods by salting.

Diets high in salt increase the risk of stomach cancer, until recently the most common cancer in the world. It was believed that the problem was confined largely to those regions in the world, such as Japan and Portugal, where traditional diets include a lot of food such as fish preserved by salting. We know now, however, that *all* diets that are high in salt, whether from salted foods, or the salty foods that are so common in British diets, increase stomach cancer risk. Diets high in salted or salty foods also increase the risk of high blood pressure and stroke.

Common salt is made up of sodium and chloride, and the adverse effects of high levels of salt in the diet are generally attributed to sodium. Most of the salt in our everyday diets comes from the wide range of the processed foods we buy; only a relatively small amount is added in cooking or at the table. Foods high in salt include cooked meats, bacon, kippers, sausages, cheese, and bread, some breakfast cereals, and savoury snacks such as crisps, salted biscuits and nuts. Baked goods such as cakes are made with a raising agent (often sodium bicarbonate), and generally have a relatively high sodium content. Salt from all these sources should provide less than 6 grams per day (equivalent to 2.4 grams of sodium) for adults. We consume far more salt than we need: typically, eating just a few slices of bread each day will provide more sodium than the body requires.

We can reduce the amount of salt in our everyday diets in a number of ways. First, avoid salted and salty foods, or eat them in small quantities, or find lower-salt alternatives. Second, use less salt in cooking: herbs and spices can provide alternative flavours. You do not need to add salt when vegetables are boiled or steamed. Most people will not immediately like the taste of some dishes such as soup without the addition of some salt, but slowly reduce the amount of salt you use in cooking over several weeks and you will adapt easily to the new taste. Once you are used to food with less salt, much restaurant food and ready prepared food will taste too salty.

The incidence of stomach cancer is now decreasing quite fast in most parts of the world. The key reason for this almost certainly is the use of refrigeration to preserve foods instead of salting them, as in the past. In Britain, however, stomach cancer is still the sixth most common cancer.

Indirectly, refrigeration also helps prevent cancer generally, not just stomach cancer, because it allows fresh vegetables and fruits to be available all year round. The British food chain now uses refrigeration at all stages from the farm, through manufacture, to distribution, retailing and, of course, in the home.

Safe storage

Storage
Do not eat food which, as a result of prolonged storage at ambient temperatures, is liable to contamination with mycotoxins

This recommendation has little relevance in countries like Britain, but is important elsewhere in the world. Mycotoxins, fungal contaminants found in grains, peanuts and other foods when they have been stored for long periods in warm, damp conditions, notably in Africa and Asia, are an important cause of primary liver cancer. In Britain and other developed countries, the conditions in which food is stored are subject to careful regulation, and imported foods are checked for mycotoxin residues.

Additives and residues
When levels of additives, contaminants and other residues are properly regulated, their presence in food and drink is not known to be harmful. However, unregulated or improper use can be a health hazard, and this applies particularly in economically developing countries

Ask most people to say something about diet and cancer, and the chances are that they will refer to the dangers of cancer-causing chemicals in food, and will be thinking of the pesticides and other chemicals used on farms. It is very commonly thought that many industrial and agricultural chemicals that enter the food chain and are be found in food, generally in minute quantities, are important causes of cancer. This is unlikely. It is also unlikely that other chemicals which are deliberately added to food to preserve it, or as colourings, or flavourings, are important in causing cancer.

Among these additives and contaminants are pesticides, herbicides and other agricultural chemicals known to be toxic when people are victims of industrial accidents or as a result of overuse or abuse. Some of these chemicals, very small amounts of which can be detected in food, have been classified by an international organisation, the International Agency for Research in Cancer, based in Lyon, France, as Class 1 carcinogens (known to be carcinogenic to humans) or as Class 2A or 2B (probably or possibly carcinogenic to humans).

Overuse and abuse of toxic chemicals, or industrial accidents in which large amounts of such chemicals are released into the environment including the food chain, are of course likely to be a human health hazard. But the panel responsible for the WCRF report, in common with other panels responsible for assessing the evidence, concluded that in countries like Britain, where the presence of chemicals in food is effectively monitored, there is little evidence from studies of humans that these significantly affect human cancer risk.

Indeed, there is an argument that pesticides and other biocides actually protect against human cancer, by making vegetables and fruits readily available and generally affordable all year round.

The fact is that much of the evidence showing that chemicals such as pesticides increase the risk of cancer has been obtained by dosing animals with quantities of these substances vastly in excess of any amount likely to be found in food. This is not necessarily evidence of any risk to humans,

partly because people are not rats, and also because the human body is equipped to break down and neutralise the small amounts of carcinogenic substances that food naturally contains.

Overuse, abuse and spillage is another matter. There is always a possibility of accidental contamination of food by abnormal quantities due to accidents at the farm or faulty processing in the factory. Monitoring and enforcement of safety limits for chemical contaminants and additives need to be maintained. At present, however, the best evidence is that when levels of additives and contaminants in food are properly regulated their presence in food is not known to affect cancer risk.

In spite of this, we should not be complacent. There are not many studies of the relationship between the additives and contaminants in our food, as we eat them, and the risk of cancer, nor do we know much about the long-term effects, or the so-called 'cocktail effect' of mixtures of various additives and contaminants in our foods. These are all areas that need research in the future.

Good cooking

Preparation
Do not eat charred food. For meat and fish eaters, avoid burning of meat juices. Consume the following only occasionally: meat and fish grilled in direct flame; cured and smoked meats

Meat and fish that have been grilled or barbecued may increase the risk of cancer of the stomach. Diets including a lot of 'well-done' red meat, and meat and other foods that have been grilled, barbecued or fried may increase the risk of colorectal cancer. The best advice is to use direct-flame methods of cooking meat and fish only occasionally, and to

Is 'organic' food better for you?

It is commonly thought that chemical contamination of foods and drinks is a significant cause of human cancer. This is unlikely. This view is derived partly from the mistaken belief that cancer is caused by exposure to single carcinogenic agents.

Fear of the effects of these chemicals in food is understandable because they are not meant to be present. Some are very toxic in high concentrations, and some cause tumours or genetic damage when given to experimental animals in very high doses – far in excess of any amounts normally found in food. Some of these chemicals are known to accumulate in fat-containing foods, in human fatty tissues and in breast milk. Chemicals dumped in rivers or seas may also accumulate in fish and seafood.

Expert reports which assess the role of these chemicals in human cancer risk compared with the diet as a whole have generally come to the view that, in foods, these chemicals are relatively unimportant. At present, there is no substantial evidence from studies of humans that chemicals found in food and drink increase the risk of cancer.

The market for organic produce depends on the public belief that the threat from chemicals is real, and that it is worth paying extra for organic food which contains less of them. Organic food is produced by farmers under strict rules without the use of fertilisers, pesticides or other chemicals, and by less intensive farming methods. Organic food varies in its composition from food produced by established methods of intensive farming: it should contain lower levels of artificial chemicals than food produced in the usual way; and it may also have a different taste, which some people prefer (it is often said that food produced by 'extensive' farming methods is tastier). However, there is no definitive scientific evidence to suggest that organic foods are preferable on health grounds.

---

discard any part of the meat, fish or other food that is burned or charred.

Curing and smoking foods have both been used for centuries as ways of preserving fresh food. Now food can be kept fresh by refrigeration we eat much less cured and smoked food – mostly as delicacies. Cured and smoked foods, such as smoked fish, ham, bacon, salamis and sausages, contain nitrous compounds – a group of chemicals known to be carcinogenic. And, of course, cured meats are often also very salty. Eating a lot of cured meats may increase the risk of colorectal cancer. Again, the best advice is to eat less of these foods.

Low-temperature methods of cooking such as steaming, boiling, poaching, stewing, and other methods such as braising, baking, microwaving or roasting, are the best. Grilling meat is often recommended for the prevention of heart disease because it allows fat to drip from the meat and so may reduce overall fat intake. Grill food lightly under an electric grill or regular gas grill (which has an indirect flame), but avoid burning or charring it. Fry food lightly, but again avoid burning or charring the food. If you are keen on barbecues there are some exceptions: whole fish may be barbecued if the burned skin is discarded before eating, and corn on the cob may be cooked in its leaves on a barbecue (discard the burnt leaves before eating it).

No need to supplement

Dietary supplements
For those who follow the recommendations presented here, dietary supplements are probably unnecessary, and possibly unhelpful, for reducing cancer risk

The diets recommended here provide all the vitamins, minerals and other micronutrients the body needs for general good health. Most of these come from the vegetables, fruits and cereals we eat. We know that vegetables and fruits, rich sources of vitamins, minerals and many other compounds, protect against cancer, and there is good evidence that diets with plenty of vitamin C and carotenoids help prevent cancer. So you might well suppose that taking these micronutrients as dietary supplements – in the form of pills and powders – might also prevent cancer. However, a careful look at the scientific evidence suggests that it is always best if the nutrients we need come from foods and drinks. Indeed, large human trials in which some micronutrients were taken as supplements have even shown evidence of increased cancer risk.

Attempts to help prevent lung cancer, for example, by giving people antioxidant vitamins in the form of pills have ended by increasing rather than decreasing the risk of disease or death. In Finland 29,000 male smokers were given either a daily pill containing beta-carotene and vitamin E, or a daily dummy pill. After six years, when the results of the trial were studied, it was found that there were 18 per cent more deaths from lung cancer among the men who took the vitamin pill, and the overall mortality of those who took the vitamin pill was 8 per cent greater. Another trial of beta-carotene and vitamin A taken as a pill by 18,000 men and women was stopped early after four years when it was found that the pill increased the risk of lung cancer by 18 per cent and the overall mortality by 17 per cent.

Why this should be is not yet clear. Taking beta-carotene, or some other vitamins, in the form of a pill may prevent the absorption of other similar but more important micronutrients from the diet. Or an abnormally high intake of beta-carotene, or of vitamins E or A, may preserve cancer cells that would otherwise die.

The best advice is that we get the vitamins, minerals and other micronutrients we need from the foods in healthy balanced diets.

What about poultry, fish, milk, dairy produce...?

You will see that not every food and drink we may regularly consume is included in the recommendations. This is simply because, for many foods and drinks, the evidence from human studies is limited or, in some cases, confusing. The best advice, again, is to use common sense, within the general framework of the recommendations.

Poultry, fish and game

Take poultry such as chicken, fish, and game animals and birds, for example. There is not much evidence that these foods of animal origin either decrease or increase the risk of any cancer, because most human studies have researched the red meats – beef, lamb and pork – and foods containing red meats. But there is some reason to believe that poultry, fish and game are better choices than red meat.

Domesticated poultry is generally less fatty (especially if the skin is discarded before eating), and game and fish are generally higher in unsaturated fats. The flesh of animals, birds and fish that were active when alive, running, flying and swimming free, is generally much lower in fat than the flesh of domesticated animals. Also, eating fish regularly is recommended as a protection against heart disease.

So does this mean that it is OK to eat up to 80 grams (3 ounces) of red meat a day and also to eat lots of other meats, birds and fish? No: because the recommendations should be taken together, and the key recommendation is to enjoy diets based on foods of plant origin. On the whole, we should eat poultry, fish and game instead of red meat.

Milk and dairy products and eggs

The same kind of common sense applies to dairy produce such as milk, cheese and butter, and to eggs. Again, there is not much evidence linking these foods with cancer: milk and dairy products may increase the risk of prostate and kidney cancers, and eggs may increase the risk of colorectal cancer. Cholesterol, of which eggs are the main source in our diets, may increase the risk of lung and pancreatic cancers. Diets high in saturated fat possibly increase the risk of a number of cancers, and dairy foods, in common with red meat, contain a lot of saturated fat. Diets that are a lot lower in fat than typical British diets, and diets low in fat and saturated fat are also recommended as protection against heart disease. So limit consumption of eggs and of dairy foods, and always choose low- and no-fat varieties of dairy foods.

Burgers, cakes, biscuits, chocolate, confectionery . . .

Advice on meat and fat of course also applies to meat, and other, products that are high in fat, such as pies, pasties, sausages and burgers. Advice on fat and sugar also applies to foods that are fatty and/or sugary, like the snack foods so common in Britain – cakes, biscuits, chocolate and confectionery, and sugared soft drinks. Eating or drinking these once in a while is, of course, no problem but, in general, the less of such foods and drinks you consume, the better. Remember that manufacturers exploit the body's natural desire for fat, sugar and also for salt. It can be a bit of a struggle, consuming less of these foods, or cutting them out of your diet, and it may take three or more months to change to and enjoy a diet low in fat, sugar and salt, but you will feel better for it.

Nuts and seeds

There is very little research on whether nuts and seeds affect the risk of cancer. This is partly because they usually form a very small part of our diets, and so no effect one way or the other can be detected. Nuts and seeds are fatty, but they are also full of nourishment from vitamins, minerals and other bioactive compounds, and their fat is generally very unsaturated. So, on the whole, nuts and seeds are fine.

Coffee and tea and other drinks

It was once thought that coffee might increase the risk of cancer of the kidney and bladder. There is some evidence that heavy coffee drinking (more than five cups a day) may increase the risk of bladder cancer, but on the whole, the best evidence now is good news for moderate coffee drinkers. There is also some evidence that regular consumption of green tea (the tea that the Chinese drink regularly with their meals and that is served in Chinese restaurants) may reduce the risk of stomach cancer; generally though, tea drinking seems to be unrelated to cancer risk. Certainly, coffee and tea are better choices than alcoholic drinks.

There is little information specifically on soft drinks, and artificial sweeteners such as saccharin and cyclamates – once thought to increase cancer risk – are probably harmless. However, many soft drinks also have a lot of added sugar. Avoid these and choose the 'diet' varieties, which are also preferable to alcohol.

Don't smoke tobacco

Tobacco
Do not smoke or chew tobacco

Strictly speaking, a report on food, nutrition and cancer might contain no reference to smoking or other uses of tobacco. However, smoking is the chief cause of lung cancer, and a major cause of heart and blood vessel disease.

Smoking is also the most important single cause of cancer of the mouth and throat, and acts synergistically with alcohol. Alcohol by itself is a cause of mouth and throat cancers, as is smoking (and other uses of tobacco), and 'synergistically' means that the risk of these cancers is multiplied when drinkers also smoke.

So it is not really possible to separate tobacco from dietary factors. Besides, smoking tobacco is such a major cause of cancers that any report on diet which excluded reference to tobacco might appear to be minimising its importance. Smoking also contributes to cancers of the pancreas, cervix and bladder, and is a major cause of bronchitis and emphysema.

Smoking is responsible for some 100,000 deaths annually in the UK. Diets containing plenty of vegetables and fruits provide some protection against lung cancer, and smokers who will not or cannot give up will benefit from the dietary advice given here, but smoking is extremely damaging to health. Of all the measures that may be taken to improve general good health and protect against disease, not smoking, or stopping smoking, will give most benefit to most people.

4 You are what you eat

WE NOW KNOW that what we habitually eat and drink – our diet – is crucial in determining our risk of suffering serious disease, in particular heart disease and many cancers. We know too that not only food and drink, but also other factors associated with diet, in particular how much we weigh – our body mass – and how physically active we are in our everyday lives, affect cancer risk.

This broader approach to food and nutrition makes sense. Obviously, our body mass is itself partly determined both by the amount of food and drink we habitually consume, and by our level of physical activity. The more active people are, the more they can eat and drink without gaining weight, whereas people who are very inactive may consume only small amounts of food and drink and yet become fat.

There are other reasons for reviewing the scientific evidence on body mass and on physical activity. First, there is good evidence that high body mass, which is the scientist's polite way of referring to overweight and obesity, itself increases the risk of a number of diseases, including some cancers. So it is important to establish what dietary patterns make it more likely that you will become overweight. Second, there is also evidence that physical activity reduces the risk of a number of diseases, including heart disease, and conclusive evidence that people who are active throughout life are less likely to suffer from colon cancer, the second most common cancer among both men and women in Britain.

This chapter tells you about the World Cancer Research Fund's recommendations on weight and physical activity, and how by making changes to our lifestyle we can become fitter and healthier.

Weight control

Keep your weight in check
Avoid being overweight, and limit weight gain during adulthood to less than 5 kilograms (11 pounds)

This recommendation is a goal for most people in countries like Britain. Scientists use a term called the Body Mass Index (or BMI) to describe whether people are the right weight for the best possible health, or if they are overweight, or underweight. Your BMI depends not only on your weight, but also on how tall you are. The box over the page explains how to calculate your own BMI. We are an ideal weight when our BMI is between 18.5 and 25.

It has been established for a long time that obese women are more likely to suffer from cancer of the womb (the endometrium). Being overweight probably also increases the risk of breast cancer in women after the menopause, and also kidney cancer; and overweight people may be more likely to suffer from cancer of the colon.

To calculate your Body Mass Index (BMI)

BMI = Weight (in kilograms)/
[Height (in metres) x Height (in metres)]

You need to know your weight in kilograms (W), and your height in metres (H).

Divide your weight by your height (W divided by H).

Divide the result again by your height (H). The result is your BMI.

The risk of heart disease, high blood pressure, diabetes (of adult onset) and gallstones are all increased by being overweight. The combination of being overweight and physically inactive is now thought by leading scientists to cause a series of diseases known cryptically as 'Syndrome X'. The theory, backed by a lot of evidence, is that chronic energy imbalance, which shows itself as overweight and obesity, also upsets our body chemistry in a number of ways, including causing abnormally high levels of fat, sugar and insulin in the blood. Excess energy in the diets of overweight people may also boost the growth and division of the cells in our bodies. This combination of factors may create conditions that promote cancer, notably hormone-related cancers such as breast cancer and cancer of the womb. Being overweight may increase cancer risk in other ways too: people who are overweight may store carcinogens in their body fat and so cells throughout the body are at risk for a longer period.

Why does excess body fat promote breast cancer? Female hormones are produced in fat tissue and so fat women are likely to have more female hormone circulating in their bodies. This extra female hormone increases the growth of cancer cells in the breast and womb, an effect which is most obvious in women after the menopause when overweight is directly linked to an increase in the risk of breast cancer.

Being both overweight and physically inactive seems to increase the risk of cancer in general. Studies in the USA show that men who are obese are 30 per cent more likely to die from cancer than men of average weight. The figure for women is even more striking: obese women in the USA are 50 per cent more likely to die from cancer.

It is not only obesity but also being overweight that increases the risk of chronic diseases. The risk of some cancers and of heart disease and other serious diseases is well known to increase when people are obese, with a BMI of above 30, and even more among grossly obese people with a BMI above 40. The risk of cancer also increases among people who are overweight while not being obese: those with a BMI between 25 and 30. It is of course also true that relatively young people who are overweight are liable to become obese later in life. All in all, it is best to maintain a BMI between 18.5 and 25 and, better still, between 21 and 23.

So the best advice for reducing the risk of cancer and other serious diseases is to maintain a healthy body weight throughout life.

There is another factor that relates to our risk of cancer – how much weight we put on in our adult lives. Weight *gain* itself, independently of body mass, probably increases the risk of breast cancer: that is to say, a woman who is slim when young and becomes overweight (short of obese) in later life, is more likely to suffer breast cancer. There is some suspicion that this may be true of other cancers too. So, as well as maintaining a healthy body weight, we should also avoid gaining more than 5 kilograms (11 pounds) in adult life.

How plant-based foods reduce hunger

The plant-based diets recommended here help reduce hunger in at least two ways. The high levels of fibre and water found in vegetables, fruits and cooked starchy staples make what we eat more filling and so more satisfying. Also, the energy in relatively unprocessed foods is released gradually, maintaining blood sugar at a more regular level.

When sweetened foods, or even fruit juices, are consumed, a rapid increase occurs in the level of sugar in the blood, and this level declines again fairly rapidly. When you eat sweetened foods you are liable to feel hungry again quite soon after eating.

On the other hand, when whole bulky foods like foods from cereals, such as wholegrain bread, rice and pasta, or pulses such as beans or lentils, are eaten blood sugar rises more slowly and the rise lasts longer. Whole foods and complex starches provide energy over a longer period and satisfy the appetite for longer. So do bananas, a favourite food of Wimbledon champions.

The starch and sugar in vegetables and fruits is contained within plant cells that have to be broken down by digestive enzymes in the stomach and colon before all the energy is released. And much of the energy in cereals and other starchy foods is not digested until it reaches the colon, where bacteria break down the complex carbohydrates. The slow journey through the colon takes some hours. Digestion proceeds slowly and energy is released steadily into the circulation over this period of time. In this way whole foods maintain blood sugar at a relatively high level between meals: we have less desire to eat snacks.

Suppose you have already gained more than 5 kilograms since you were twenty? This is true for many people, and probably for most people who have tried to lose weight. This doesn't mean that you are doomed – of course not: it is never too late to follow sensible dietary recommendations, just as it is never too late to stop smoking.

The number of people in Britain who are overweight has increased in the last two generations, and has increased more rapidly in the 1980s and 1990s. There are two simple reasons for this. First, most people are becoming less and less active. A generation or two ago, most children walked to school: no longer. The television and computer games generation tends to take little exercise. Adults, too, are less and less active. (There is more about the need for physical activity later in this chapter.)

Second, the food and drinks we regularly consume are becoming 'calorie-dense', that is, they contain more and more calories (energy) per unit of weight. And this calorie-dense food is usually fatty and/or sugary, and is often a poor source of the fibre, vitamins, minerals and other dietary constituents that are vital for health and as protection against disease.

Biscuits, cakes, pastries, chocolate, confectionery, sugared soft drinks, meat pies and sausages, and bread with sweet spreads are all obvious examples of calorie-dense foods often eaten as snacks as well as at meals.

Indeed, any diets that include few vegetables and fruits and only small amounts of starchy foods like potatoes, rice and pasta, will be calorie-dense. Calorie-dense diets provide a lot of calories in a small volume and they have little bulk. People who eat these diets are much more likely to put on weight, to become overweight and obese and, as a result, to be at higher risk of a number of serious diseases.

No need to count calories

You don't have to count calories in order to lose weight. For half of all slimmers, the most popular way to lose weight is to avoid certain foods and drinks (according to a MORI poll undertaken for *The Sunday Times*). Most slimmers also found avoiding certain foods to be the *best* method. Only one in seven slimmers tries counting calories, and this works for only half of them!

Most slimmers avoid sweet and fatty foods, as recommended here. However, some cut out starchy foods: this is bad for health and not effective. When we cut out starchy foods we lose water normally retained in the body. Because water is heavy the loss in weight during the first week or so encourages slimmers to believe they are making progress. Unfortunately this weight is put on immediately they start eating a normal diet again.

One in seven men who slim finds that cutting down on alcoholic drinks is an effective way of slimming. Fewer women find this is effective – perhaps because they are less likely to be drinking regularly.

A third of slimmers tried taking more exercise and an encouraging two-thirds of these found that it was an effective way of losing weight, according to the MORI poll. This is particularly important, because in the past slimmers have often been given the advice not to bother with exercise.

How to get to the right weight and stay there

The first tip is to start to follow the goals for healthy diets that we recommend in Chapter 3. Use the recipes in Section 2 to help you. If you are overweight, the increased bulk of this diet will help you to lose excess fat, but the change will not happen immediately. Maybe you have put on the extra fat over ten years or more. Be kind to your body, and be prepared to take a few months losing the fat. Aim for no more than half a kilogram (about 1 pound) a week.

For most people, the secret of losing excess body fat is not to eat less food, but to improve the quality of the food eaten, and to become more physically active. High-quality food is mostly of plant origin: include plenty of vegetables and fruits, cereals and pulses in your diets. Low-quality diets, that tend to make you fat and also increase your risk of heart disease and cancer, are high in calories and low in nourishment.

Unfortunately, much of the food that is most convenient to eat is high in fat and/or sugar and is calorie-dense. Part of the secret of a healthy life is to avoid these foods. This is often easier said than done, because food manufacturers have found ways to take advantage of our natural hungers for fat, sugar and salt; and alcohol, of course, is or at least can be addictive.

Eating and drinking are social and emotional activities; another reason why attempts to lose weight by trying to change your diet often do not work. It is all too easy to go along with what other people are eating and drinking, and when. However, if you become more active, your body fat will decrease even while you are eating the same amount of food. You may even find you eat more – of the healthy and nutritious foods, of course.

A lot of people can lose weight by eating fewer snacks, by putting less food on their plate, and by avoiding second helpings. But some of us have much less regular eating habits. If we reduce the amount we eat at one meal it seems that we just eat more later in the day, or after two or three days we have a binge. Here are some tips for those of us who find it difficult to change our habits.

● Do you eat snacks all day and then persuade yourself that you have not eaten anything? Aim to eat three meals a day and to plan any snacks.

● Do you eat sensibly at regular times but find you aren't able to stop? Aim to eat more slowly and avoid second helpings.

● Do you eat or drink more when you are anxious, hurt, angry, depressed, bored or excited? Find another way of dealing with your feelings. Instead of eating or drinking, relieve boredom with activity, and relieve stress or anxiety with exercise or relaxation. Learn to handle anxiety and anger by being carefully assertive.

● Learn to skip courses in restaurants, organise fruit snacks for hungry moments, avoid people who are going to encourage you to eat or drink too much, or at least make sure you don't meet them in a restaurant.

● If particular foods such as chocolate are too tempting, then keep them out of the house and ask people not to give them to you.

● Do you drink alcohol with meals and find you drink too much? Always have water on the table, and have a non-alcoholic drink at the beginning of the meal to quench your thirst.

● If leftovers are a temptation for you, make sure they go straight into a soup, into the freezer, the fridge or the bin.

● Read labels on food so that you learn which foods have the most calories and contain a lot of fat and/or sugar.

● Do not just blame yourself for constant nibbling. Work out exactly what you have eaten – is it two or ten snacks during the day? Decide that you are going to cut your snacks down by a specific number and which snacks you will leave out in future.

● If you drink alcohol, don't be vague and just say you will drink less. Limit yourself to one drink today, tomorrow and the next day.

● Keep eating separate from other activities. Do not snack while watching tv or reading or while you are rushing around doing something else. Eating should be a deliberate activity so you can keep track of what you are doing. Try to sit down and eat in a leisurely way, even if it is only a snack.

● If you find you are eating fast, and usually finish your food ahead of companions, try putting down the utensils and pausing from time to time. Give yourself time to chew more thoroughly.

● Learn to leave food on your plate. This means not only that you will eat less but you will master your food. It is important to have a sense of control over what you are eating, to be able to take it or leave it. Leaving some means you are no longer a victim of your own impulses, or of other people trying to persuade you to eat or drink too much.

As well as changing what you eat, start to increase your physical activity – see the next part of this chapter. This will increase your energy consumption and should reduce the amount of energy you store as fat. Become more interested in your shape than your weight. Lean tissue contains a lot of water and is heavier than fat: if you are naturally fit and able to become much more physically active quite quickly, you may well find that your waist and other measurements decrease, and skirts or trousers that were tight become comfortable, even without you losing weight.

The special case of breast cancer

Reviewing the evidence on the relationship between body size, weight and breast cancer has needed special care for a number of reasons.

Breast cancer, like some other cancers that are now very common in Britain, is more common in economically developed countries. When women migrate from countries

How and why vegetables and fruits are naturally satisfying

Vegetables and fruits are excellent snacks for everybody, and for people who want to lose excess body fat in particular. They are bulky, usually contain plenty of fibre when eaten whole, and are digested slowly. They fill you up, whereas calorie-heavy, fatty or sugary foods are less satisfying and indeed often make you hungry for more.

The fact that bulky whole foods are satisfying has been demonstrated dramatically by Dr Kenneth Heaton and colleagues at Bristol University. They gave ten volunteers either a whole apple, or the same amount of apple made into a purée or into juice. It took the volunteers an average of seventeen minutes to eat an apple, six minutes to eat the purée and only one and a half minutes to drink the juice.

The volunteers said that the whole apples were the most satisfying, and Dr Heaton found a good reason for this when he checked the volunteers' blood sugar levels. Their blood sugar rose whether they had had juice, purée or a whole apple. For those who drank apple juice, insulin in the blood rose to twice the level for those who ate a whole apple. About two hours later the blood sugar of the volunteers who ate whole apples was back to normal but, for those who had drunk the juice, the blood sugar level had plummeted below normal, to a level that the body is designed to associate with hunger.

This classic experiment shows that whole foods take longer to eat and longer to digest, and they maintain the blood sugar at a high level for longer, and so are more satisfying. Foods and drinks consumed in a refined or extracted form are less satisfying and can actually create hunger. This is, of course, no secret to snack food and drink manufacturers!

Other whole foods such as wholegrain bread or pasta, pulses such as beans and lentils, and of course whole or minimally processed starchy fruits, roots and tubers also have this healthy effect on the body and therefore are very sustaining foods.

Vegetables and fruits are an ideal snack because they have a very low calorie-density: around 35 calories per 100 grams on average. And as well as being high in fibre, they are usually rich in vitamins and minerals and other compounds that may protect against diseases including cancer.

where the rates of breast cancer are low, to countries where rates are high, in time they – or their daughters – are more likely to suffer from breast cancer, and eventually their risk of breast cancer is much the same as that of the country they have moved to. This suggests that environmental factors like diet and lifestyle are closely related to the risk of breast cancer.

Breast cancer is a special case for other reasons too. For many years scientists have known that the risk of breast cancer is higher among women whose first periods (menarche) started early in life, and also among women who grew quite quickly when they were girls. For this reason, tall woman are generally more likely to suffer breast cancer. Until recently these factors were not considered part of the diet and cancer story, but they are: a key factor that determines age at menarche and speed of growth in early life is diet.

The average age of girls at the time of their first period has been declining in economically developed countries such as Europe and the USA since at least the beginning of the century; and at the same time the incidence of breast cancer has been increasing. In Britain now, in common with the USA, girls' periods usually start around the age of twelve or thirteen, whereas, in parts of the world like rural China, where breast cancer is uncommon, girls begin their periods much later, between the ages of fifteen and seventeen. There is reliable evidence that this later time of sexual maturity is more biologically natural: less than 200 years ago girls in Britain and other European countries had their first periods at the age of fifteen or even older.

The diets of babies, younger children and pre-adolescents, like the diets that most adults eat in countries like Britain, are high in fat, sugar, and foods of animal origin that are high in protein. Such diets were recommended for babies and children until the 1950s and 1960s, because the acute public health problems before the 1939–1945 war were those now more often associated with Africa and Asia – under-nutrition leading to small, weak adults and even to deficiency diseases such as rickets. Diets high in fat and animal protein do indeed promote growth in early life. But these very same diets probably also promote chronic diseases such as heart disease and cancer later in life.

Why this should be is not yet fully understood. In the case of breast cancer, it is fairly likely that the relatively high levels of hormones circulating in the body of women who are bigger and taller, and whose period of sexual fertility is longer, increases growth of cells in the breast and therefore makes cancer more likely. As a simple analogy, it may be that girls who become sexually mature early, whose bodies grow fast, and who therefore become bigger, taller adults, have a greater risk of cancer, rather as a car constantly driven with the foot on the clutch and accelerator is more likely to burn out.

Why should rapid growth in early life promote breast cancer in particular? The first steps towards cancer are changes (known as mutations) in DNA, the genetic material within each cell. Mutated, potentially malignant cells require a period of rapid growth to evolve into cancer cells. Thus the breast, and also the womb, that grow very rapidly during puberty, are particularly vulnerable to cancer. Premalignant 'seed' cells may become well established in these and some other body organs during this rapid phase of growth. However, these seed cells must undergo further changes before they turn into cancer cells, so it may be many years before they develop into malignant tumours.

These further stages towards cancer may occur when diets contain only small amounts of vegetables and fruits, and thus are deficient in dietary constituents such as antioxidants, that protect cells against mutation. The calorie-dense and protein-rich diets that promote growth in early life may also be relatively poor in vitamins, antioxidants and other micronutrients, thus providing the conditions under which potential cancer cells form and multiply rapidly.

The complicated links between body weight, height, diet and also exercise are best, though not fully, understood for breast cancer.

How physically active girls and women are also affects their body weight and the time of the first menstrual period. Girls who play a lot of active sports have their first period later than average, according to research from Germany. A number of other studies have found that women who are more physically active have less risk of developing breast cancer. One study of college athletes in the United States found that they are less likely than other college students to develop breast cancer. Another study found that women in more active occupations are less likely to develop breast cancer. It seems that sport or exercise may burn off excess energy, make girls slimmer, and reduce the risk of cancer cells becoming established in the body. Exercise may also decrease the growth of breast cancer cells by decreasing production of female hormones.

The evidence that breast cancer is a special case, as described here, makes a crucial difference to public health messages designed to prevent breast cancer. Put bluntly, because breast cancer risk is increased early in life, the women who need to be targeted are not adults but their daughters.

Activity and exercise

Keeping physically active
If occupational activity is low or moderate, take an hour's brisk walk or similar exercise daily, and also exercise vigorously for a total of at least one hour in a week

This recommendation is a goal for everyone who, probably like most of the readers of this book, have jobs that are essentially sedentary, whose travel is mostly in vehicles, and who mostly watch rather than participate in sports and entertainments. If we follow this recommendation we can be as physically active as people whose occupations involve regular physical work, while at the same time enjoying lifestyles that include working in offices, using our cars, having labour-saving machinery, and enjoying television and movies.

Our bodies are designed to be active throughout life, and a mass of research now shows that people who lead inactive lives are at higher risk of a number of diseases, including excess body fat (obesity) which itself further increases the risk of disease. Regular exercise helps to regulate metabolism, improves the function of the heart and the strength of muscles and bones. Lack of exercise leads to wasting of muscle and bone. In general, regular physical activity increases life expectancy while overweight reduces it.

It has been known for a long time that regular physical activity protects against coronary heart disease. We now also know

Case history

Everybody is different and everybody's circumstances are different, of course.

Here, for example, is what Geoffrey Cannon, the director of the project responsible for the WCRF report, does to build moderate physical activity into his everyday life. He lives and works in central London, and in the early 1990s realised that it was irrational for him to own a car. Most days he cycles to and from work, a round trip taking 35 minutes. Sometimes he walks briskly for 20 minutes to an underground station and, at the other end, walks up the escalator. At work he has made a vow never to use the lift, and walks up and down stairs to talk with colleagues in their offices. When he has appointments in central London, he usually walks. He makes a point of carrying bags of food on foot, or on his bicycle. Activity like this adds up, and as well as being fitter, he reckons that taken together, he is saving money, and also saving time, compared with a car-orientated working life.

from studies published in the 1980s and 1990s, that regular physical activity certainly protects against colon cancer, the second most common cancer in women, and the third most common cancer in men in Britain. Regular physical activity may also reduce the risk of lung cancer and breast cancer, the most common cancers respectively among British men and women.

One explanation for the benefit of physical activity in preventing colon cancer may be that it stimulates bowel action and emptying of the colon. As a result any carcinogens remain in the colon for a shorter time and so are less likely to induce cancer. Also, physical activity has a favourable action on the immune system, and on the level of hormones circulating in the body, which may also discourage growth of cancer cells.

Regular physical activity at work and play seems to protect against cancer in general. The benefit of exercise in reducing the risk of cancer in general may come from maintaining a higher proportion of lean tissue to body fat, which may discourage development of cancer cells. Physically active people are also able to consume more food and so obtain more nourishment from food.

People who are physically active are less likely to become overweight or obese. Readers may well think that this conclusion is common sense, and so it is: in countries where most work involves physical activity, like China, most overweight and obese people are found in the cities, where they live lifestyles similar to those we lead in Europe and North America. People who are physically fit and whose bodies contain a relatively high proportion of lean tissue burn energy from food faster than people who are sedentary and therefore physically unfit, and whose bodies therefore contain a relatively high proportion of fat. This relationship between being physically active and maintaining the right weight is important because, as already discussed in this chapter, high body mass certainly increases the risk of cancer of the womb, probably increases the risk of breast cancer after the menopause and of kidney cancer, and may also increase the risk of colon cancer.

What does the recommendation really mean, and how can you achieve it?

The goal includes both moderate and vigorous physical activity, and there is an important distinction between them. Put simply, much moderate physical activity, such as walking, cycling, dancing and housework, is usually done in normal everyday clothing, whereas for vigorous physical activity, whether exercise or sports, such as swimming, running, football, hockey, gym work or skiing, you usually need to wear special clothes.

Ways of walking for one hour

Some people will be able to get an hour's brisk walk each day by travelling to work and back on foot. This may take little more time than travelling by bus or train when time spent waiting is taken into account. Here are some other ways you can do it:

● Walk all the way to work – say half an hour – walk another half hour during the lunch period, and then take the bus or train home.
● Walk for half an hour in the lunch break and then take another half-hour walk just before going to bed.
● Get off the bus or train a stop or two before your destination and walk the rest of the way to work or home.

One of the reasons for the boom in aerobics and road running in the early 1980s was the overwhelming evidence that vigorous activity protects against heart disease, which indeed it does. But it's mostly only young and naturally fit people who are willing and able to build many hours of physical training into their lives. It is unrealistic to expect busy men and women with professional and domestic responsibilities to spend a lot of their spare time in the gym or on the road. Happily, in the 1990s it became apparent that moderate physical activity also reduces the risk of heart disease, and a number of important cancers. Normal able-bodied people, old as well as young, can reduce their risk of the most common killer diseases, by choosing to build regular walking, cycling or work in the house and garden into their lives.

Moderate activity

Maybe you are inactive and do not feel able to start because you are relatively overweight or unfit. Do not be put off by thinking that you

Additional weekly activity

There are many types of exercise and sport you can do for your additional hour of vigorous exercise each week. These are just some examples. Very vigorous activity can have the same effect in less than an hour.

1 hour of vigorous activity
- Swimming breaststroke (at about 40 m/min)
- Running (at about 8 km/h)
- Cycling (at about 18 km/h)
- Tennis
- Brisk hill walking (at about 6 km/h)
- Canoeing (at about 7 km/h)

45 minutes of more vigorous activity
- Swimming crawl (at about 50 m/min)
- Running (at about 10 km/h)
- Cycling (at about 21 km/h)
- Squash

30 minutes of very vigorous activity
- Running (at about 13 km/h)
- Cycling (at about 25 km/h)
- Basketball
- Soccer, Rugby, Handball

have to put on a track suit and work out. Walking is the simplest moderate physical activity. Walk briskly, within your limits. Brisk walking should bring on a light sweat and make you breathe faster. Check your heart-beat sometimes: you will find that it speeds up from maybe 70–80 beats a minute at rest, to 120–150 beats a minute immediately after your walk. If you are not used to any sort of exercise begin with a modest plan of just ten or twenty minutes walking a day and extend it gradually. If this is too much, begin with a few minutes and build it up slowly week by week.

The problem for many people, and particularly for those who are overweight, is to find a way to increase their physical activity without becoming too tired or even sustaining some injury, such as strained joints. For most sedentary people, walking for a whole hour a day at first is too much; and this amount of walking needs planning into your day.

Begin with a distance which is not too ambitious and repeat the distance daily for a week. Build walking into your daily routine. Walk some, most or all of the way to and from work; go for a walk in a local park at lunchtime; take the dog for longer walks at weekends: whatever works best for you. Bear in mind that it usually takes around three weeks to create new habits. Be patient with yourself! Wear comfortable flat shoes. Consider buying a pair of trainers that cushion the feet; these are ideal for walkers as well as runners. Shoes which have an air sole that absorbs vibration may be an advantage. This type of footwear is particularly helpful for people who suffer from pain in the legs or back. Good trainers are expensive but you will not regret the investment.

Plan walking routes that are as interesting as possible, and enjoy your exercise. After the first week gradually extend your walk. You will find that your stamina gradually increases as you do more. If you have sore muscles after walking do not worry. It shows that you are using them and that they are adapting to the new demands on them. If you rely on walking for your recommended moderate physical activity, you will eventually be walking for three or four miles a day.

Cycling is in many ways the best physical activity. It is a cheap, convenient and energy-saving alternative for relatively short-distance travel. The weight of the body is supported and the possibility of damage to the knees and hips is minimised; an important consideration for those who are overweight. More and more people now are cycling to and from work, most days, for round-trip distances of maybe five to twenty miles, taking maybe 20–75 minutes. Whether cycling counts as moderate or vigorous, of course depends on how fast you cycle! In general, the fitter and more skilled you are, the faster you can cycle, and the more calories you burn for any given length of time.

For most people, the main problem with cycling nowadays is the traffic on roads. Vehicles themselves are threatening to the inexperienced cyclist, and traffic fumes are noxious. Happily, many cities and towns in Britain, as well as in the USA and Europe, are responding to pressure from organisations representing the interests of cyclists, and are creating dedicated cycling paths not only in parks, but also in busy streets. This is an example of how reducing your risk of cancer and of heart disease involves you as a citizen as well as an individual. Cycling on a stationary cycle is also a good form of exercise. Cycling on a stationary bike appeals to some people because they can watch tv, listen to music or read at the same time. Stationary cycles can take up a lot of space at home, and a good one is expensive; try one out for a while at your local exercise centre before buying one.

Swimming is an excellent physical activity, particularly good for people who are overweight or have problems with joints, because it takes the weight off the legs and uses almost all of your muscles. People with arthritis find swimming especially beneficial because it helps make the joints more mobile. Even for those who cannot swim, exercise in a pool may be the best way forward if they have joint or weight problems. These pool exercises are done in the water holding on to the rail so that the body can be fully flexed in various ways while holding on. Join an exercise class at your local pool so that you can be taught the best exercises.

The secret of keeping physically active is to

Lesson of the Irish brothers

The amount of everyday activity a person engages in makes a great difference to the amount of food needed to fuel the body. This is shown by the story of more than 1,000 Irish brothers who have been studied as part of a major research project.

The Irish brothers were chosen in pairs. In all cases, one of the pair lived in Boston, Massachusetts, and the other brother lived in Ireland. The brothers living in Ireland consumed, on average, 700 calories more each day than their Boston brothers. Yet the brothers who were living in Ireland and eating more weighed on average 5 kilograms (11 pounds) less. Why? The reason was that the Irish brothers were physically more active than their Boston brothers. The lesson of the Irish brothers is that, when you are physically active, you can eat more and yet weigh less.

---

build it into your everyday life. Most books and magazine articles encouraging you to be active suggest that you have to find a lot of extra time every day for exercise, almost as if it is another job. The cleverer approach is to take every opportunity you have during each day to replace inactivity with activity.

The Health Education Authority and other expert bodies in Britain now confirm that moderate physical activity does indeed protect against disease; and also, that a recommendation for an hour's activity a day can be met by adding up short bouts of activity throughout the day. Activity can also include housework, gardening, dancing and actively playing with children. These are all things which many of us do anyway. Begin by making an audit of the time you spend, for example, walking around the house or garden, to the shops, or anywhere else. Note down all your physical activity and increase it at a rate that is comfortable for you. Using this approach you can increase your activity so that it remains a natural part of your life.

Vigorous activity

There's no exact division between moderate and vigorous physical activity. Walking becomes vigorous activity when you begin to jog and run. Swimming and cycling become vigorous when you are ready, willing and able to go fast. Likewise, skiing, dancing, and squash or badminton.

Once you begin to exercise vigorously, your metabolism begins to do some of the slimming for you. Calories are burnt up in muscles during exercise, and exercise also boosts the body's basal metabolic rate (the rate at which the body normally burns energy), so that 24 hours later the body is still using more calories than it would be if no exercise had been taken. This means that with regular exercise your raised basal metabolic rate will enable you to lose weight while eating the same amount of food, or else enable you to eat more food

without putting on weight.

If you continue with regular exercise, fat will be replaced by lean body tissue, and your body will burn more calories and produce more heat, because muscle tissue burns more calories than fat. Exercise has the extra advantage of producing a better body shape even if your weight changes comparatively little. This is because fat is being replaced by muscle which provides a firmer more attractive support to skin, particularly around the face, neck and hips.

Exercise is also good for mood. Substances called endorphins, which are similar to morphine, the opiate painkiller, are released in the body during exercise. These substances produce what has been called a 'runner's high' and marathon runners have been found to have particularly large amounts of endorphins in the blood. As you increase your physical activity you will notice it brings other benefits such as helping you to relax and sleep well.

SECTION 2
5 The best of all foods

OUR RECOMMENDATIONS are state of the art. If you adopt them your diet could not be more healthy. All you need now are practical suggestions and a strategy to make it easy. This section gives you lots of practical advice on choice of food, the best methods of cooking, healthy recipes, and a strategy.

The simplest way to see how our recommendations work in practice is by trying our recipes. The recommendations are not difficult to implement if you give as much thought to planning the vegetables and starchy staples in each meal, as you would to meat, fish or eggs. Begin by changing what you eat for breakfast. Most people choose their own breakfast and do not have to eat what someone else has chosen for them. Consider whether you should be eating a healthier breakfast (see page 71). Next, think about the snacks you eat (see page 73).

Many people eat a lot of snacks, and we each make our own choices. However, the key to changing to a healthy diet is what you eat at the main meals of the day. We suggest you decide on a strategy for putting our recommendations into practice.

Many of us have eaten foods from around the world in restaurants or from the variety now available in supermarkets. This chapter selects some of the best dishes from around the globe that meet our recommendations for a healthy diet. You might also like to choose a strategy for changing what you eat. Here are three:

Best of British
If you like an essentially British diet, stick to it but adapt it gradually to the recommendations. For example, put more vegetables and less meat in your Lancashire hotpot, look for vegetable side dishes to serve as extras with meat dishes, cut out sugary and high-fat desserts and serve fruit puddings instead.

The Mediterranean diet
If you like Mediterranean food, this is an easy strategy to implement. Mediterranean vegetables are in the shops all year round; pasta and rice are readily available. Use the recipes section as a starting point. Look on the back of pasta, rice and bean packets in the supermarket for more ideas. Italian food is probably the easiest to start with because we are all familiar with so many Italian pasta dishes.

Go global
Draw inspiration from some traditional diets that meet our recommendations. Chinese, Japanese and Indian cuisines, for example, contain a high proportion of rice, giving the emphasis we recommend to starchy staples in the diet. They also use a large variety of vegetables, together with herbs and spices, to make a relatively small amount of meat go a long way. Many healthy and attractive dishes are also found in the cooking of the Middle East, the place where wheat was first cultivated.

Whichever strategy you choose, make the changes slowly, step by step, so that you have time to adapt to changes in taste and to a bulkier diet. As your dietary fibre intake increases, also make sure you increase the amount you drink.

You may prefer just to look at our recipes and try some of them out. Study our recommendations and cooking advice and develop new recipes of your own. Think what you most like to eat, and check our recipes for new ideas. With experience you will see how our recipes implement our recommendations, and then you can experiment further.

Simple ways to change your diet now

● Eat a fresh fruit as part of your breakfast. Start with the fruit as you may not have room for it otherwise.
● Eat two vegetables with your main meal – and don't add any butter to them.
● Alter your snacking habits. Eat fresh or dried fruit instead of biscuits or crisps.
● Treat yourself to freshly squeezed orange juice, or other fruit juice, instead of alcoholic drinks.
● If you have a light takeaway lunch choose either a sandwich made with wholemeal bread and salad, or a boxed meal which includes a salad.

Changing diets – your own and your family's

If you cook the family food then you will be making the changes for yourself and your family. Change the family food cautiously – seduce rather than dictate. However delicious the new food, it will take your family a while to get used to it: gradualism is the answer. You

can begin by serving an extra vegetable dish, for example, with the favourite meat dish. Introduce a new flavouring in small amounts at first. Use your power as the cook wisely.

If others usually cook for you, you will need to persuade someone else to cook the healthier food you want to eat. You can make a start by changing what you put on your plate: ask for more vegetables and potatoes, and smaller portions of meat.

Forego any sweets and high-fat desserts. Choose some fruit if it's available or keep your own supply to have a snack later. Help the cook where you can. The best way is probably to get more involved and cook some weekend specials. And as a non-cook, change to a healthier breakfast and eat fruit as snacks – see suggestions for breakfast and snacks below.

Strategy 1: Best of British

Misleading ideas about protein and its importance in the diet suggested to British people during and after the two world wars that meat was more important in the diet than it really is. The emphasis placed by government advisers and teachers of nutrition on protein and meat fitted with the style of cooking which came to be seen as quintessentially British.

However there is another style of traditional British cooking which, at its best, makes good use of potatoes, and root and other vegetables, to produce simple but nourishing fare. When vegetables and meat are combined in a stew, for example, there does not need to be a lot of meat to make a successful dish. In the past ordinary people often could not afford to be as generous with meat as we have become now.

Classic English dishes can easily be adapted to meet our recommendations for healthy eating. Shepherd's pie, Lancashire hotpot,

Take care with salt

Most of us have too much salt in our diets and need to cut down. Most ready-prepared foods include quite a lot of salt. Cooks add salt to the majority of dishes during cooking. However, the amount of salt can be reduced in many dishes, or even left out altogether. Most people adapt quite quickly to a lower level of salt in food. Salt has not been listed as an ingredient in the recipes in this book because each cook will want to decide how much to add and may decide to omit it altogether. Use herbs and spices to season foods instead of salt wherever possible. Once you are used to a lower level of salt, prepared foods will taste too salty. Adding freshly cooked vegetables to the meal may help reduce the saltiness.

Cornish pasties, steak and kidney pie can all include more vegetables, less meat and plenty of starchy staples such as potatoes. Several recipes for these dishes are included in the recipe section.

Roast meat may also be included on a healthy menu, but choose poultry or meat from non-domesticated animals more often than red meat. If you do roast red meat, remove the roast from the oven while still on the rare side and serve a substantial vegetable side dish, as well as one or more boiled or steamed vegetables. Give each person smaller portions of meat, the meal will still be a success.

'Meat and two veg' makes a good meal provided the portions of vegetable are substantial and not overcooked (too often the vegetables are doused in butter in an attempt to make them more interesting). Some people take two veg to mean potato plus a vegetable. Potato is the starchy staple food in the meal, so you should serve two different vegetables as well as the potatoes.

Avoid English puddings made with suet, white flour and treacle – a combination of ingredients which provides the maximum amount of energy in the least healthy combination. Classic English desserts such as fruit crumble can easily be adapted to make them less sweet and less fat (see page 126), and summer pudding can now be served all year round (see page 127).

Our collection of recipes includes adaptations of a number of traditional English recipes. These classic English dishes can be altered without difficulty to meet our recommendations.

Strategy 2: The Mediterranean Diet

Broadly speaking, Mediterranean food is healthy, and if you follow a Mediterranean style of eating with our recommendations in mind, you can be doubly sure that you are eating the right diet. You may choose to use Mediterranean food as an occasional inspiration or choose to base most of your eating on the Mediterranean style.

Mediterranean food can be as simple or sophisticated as you like. It provides delicious dishes that can be made quickly as well as the more elaborate but still healthy dishes for special occasions. If there is a disadvantage in the Mediterranean diet it is that Mediterranean vegetables are more expensive in Britain, particularly in the winter. However, if you eat less meat, as will be the case if our recommendations are followed carefully, then a switch to a Mediterranean-style diet is unlikely to cost you more; you may even save money.

Mediterranean food has a long history, going back at least 4,000 years to the Minoan civilisation of Crete where the giant jars that were used by the Minoans for storing olive oil

Reduce the amount of fat you eat

Most of us have far more fat in our diets than is recommended: we need to eat less of it. Diets high in fat possibly increase the risk of certain cancers and increase the likelihood of becoming overweight, as well as increasing the risk of heart disease. Fat contains more calories in a given weight than other types of food: if it is replaced weight for weight by other foods, calorie intake will fall. The type of fat eaten is also important to the prevention of cancer and heart disease. In general vegetable oils and soft margarine should be preferred to animal fats. But remember it is important to reduce the overall amount of fatty foods we eat, even if the fat is of vegetable origin.

● Milk is a major source of fat. This is because we tend to consume it in quite large amounts, rather than because it is a high-fat food. Use semi-skimmed or skimmed milk instead of whole milk. If you eat a lot of yoghurt, choose low-fat varieties, and eat cream only occasionally.

● Meat and meat products contribute very significant amounts of fat in the diet. Choose lean meat that is not marbled with fat and eat no more than the recommended daily amount of meat, 80 grams or 3 ounces cooked weight.

● Reduce the amount of butter or margarine you use on bread, toast or biscuits. Alternatively use a low-fat spread – but still only sparingly. Often you don't need a spread at all, for example for baked beans on toast, or bread with soup.

● Whenever possible make jumbo chips rather than French fries. Jumbo chips, made by quartering potatoes lengthways, are delicious and absorb much less fat when cooked. Try oven chips (which can also be cooked under the grill) which have a much lower fat content than deep-fried chips.

● Reduce the amount of cakes, biscuits, croissants and pastries that you eat because they often contain a lot of added fat. Eat bread, fruit and vegetables instead.

● Use low-fat methods of cooking (see cooking methods).

● Choose a vegetable oil such as rapeseed or olive oil for cooking (see page 68).

● Choose ready-prepared meals carefully. By reading the labels and comparing them with similar products, you can choose the ones with a lower fat content.

can still be seen today. However, many of the foodstuffs that we think of now as Mediterranean have their origin in South and Central America. These include such staples as potatoes and maize, as well as tomatoes, peppers and various types of beans. Other foods such as rice and citrus fruits came to Greece from the East long after the classical period. So the Mediterranean cuisine has evolved, constantly experimenting with new foods and adding them to its repertoire. This has been possible because the Mediterranean climate provides a long, hot growing season which allows both temperate and tropical foods to be grown.

Over thousands of years, migrants carried their food and their agricultural experience all round the borders of the Mediterranean sea.

Greeks established cities in Italy, North Africa and Asia Minor, where they learnt from local people and carried the new ideas to friends and relatives in other places. Nevertheless distinctive styles of Mediterranean food have developed in different countries. Rice has a primary place in Spanish food, just as pasta has the first place in Italian food, while for the Greeks bread and cracked wheat (bulgur, burghul or pourgouri) are generally more important.

Medical evidence tells us that the everyday diets of Greece, southern Italy, southern France and southern Spain are all healthy and so we may choose dishes from any of these countries. Although Albania is the poorest country in Europe, it has an unusually healthy adult population, particularly in the olive-producing regions. There is a high mortality among young children in Albania because of poor control and treatment of infectious diseases, but after that the average Albanian, despite great poverty, is likely to live longer than the average northern European. With this thought in mind it makes sense to try out the Albanian national dish, raisin pilaff.

What do these countries have in common that makes their food so healthy? Olive oil, tomatoes, garlic, onions, herbs and plentiful vegetables all come to mind immediately.

The healthiest diet is the simple diet of Mediterranean peasants who are making the best of the food they grow for themselves. Meals are often very simple, consisting of just one dish such as soup. In many Mediterranean households soup is served several times a week and, eaten with quantities of crusty fresh bread, is often the main dish. These soups use the fresh vegetables that happen to be at hand, and leftovers.

Minestrone soup or ratatouille served with crusty fresh baked bread, fresh pasta with a delicious home-made tomato sauce and a sprinkling of cheese, or a generous dish of macaroni and beans (*pasta e fagioli*) are the staple dishes of the southern Italian peasant. Such dishes, made in the proper way with fresh ingredients and with correct seasoning, will delight the most sophisticated palate as well as being enjoyed by hungry schoolchildren. Eaten with bread, these dishes provide plenty of unprocessed starch, plenty of vegetables, and are relatively low in fat.

But we must remember that eating Mediterranean food does not provide an automatic passport to health. Some people living in Greece, southern Italy, Spain or France die of heart disease, breast cancer and other conditions that the Mediterranean diet generally makes less likely. This is because in cities everywhere people turn to a richer, more international, more convenient type of diet. Many middle-class Italians in the south have begun to choose a more northern Italian or more international cuisine, to eat more meat, more fat and fewer vegetables and starchy staples. As a result their risk of getting cancer or heart disease is increasing. If we adopt a Mediterranean diet we must take care to select the traditional dishes which comply with our recommendations.

Fruit is the traditional dessert in Mediterranean countries. Ice-cream, creamy cakes and sweet desserts are occasionally offered on special occasions but are usually eaten as treats between meals. Greek rice pudding (see recipe page 131) can be recommended, and there are recipes which include fruit. Cakes and biscuits have little place in the Mediterranean diet; they do not have to be excluded completely from a Mediterranean diet, but they should not be eaten every day. Home-made cakes and biscuits often have a much lower fat content than bought ones.

Strategy 3: Go Global

Explore different types of food from countries round the world to find a style that you enjoy. You may find it much easier to eat a healthy diet if you adapt your present eating style more radically and cook in an entirely different way. Alternatively you may just want to build up a larger repertoire of healthy recipes harvested from the kitchens of the world.

Certain styles of cookery lend themselves naturally to the production of healthy food. Chinese cookery, for example, is easily learnt and is adapted to producing the kind of diet recommended. Cooking in a wok is an excellent way of preparing vegetables with the small quantities of meat or seafood which are used to add flavour and nutritional value to rice or noodles, a Chinese type of pasta. Noodles are made from a wider variety of ingredients than European pasta: they may be based on rice, wheat, buckwheat or mung beans.

The four styles of cooking discussed here are excellent vehicles for a healthy diet. Chinese food is well liked and lends itself easily to healthy proportions of meat or fish, vegetables and rice. Indian food, because of its exotic spices, provides a range of new and exciting vegetable dishes. Japanese food is very different, and will seem unusual for cooks from other traditions. Middle Eastern food is immediately attractive and easy for us to assimilate. The recipe section gives just a few recipes from each country, but there are sufficient to make two or three different meals in each style.

The Middle Eastern tradition of cookery

In the eleventh and twelfth centuries Baghdad was the foremost cultural centre in the world, and a unique style of cookery and food preparation developed. This style, which was at its most elaborate in the courts of the Caliphs, developed from simpler forms used by Bedouin and other tribes of the Fertile Crescent. This area encompasses modern-day Lebanon, Syria, Jordan and Iraq and produces a great range of fresh vegetables, beans, grains, and fruit including figs, dates, oranges, lemons and apricots. Wheat is the staple crop and bread the staple food. Little meat or animal fat is eaten. Half of the fat used is olive oil and other seed oils.

Evidence from Israel attests to the health of Jews coming from the Yemen, who eat a Middle Eastern diet, compared to immigrants from the United States who eat a Western-style diet and are more vulnerable to heart disease and cancer. (What we generally think of as Jewish food is based on a Central European cuisine and is rather rich. It is not recommended as a regular diet.)

The diets still consumed widely in the Middle East today comply with our recommendations, so we can turn to the Middle East as a source of inspiration for healthy food. It is a great culinary tradition which deserves to be much better known.

The peasant farmers of the Fertile Crescent produce a wealth of produce that makes eating a healthy diet easy. But healthy eating is also an essential part of the Arab philosophy which declares that there must be perfect concordance between the elements of the human body and the universe. The subject of cookery was taken seriously and recipes were recorded by poets, astrologers and even the Caliphs. The sensual traditions of this court cuisine survive today in modern Arab cooking.

Middle Eastern foods may be flavoured with combinations of herbs and spices, orange-blossom water, rose water and sesame seeds. Relatively little sugar is eaten; the natural sweetness of dates, raisins, dried apricots and prunes is used to enhance dishes. Arab cooking has always used meat sparingly. For poor people in town or city, meat is still a luxury eaten only on special occasions. But even the rich traditionally use only half a pound (about 225 grams) of meat to feed four people in a stew or stuffed vegetable dish, and meat is seldom eaten twice in the same day.

In Middle Eastern countries people consume about twice as much wheat as we do in Britain or other European countries. Much of the wheat is eaten as unleavened bread like pitta. Wheat is also eaten as bulgur, burghul or pourgouri (cracked wheat), which is used to thicken soups and stews and served as a side dish with yoghurt. Chickpeas, lentils and other pulses are an important part of the diet. The long growing season in Middle Eastern countries ensures the year-round availability of fresh fruits and vegetables.

The ingredients for Middle Eastern food are relatively easy to buy in Britain nowadays. The vegetables used are broadly similar to those used in Mediterranean food, and pulses such as chickpeas, black-eyed beans, and cracked wheat can generally be bought in the larger supermarkets or in health-food stores.

We are much indebted to Claudia Roden, a great cook and fine writer, for the Middle Eastern recipes. Claudia Roden's recipes are wonderfully flexible. She recognises that many cooks make it up as they go along, and presents plenty of options. In some places we have modified the recipe by including less fat or oil and also by using less meat. And of course, if you are in a hurry, there is no reason why you cannot use high-quality prepared ingredients.

The Indian tradition of cookery

The Brahmin tradition in India forbids the eating of meat and even eggs. Although Brahmins are a small minority of the population, their philosophy has had a great influence, and many Indians are vegetarians. As a result the Indian cuisine has developed ingenious ways of cooking vegetables, making use of fragrant flowers, seeds, barks and roots to provide an extraordinary range of pungency and fragrance. Many Indians, particularly Muslims, also eat meat, and so the cooking of meat has developed alongside the vegetarian tradition, making use of the same delicious aromatic seasonings.

In the West these fragrant sauces are known collectively as 'curry', a word which simply means 'sauce' in the Tamil language. To use one word to cover so many different seasonings does injustice to the variety and subtlety of Indian cooking. A wide range of curry sauces may be bought ready made in jars or ready ground as powders. However, most of the spices used to make these sauces have an important aromatic quality which may be lost or altered during processing and storage. For those who eat Indian food occasionally the

Spices and health

Most diets around the world include herbs and spices that have aromatic, pungent, or other flavours, aromas and colours.

Herbs often have high levels of carotenoids and vitamin C. But as we consume them in relatively small amounts, they do not make a large contribution to our diets. Herbs and spices also contain a vast range of other bioactive compounds whose functions and effects on health are now beginning to be investigated. Many herbs and spices have medicinal properties, which lead us to think they may also affect our cancer risk.

However, so far, studies on herbs and spices and cancer risk are limited and rather difficult to interpret, partly because herbs and spices are used in such small quantities, and their use varies widely in different populations. More research needs to be done.

ready-made sauces are convenient, but the flavour will be fresher if sauces are made up from individual ingredients.

Rice, chapatis and various breads are the most important starchy staples in the Indian diet. Potatoes, green bananas and starchy roots are also used, particularly in certain regions. Rice should be cooked by the absorption method (see page 62) which retains the vitamins and other micronutrients.

Ghee, the traditional cooking fat used in India, is made from clarified butter and/or heavy vegetable oils which contain a high proportion of saturated fat. Cream, which is also high in saturated fat, is also included in many Indian dishes eaten in the West. A high intake of saturated fat is associated with an increased risk of certain cancers and heart disease, and so ghee and cream should be used sparingly to add flavour, if at all. Vegetable oils such as rapeseed oil may be used instead of ghee, but added only in modest amounts. Yoghurt, which is used in many Indian recipes, can generally be substituted for cream.

The Chinese tradition of cookery

China has a rich and varied culinary tradition that has developed over thousands of years. In traditional pre-revolutionary China, eating was an important interest of the rich, an activity which many enjoyed for its own sake. At the same time, poverty and famine schooled Chinese cooks in the art of making use of every possible edible item. Another major influence has been the Buddhist vegetarian tradition, which makes creative use of seasonings to make vegetables more interesting. China's vast size encompasses a wide range of climates, and an equally great range of produce. Cookery in the different parts of China varies considerably, giving rise to several regional types, for example Szechuan and Cantonese. The use of particular spices, certain cooking methods such as stir-frying, and of rice gives Chinese cookery a character of its own which is immediately recognisable.

Traditional Chinese cookery uses only small amounts of meat. This is generally served chopped or shredded with vegetables and with boiled or fried rice as the staple starchy food. In northern China rice is often served in the form of steamed cakes. A clear soup, often made with chicken stock, may be served with the meal. The sparing use of meat in Chinese cooking, together with the Buddhist tradition of vegetable cookery, means that it is easy to eat healthy diets based on Chinese food. In some parts of China vegetables and fruits provide about 10 per cent of dietary energy, over twice that in northern Europe. Green tea, which, like soup, may be drunk throughout a Chinese meal, may provide some protection against cancer.

Certain Chinese foods do increase the risk of cancer, but these may easily be avoided. In parts of China salted meats (sometimes called 'wind-dried') and salted fish play a large part in the diet. Cantonese-style salted fish, which is a regular part of the diet of people who live on boats throughout China, increases the risk of cancer of the cavity behind the nose (the nasopharynx). Salted foods also probably increase the risk of stomach cancer and so are best not eaten regularly. Monosodium glutamate is often used to flavour Chinese food; it adds sodium to food in the same way as salt (sodium chloride), so avoid using large amounts of it. Some varieties of soy sauce contain monosodium glutamate, so do read the label carefully.

The Chinese food served in restaurants in the West generally differs from true Chinese food in several ways. Dishes are often modified and only certain styles of cooking are used. Many traditional Chinese dishes require a long time to cook, for example, by long simmering in earthenware casseroles, but these dishes will not be found in most Chinese restaurants outside China. The most common way of cooking in Chinese restaurants is with a wok. Food may be fried quickly in a wok using only a little oil. This method is well suited to the cooking of vegetables, leaving them deliciously fresh and crunchy.

Chinese cooking may be commended for its balanced use of vegetables, meat and rice in a way which generally meets our recommendations. Our only caution is that salt fish and other salted foods should be avoided and care should be exercised in any use of monosodium glutamate or ingredients containing it, such as soy sauce.

The recipes section has just a few simple Chinese dishes which will be familar to anyone who has eaten in a Chinese restaurant. These are dishes which are eaten in China but are also particularly popular in restaurants in the West. Few special ingredients are needed and the dishes are easy to cook. Specialist ingredients such as noodles and fresh root ginger are available in most supermarkets. These dishes provide an introduction to cooking Chinese food and illustrate how well suited it is for implementing a healthy diet. You do not need a wok to cook these dishes, but a wok does make it easier. The best way to cook rice is by the absorption method (see page 62).

The Japanese tradition of cookery

According to Japanese mythology, the benevolent gods gave rice to mankind. They also gave the soya bean which in its many forms is another essential of Japanese cooking. Soya beans are used to make the soy sauce which is added to most dishes. Soya beans are also used to make fermented miso paste which has many uses, and tofu or white bean curd, which is rather tasteless in itself but which carries flavours well and has many culinary uses. Tofu is also an excellent, virtually fat-free, source of protein.

Japanese cookery has been influenced by centuries of Buddhism which in its strictest form demands a vegetarian diet. This explains why the Japanese have become so expert in cooking vegetables. Fish is the other major ingredient of Japanese cooking. Everything from the sea that might be eaten is eaten by the Japanese – from the smallest crustacean to tuna, swordfish and several varieties of seaweed. Fish is often eaten raw. Finely sliced and beautifully presented, the raw fish is dipped first in soy sauce and then in wasabi, a type of horseradish paste. Large helpings of rice are served at all meals.

In Japanese literature the poor man's bean curd soup or his bowl of plain boiled rice is often used as a symbol of hardship and poverty. But it also stands for the virtues of a simple life – and generally a healthy one. The basic Japanese diet, with a large quantity of rice with some vegetables and fish, is also very close to our recommendations. Avoid, however, dishes which contain salted food or have an especially high salt content.

Japanese dishes are always beautifully arranged and presented with great care. The appearance of the dish is considered to be as important as the taste. The Japanese style of presenting food is becoming more familiar to us through the increasing number of Japanese restaurants. This style has its own aesthetic and spiritual value for many people and is satisfying to reproduce. However, the major health benefits of Japanese food may be gained from the food itself – you do not need to emulate the style closely. Buying special ingredients such as miso, wasabi, or dried seaweed, which are essential for certain Japanese recipes, may be difficult; some may be found in large supermarkets, but health-food shops are generally more likely to stock these items.

Try the dishes in the recipes section to give you a taste of Japanese food. We are indebted to Momoko Williams for help with these recipes.

Essential ingredients of a healthy diet

Vegetables and fruits, together with starchy staples such as potatoes, pasta, or rice, are the most important ingredients of healthy diets. Meat, fish, poultry and eggs are not essential if we eat plenty of vegetables and fruits, pulses and legumes, although, of course, most of us enjoy them. Most of us eat too much fat, meat and eggs in proportion to starch. We also tend to think of meat or eggs as the central part of a meal. To eat a healthier diet, change the way you plan a meal. Do not neglect the starchy foods, but try to think of ways that will make them more attractive.

The following sections describe the special culinary and nutritional virtues of the major foods to help you choose dishes which will make good use of the most suitable ingredients.

Great ways with vegetables

For the healthiest diet, we should eat plenty of vegetables and fruits – five or more portions a day – every day, all year round. We should also eat a variety of vegetables because different vegetables have different amounts of the various micronutrients that are important for basic health and the prevention of disease. We can also eat vegetables cooked or raw.

Various groups of vegetables are particularly important in reducing the risk of cancer:

● green vegetables
● vegetables of the cabbage family (cruciferous vegetables)
● vegetables of the onion-garlic family (allium vegetables)
● carrots
● tomatoes
● raw vegetables (salads)

Buy vegetables when they are in season, because they are then at their best and at their cheapest. Although the growing season in Britain is short, particularly in the north, relatively cheap supplies of vegetables now come year-round from Spain, Italy and much further afield. Even so, cucumbers and lettuce are best and cheapest in summer, and root vegetables such as turnips and parsnips best and cheapest in autumn and winter.

Green vegetables

Cabbage, Brussels sprouts, broccoli, spring greens, kale, kohlrabi and cauliflower are all cruciferous vegetables (and sometimes also known as brassicas). They are generally good sources of fibre, vitamin C and carotenoids.

Cauliflower is a good source of B vitamins, vitamin C and fibre.

Common spinach, and the leaves of beet spinach or Swiss chard, are all called 'spinach'. They are good sources of beta-carotene, vitamin C and fibre. Lettuce, particularly the dark outer leaves, is also a useful source of vitamin C and carotenoids.

Steam rather than boil cabbage and the other brassicas – this helps retain most of the micronutrients. If you do boil them, use the minimum amount of water, and cook for a short time only. Cut them into strips for stir-frying or add to soups and stews. Cook cabbage only briefly, or add at a late stage to soups and stews. Spinach is best cooked in very little water. If the leaves are newly washed and drained no water need be added, there is enough on the leaves to cook them well. Serve spinach hot or cold with a little olive oil and lemon juice to make an excellent salad dish.

The classic salad uses lettuce, but cabbage may be used to make a delicious winter salad if it is cut very finely. Spinach leaves also make an excellent raw salad.

Although it is best to use vegetables soon after buying them, cabbage may be stored in a plastic bag in a refrigerator for a few days and still retain most of its vitamin content. Other brassicas will keep for days or weeks if wrapped and put in the fridge. Broccoli florets slowly change from green to yellow as the flower develops – once yellow they are past their best. Cauliflower becomes smelly after a week or two, and Brussels sprouts may become yellow and mouldy.

Carrots

Carrots are an excellent source of the deep yellow micronutrient, carotene.

Eat carrots raw, sliced or grated, or cooked by boiling, steaming, stir-frying, braising or roasting. A winter salad made from grated carrots with a scattering of sultanas and nuts is a classic healthy dish, delicious because of its moist texture and slightly sweet flavour. Carrot soup is an equally nourishing and enjoyable dish.

Most carrots bought in supermarkets today have been washed to remove earth. This process allows fungi to establish themselves on the surface, and as a result washed carrots do not keep indefinitely in the refrigerator. Discard carrots if the fungal growth is at all extensive. Unwashed carrots, which you can sometimes buy from local or organic suppliers, keep for a long time if put in a plastic bag with holes that allow some circulation of air, and then into a refrigerator or cool storage place such as a larder.

Peeled carrots may be kept for up to two days in water in the refrigerator. Carrots, whether cooked or raw, do not freeze well, and are limp when defrosted. From the strictly nutritional viewpoint frozen carrots are as good as raw carrots although they have lost the crisp quality that makes them so satisfying to eat.

Garlic and onions

Garlic has an important place in Chinese and Indian food, and is at the centre of Mediterranean cooking. It is impossible to imagine the cooking of southern France, particularly the cooking of Provence or the Languedoc, without garlic, and it is an indispensable part of the Spanish cuisine. Indeed *à la provençale* describes a dish containing olive oil, garlic, and generally tomato, flavoured with Provençal herbs such as oregano.

Onion soup provides all the best qualities of onions in one gloriously potent dish. However, recipes for traditional French onion soup can contain a lot of butter and cheese and so be high in fat. Another dish popular in the Italian south, that does not stint on onions, is *fegato alla veneziana*. It consists of liver and onions but, as eaten by the ordinary Italian, the onions rather than the liver are the principal ingredient.

Tomatoes

The tomato was brought to Europe from Central and South America and has found a major role in southern European cooking, although it has been grown on a large scale for little more than 100 years. Today the tomato is as much an essential part of Mediterranean cooking as garlic, onions or oregano. Indeed, when these ingredients are combined we have the classic tomato sauce which, served with pasta, is a staple food throughout Italy. Tomatoes provide the perfect foil to garlic and onions; they both thicken the sauce and carry the flavour.

In late summer, many Italian families make tomato sauce which is bottled for use during the winter. Cooks should not feel that they are using a shortcut when they use tinned or bottled tomato pulp or paste. These are staple ingredients of Mediterranean cooking in the winter, when fresh tomatoes are not available,

> ### Tomato salad
> A quick and delicious meal may be made in summer from a plateful of sliced ripe tomatoes sprinkled with olive oil and lemon juice, or vinegar. The juice of the tomatoes mingles with the oil and lemon juice, complementing and enhancing the flavours. Serve this juice with the tomato slices and dunk your bread in it. When you have ripe, full-flavoured tomatoes and a good cheese, perhaps generous shavings of Parmesan, there can be no better simple meal. If you think it is too simple to present to guests, then make a salad *'tricolore'*, by adding avocado and mozzarella cheese (and lettuce if you like).

or considered too expensive for use in cooking. For the most authentic Mediterranean flavours, use the plum tomatoes that are especially favoured by Mediterranean cooks.

Fruit

Fruit is the traditional dessert in Mediterranean countries and is eaten at the end of most meals. In Japan, China and the Middle East, fruit is the most common dessert. People in the Mediterranean and China, in particular, eat much more fruit than northern Europeans and this is probably one of the reasons for the success of the Mediterranean and Chinese diets in reducing risk of cancer and heart disease.

There are many ways of presenting fruit. Present different fruits whole in a bowl, or prepare fruit in enticing ways that allow us to eat a smaller portion of a large fruit or to sample more than one fruit (see recipes for Greek fruit plate, *Macedonia di frutta* and Japanese fruit dessert, pages 129–130). These ways of presenting fruit make it easy for us to eat fruit and to eat more of it.

In Britain, until recently, only bottled fruits and relatively poor-quality apples and pears stored without refrigeration were traditionally available during the winter. Oranges first became available as relatively expensive imported items during the winter. And many people still consider that fruit is an unnecessary luxury food item.

With the help of rapid distribution and greatly improved refrigerated storage methods, fresh ripe fruit is now available throughout Britain all year round. Even so, for the best flavour, and the best price, it pays to follow the seasons. Fruit is often at its best when it is cheapest.

In Britain, we can follow the best seasons for the various fruit that come to us from southern Europe and the world over, but it can be difficult to be sure when particular fruits and vegetables are at their best. A good greengrocer will be able to tell you which fruits are in season and what are the best buys. In supermarkets care needs to be taken to get good value. It is convenient to pick up a packet of eight or ten kiwi fruit or peaches, but the best fruit is generally picked individually from an open box or a large pile. Examine the fruit to ensure that it is suitably ripe and in good condition. You can usually buy cheap fruit from street markets, but be careful you choose the fruit yourself and are not given bruised fruits from the back of the stall! Here are a few tips:

Apples

There is a short season in the early autumn when fresh English apples such as Worcesters, Russets and Coxes can be bought. After that apples such as Coxes, Braeburns and Granny Smiths are sold in excellent condition out of cold storage. These European apples last well until the middle of the summer when the new crop of New Zealand apples comes on to the market and are often preferable in flavour and firmness to last season's European apples. To keep apples firm and crisp store at home in the refrigerator.

Pears

Comice, William and Conference pears all keep very well during the winter, even in a cool larder. Commercially they are kept in cold storage and so are generally available in the shops in a hard unripe state. Buy them like this and keep them in the warmth for two or three days and they will be perfect. Keep them in the refrigerator if you want to slow down ripening.

Oranges

The best oranges are the navels that start to come to Britain from Spain and Morocco in November. Their flavour is much better than other oranges which have a longer journey and are not so fresh. About the same time excellent mandarin oranges (easy-peel citrus) become available from North Africa. These and other citrus fruits are in perfect condition all winter. By the end of the summer, when the navels are finished, good oranges are difficult to get in Britain.

Grapes

Grapes from Italy, Greece and Spain are best in September and October. After that they are more expensive. The cheaper varieties are often spoiled by fungal growth around the stalk. In winter the more expensive varieties of grapes that come from South Africa are best. A reddish brown, seedless South African variety called Red Flame is particularly good – it is sweet and has a good flavour. Its thin skin and absence of seeds makes it easy to eat and particularly suitable for fruit salads.

Melons

Melons of all kinds are also best in September and October. Melons bought in winter often never ripen properly.

Plums

Good plums are only available in the UK for a short season from August to October. Winter plums come from South Africa and other countries, but are very variable in quality and often do not ripen well.

Peaches and nectarines

Peaches and nectarines available in the UK are often of poor quality because they are picked while unripe and kept in cold storage. These fruit do not respond favourably like apples and pears to cold storage. The best fruit is ripened on the tree and is generally only available during the peak of the season in August and September.

Cooked fruit

Nothing can be better than fresh plums stewed with a little muscovado sugar or molasses. Dried apricots or prunes are so sweet they do not need any sugar to be added when they are stewed. Desserts made from dried prunes and apricots (see recipes, see pages 124,125) provide good winter standbys. Stewed apples, pears or peaches also make a good dessert in season, or may be used from bottles or cans in winter. Do not feel embarrassed to serve canned fruits if you have run out of fresh alternatives – they provide useful fibre and micronutrients, but choose those canned in juice rather than syrup. Include some spices for extra flavour, for example, cinnamon with pears, cloves or ginger with apples.

Baked apples are popular as a dessert in Mediterranean countries. For more flavour and a Mediterranean touch, these can be cooked with some wine added to the water in the bottom of the dish. If you want a sauce other than the delicious juice that comes from a combination of apple and wine, and an alternative to cream, then serve the baked apples with English custard, low-fat yoghurt, *fromage frais* or reduced-fat *crème fraiche*. English custard is not a fashionable sauce (it reminds people of school dinners), but it carries flavours well, is healthier than cream, and is very popular with children.

Starchy staple foods

Our recommendation is to increase the amount of starchy staple food in the daily diet to between 600 and 800 grams – at least seven portions – a day (20–30 ounces). This is considerably more than most of us eat at present and will make our diets much bulkier. In Britain, most of the starch in our diets comes from bread, potatoes, cereal and cereal products, such as rice and pasta. You can eat the recommended amount, for example, by having a portion of muesli and a couple of slices of brown bread at breakfast, a banana as a snack, a baked potato, or potato salad with a good sandwich at lunch, and a large portion of rice or pasta in the evening. At first this may seem like a lot of food, but build up to it gradually, using these foods to replace biscuits and cakes which contain a lot of unwanted fats, sugar and salt, and salty snacks. You can also replace some of the meat in your diet if you are eating more than about 80 grams (3 ounces) of cooked meat a day.

Eating sufficient starchy staples need not be a problem if you choose food which makes the starchy staple a central part of your meal. For example, pasta with sauce, rice with a stir-fry, bread with Greek dips and salad, or a modest portion of meat with accompanying vegetables and potatoes.

Bread

Bread is the staple food of Europe and the Middle East, where early agriculturalists first developed wheat. As chapatis and naan, bread is also important in the Indian diet. One way of achieving the recommendation to increase the amount of starchy foods in our diet is to eat more bread.

Wholemeal bread is best nutritionally because it contains more fibre and vitamins than bread made with refined white flour.

Eat a variety of breads. Make wholemeal bread your everyday staple, and eat other interesting breads to complement particular dishes. If good wholemeal bread and interesting speciality breads are not easy to obtain locally, buy enough for a week or two and store the loaves in a freezer. Bread will maintain its freshness very well for some weeks when wrapped in plastic and frozen. Wholemeal loaves will also keep well for some days in the refrigerator, but white bread tends to get stale faster in the refrigerator and so is better kept at room temperature.

Bread and butter are so much a part of our traditional diet we tend to think them as almost indivisible, but we can change. It may surprise you to learn that butter has little or no place in the Mediterranean diet. In the Mediterranean, people dribble olive oil on their bread and dunk their bread in the oil that is part of so many dishes. Of course, oil cannot replace butter if you want to eat bread with jam. Try it the Mediterranean way – just bread and jam, no butter.

Bread is a very versatile food. Eat more of it by making it the basis for meals. Here's how:

● Eat bread with cheese and salad, but do not use butter. If you like dribble a little olive oil on to the salad and the bread.
● Eat bread with sliced tomatoes Greek style with oil, lemon juice and black pepper. Dunk the bread in the delicious pink juice.
● Simply dip some bread into a saucerful of olive oil. This is the favourite snack of the Greek peasant, equivalent to our bread and butter.
● Eat bread as the natural accompaniment to soup and, if you like, make soup and bread your main course.
● Eat pitta bread with various traditional Mediterranean dips such as aubergine purée, cucumber and yoghurt (tzatziki), hummus, or tahini (see recipes, pages 78–80).
● Eat bread with cooked vegetable dishes, dunking the bread in the juices.
● Get a loaf of partially-cooked bread from the supermarket and put it in the oven for 10 minutes to get that newly baked flavour and crispness. Eat with ratatouille.
● If you like Indian food, eat it in the traditional way using chapatis or naan instead of a fork to help you pick up the food in your fingers.
● Simplest of all, eat bread with all your main meals – including meals with pasta, rice or potatoes.

The world of bread

Most of the bread we eat is made in factories by a mainly mechanical process. The dough, made with wheat flour, is given a short treatment with yeast, mainly to develop the flavour, before being mechanically aerated so that it will have a light texture after baking. This is modern factory bread – it may be white, brown or wholemeal. Traditionally made yeast-raised bread tends to be heavier, especially if it is made with wholemeal flour. From the strictly nutritional point of view, bread is equally good whether made by the factory process or the traditional method.

Bread contains a substantial amount of salt, and can be a major contributor to salt in the diet. Some types of bread are saltier than others: find a bread for regular use which is not too salty. Irish soda bread is made without yeast, using sodium bicarbonate as a raising agent. As a rule, soda bread tends to taste salty, and although delicious, it should not be eaten regularly. Naan, the Indian white bread, is made from a dough containing eggs, and is also raised with sodium bicarbonate; it is baked in the tandoor oven.

Granary bread is made from a flour which is partially malted and has a sweetish taste. The bran-plus loaf is made with extra bran, the fibrous part of the wheat grain. This idea was pioneered by Surgeon Commander T.L. Cleave, who found that constipation was a serious problem on his battleship in World War Two. He discovered that he could keep the sailors 'regular' by serving them with extra bran in various forms.

Other breads contain whole grains or seeds which enhance texture and flavour. Delicious Greek breads are made with added olives and onions. Special breads such as Vienna loaves or buns may be made with added milk or eggs. Foccaccia is Italian white bread made with herbs and olive oil. Ciabatta is a flat white Italian bread with large holes, also made with olive oil. Ciabatta can now be bought in supermarkets part-baked: just a few minutes' additional baking at home produces a delicious fresh crisp loaf.

The traditional French baguette with its open texture and crisp crust is made with soft wheat flour. It does not keep well and is traditionally bought fresh three times a day. Real baguettes are made in France by artisan bakers. Baguette-style bread made in Britain is most often a poor factory-made imitation: it has the right shape, but does not compare in texture and taste.

Bread may also be made with many different grains apart from wheat. Rye, maize (corn), buckwheat, oats, barley and rice can all be made into bread of one kind or another. The bread may be leavened with yeast, or with sourdough, a mixture of yeast and other bacteria, particularly *Lactobacillus*, which make a more plastic dough and provide the characteristic sour taste. Or bread may be unleavened. Greek pitta breads and Indian chapatis are unleavened and have a soft texture, whereas matzo bread is baked until it has a hard texture like a biscuit. Pitta bread, made from wholemeal flour, can now be widely obtained. It can be quickly reheated in a toaster, even from frozen, and served with the traditional spreads (see recipes, see pages 78-80).

Potatoes

Potatoes and wheat are the most important starchy foods eaten in Europe. In Britain potatoes are an important source of vitamin C because the average person eats relatively few vegetables and fruits, but a lot of potatoes. The Spaniards and the French are the great potato eaters of the Mediterranean. They eat about twice as many potatoes as the Greeks or Italians. The Spanish omelette, eggs cooked with onions and potatoes, is a staple dish eaten once a week or more by most people in southern Spain.

Eating more potatoes is a good way of increasing the amount of starch in our diets. Boiled potatoes are 80 per cent water, and contain almost no fat. Remember, they are not fattening until butter or some other fat is added to them. The solid matter in potatoes is 90 per cent starch, and potatoes are also an important source of the B vitamins thiamin, niacin and pyridoxine, and vitamin C, and other micronutrients. Contrary to what most people believe, potatoes provide a significant amount of protein. They are also rich in potassium, which is good for people with blood pressure problems.

The way in which potatoes are prepared makes a great deal of difference to the amount of fat they absorb.

● Potato chips lose a lot of water during cooking and absorb fat, up to 15 per cent of their weight. Chips are often dismissed as fattening and as a food of questionable nutritional value. In fact, they are a valuable source of unprocessed starch, micronutrients and protein. The fat content, which is what makes them fattening, is greatest when they are finely cut (French fries) or crinkle cut. To reduce the fat content, make jumbo chips for deep-frying, and the amount of fat absorbed will be considerably less. Alternatively, use oven chips, cooked either in the oven or under the grill. When possible, serve chips with a boiled or steamed vegetable that is low in fat.

● Roast potatoes the Greek way (see recipe page 89) to reduce fat content. Cut the potatoes in half lengthways and roast with vegetables and olive oil, basting from time to time.

● Boiled potatoes are the natural accompaniment to a dish that has its own sauce, and to meat or vegetable dishes which produce their own delectable juices.

● Be cautious with baked potatoes. Don't add butter, margarine or mayonnaise; try them with tuna and red kidney beans, sweetcorn in low-fat natural yoghurt, low-fat soft cheese or simply baked beans in tomato sauce.

Know your potatoes

There are hundreds of varieties of potato but only about fifteen are widely available in shops. These are some of the most readily available types:

Early potatoes

Some of our best early potatoes come from Jersey, Cornwall and Kent, but good early potatoes are also imported from Cyprus and Egypt.

Jersey Royal

Probably the best known of the early potatoes. They first become available in early April when they are very expensive, but they rapidly become cheaper as they become larger. They have flaky skins that scrape off very easily, and may also be scrubbed. Excellent flavour and texture.

Pentland Javelin

The most widely grown of the early potatoes. This variety is grown all over Britain and has a moderately waxy texture.

Maincrop potatoes

Desirée

Pink skin, yellowish flesh. Good for baking, boiling, chipping and roasting. Not a good masher.

Maris Piper

Plain skin, creamy flesh, floury texture. Good for baking, chipping, roasting and mashing.

Cara

Pale skin, pink eyes. High yield alternative to the King Edward. Good for baking.

King Edward

The best British masher, also good for roasting and for chips, but disintegrates on boiling.

Pentland Dell

Excellent roaster and masher. It tends to disintegrate on cooking, and so is a poor boiler, but the flaking makes it crisp up well when roasted.

Romano

Pink skin, yellowish flesh. Good for baking, boiling, chipping and roasting. Not a good masher.

Pasta

Pasta was brought to Italy and the rest of southern Europe by the early traders who worked the land routes to China. Italian pasta is made with semolina flour, ground durum (or hard) wheat, whereas noodles, the name used for Chinese and Japanese forms of pasta, may be made from rice, wheat, buckwheat or mung beans. Semolina flour retains most of the nutrients of the wheat, which are lost when wheat is made into plain flour by high-pressure roller mills. It is worth checking that the pasta you buy is made from semolina flour, because commercial pasta may sometimes be made from plain flour. Pasta may also be made with egg.

● Chilled freshly-made pasta is now widely available in supermarkets. It cooks much more quickly than the dried pastas and has the advantage of freshness. As well as the ribbon-shaped forms, many types of ravioli (stuffed pastas) are available. With a good sauce and a vegetable side dish, these raviolis may make a healthy and agreeable meal. Chilled pastas can be kept in the refrigerator for a few days or in the freezer at home for up to a month before using.
● Green pastas, made with added puréed spinach, are available, and some red- or orange-coloured pastas contain tomato. The inclusion of vegetable within the pasta adds flavour and some useful micronutrients to the pasta – use green or red pasta for the simplest ever healthy meal (see page 70). These coloured pastas are available chilled or dried.
● Home-made pasta is made with white flour rather than semolina. It cooks faster than semolina and becomes a sticky mess if cooked too long. Home-made pasta of this kind is less nutritious than pasta made from semolina, and some connoisseurs say that it actually has less flavour.

Simple sauces for pasta

Pasta may be served very simply and quickly without much extra cooking in any of the following ways. Amounts, where given, are for about four servings.
● *With cheese.* Toss well-drained pasta with 2 tablespoons olive oil and a similar quantity of Parmesan (or other) grated cheese.
● *With basil.* Toss well-drained pasta with 2 or more tablespoons of ready-made pesto sauce. Pesto is made from basil, Parmesan, garlic, olive oil and pine kernels, and can be bought in most supermarkets.
● *With tomato.* Serve with a tomato sauce. For speed and simplicity use a commercial bottled sauce, or see recipe on page 94. Bottled sauces vary greatly and sometimes may be rather sweet but they provide the essential nutrients. Best of all, make tomato sauce at home, and freeze it in batches for later use.
● *With garlic and parsley.* Finely chop 2 cloves of garlic and some parsley. Fry the garlic and parsley for about 3 minutes in 2 tablespoons olive oil. Add to well-drained pasta. Sprinkle with freshly ground black pepper and toss.
● *As a salad.* Toss cold cooked pasta spirals or other shapes with small pieces of lettuce, green and red pepper, tomato, avocado, olive oil and a little vinegar or lemon juice. If you like, add some canned tuna or pieces of anchovy, or a little feta or Edam cheese.

● Wholemeal pasta, which contains the wheat bran as well as the germ, is available, although it is not part of the traditional Mediterranean diet. The additional health benefit of the bran is probably small when pasta is part of a full Mediterranean diet which contains plenty of fibre from fruit and vegetables.

In Italy pasta is usually served as the main

dish in the main meal of the day. Most Italians eat pasta every day and often twice. Vegetables, salad and meat are generally served separately. A large bowl of noodles cooked in a nutritious broth is often the mainstay of a traditional Chinese meal.

Cooking pasta

The pasta should be cooked *al dente*, that is about 7–11 minutes for dry pasta, just 3–4 minutes for fresh chilled pasta. To be cooked *al dente* the pasta should still give a little resistance to the bite. Put the pasta in boiling water and stir regularly so the pasta does not stick together at the bottom of the pan. When the pasta is ready it should be drained in a colander and served without delay. The sauce may be mixed with the pasta in a large bowl before serving, the best method if the amount of sauce is limited, or put on top of the pasta to be mixed by each person at the table.

Rice

Rice is, of course, the staple food in most parts of China, many parts of India and throughout the Far East. It is also a popular staple food in Greece, Spain and Italy, although less so in France. Always choose the correct kind of rice for the dish you are cooking and understand its special qualities. English pudding rice is good for making English milk puddings, and even Greek milk puddings but is totally unsuited to most savoury dishes. An Indian curry or Greek pilaff, for example, requires long-grain rice. An Italian risotto traditionally requires a short-grain rice such as arborio. Many Japanese recipes require a special sticky or glutinous type of rice that can be 'squashed' into various shapes.

Brown rice

Some people prefer brown rice because it has not lost vitamins in the milling process as has white rice, but many people find it less enjoyable to eat and less convenient. Brown rice takes longer to cook because the grain is covered by a thin membrane of bran which resists penetration by water. Some cooks recommend soaking brown rice for 30–40 minutes before cooking. It should not be stirred until it is cooked and some cooks recommend that, after cooking, it should be left covered in the pan for 10 minutes before serving. This means that preparation of a meal with brown rice may take almost an hour, which may be inconvenient. Many people prefer the texture and taste of white rice.

Cooking rice by the absorption method

This is the best way to cook rice because it preserves the best aroma and flavour while also conserving important vitamins and other micronutrients. Once mastered, this method is easy but beginners often find it difficult. Here are some tips:

- Use long-grain rice such as American long-grain, Patna or basmati.
- Rinse the rice in cold water to remove the starchy powder which, if left, will make the rice too sticky. If time permits, soak the rice for 30 minutes before cooking.
- Use 300g of rice to 570ml of water (10½ oz rice to 20 fluid oz or 1 pint of water). Or if measuring by volume use one part of dry rice to one and a half parts of water.
- Use a heavy pan, ideally one with a glass lid which enables you to judge whether the rice is cooked without lifting the lid.
- Use a closely fitting lid. If the lid does not fit closely put some aluminium foil between the lid and the pan.
- Cook for about 15 minutes. Do not look into the pan earlier because steam, which is essential for cooking the rice, will escape. If the rice is still wet after 15 minutes, cook until dry.

White rice

White rice is often steamed (par-boiled) before it is milled, a process which causes vitamins to leach out of the germ into the grain where they are retained during the milling process. This type of rice is widely eaten in parts of the Far East. It has the reputation of protecting against beri-beri – the disease caused by deficiency of vitamin B₁ (thiamin), which appears when people are dependent on rice milled and polished by modern machinery. White rice available in the UK may or may not have been prepared by parboiling, check on the packet.

Cooking rice

Ideally, whatever type of rice is used, it should be cooked by a method which retains vitamins. If rice is boiled in a lot of water which is then thrown away, useful vitamins are discarded. Boiled rice is best cooked using the 'absorption' method. This method uses a carefully measured amount of water which is all absorbed during the cooking process, leaving fluffy grains containing vitamins (see page 62). Most cooks choose a variety of rice

that suits their purpose and find out from experience exactly how best to prepare it. Good advice can often be obtained from the packet, and you should try the sample recipes it often includes.

Pulses

Pulses, the seeds of leguminous plants, include black-eyed beans, chickpeas, dhal, broad beans, dried peas, haricot beans, kidney beans, lentils, lima beans, navy beans, peas, soya beans and split peas. They can be used to make a great number of delicious and nutritious dishes. What we know as baked beans are navy beans cooked in a tomato sauce. They are a very good source of starch and also provide a substantial amount of protein. Beans should be included among your regular starchy foods because they are an excellent source of energy, fibre and micronutrients, particularly folic acid and other B vitamins. They also complement the protein in grains and add variety to the diet.

As well as fibre, beans contain variable quantities of complex sugars which cannot be digested in the small bowel and are broken

---

Lentils and rice

Lentils and rice make a very satisfying meal which is eaten in many different forms the world over. Not only is the combination satisfying to the appetite, it is also a good combination for our metabolism because the protein in lentils complements the protein in the rice to provide the best proportions of amino acids (the building blocks of protein). This dish therefore provides all the protein we need, as well as the starch and micronutrients that we recommend for reducing cancer risk, without including any meat. We are indebted to Claudia Roden for this simple but delightful Middle Eastern version of lentils and rice.

Soak 250g (9oz) of large brown lentils for an hour, discard the water, and then cover with

fresh water and cook for 20–30 minutes or until tender. Chop an onion and fry in 2 tablespoons of olive oil until it is soft and golden. Combine the onions and lentils with some freshly ground black pepper. Add 125g (4½oz) of long-grain rice to the lentils and mix well. Add the same volume of water and simmer gently for about 20 minutes or until the rice is cooked, by which time the liquid should be more or less absorbed. Add more liquid if it dries up before the rice is cooked.

Slice 2 onions to make half-ring shapes. Fry these in 4 tablespoons of olive oil until dark brown and partially caramelised. Spread the rice and lentils on a large shallow dish and arrange the half rings of onion on top. This dish may be served hot or cold and may be dressed with yoghurt. It is a complete meal in itself.

down by bacteria in the colon. This generally produces gas which some people find particularly awkward or uncomfortable. It is, however, the normal healthy function of the colon to digest these substances and the process of doing so keeps the colon healthy.

Black-eyed beans and lentils cook relatively quickly – in 20–40 minutes. But several types of pulses, for example chickpeas, haricot and kidney beans, may take two or more hours to cook even when soaked first. It is best to soak them overnight or bring them to the boil and then leave them to soak for a few hours before boiling again until soft. Throw away the water in which these hard pulses have been soaked or boiled because it has a disagreeable taste and is particularly potent in causing wind.

Uncooked pulses may contain various chemicals produced by nature to prevent them being eaten by animals. These chemicals are mild poisons which alter the activity of digestive enzymes and may cause blood to clot. It is most unwise to eat red kidney beans, for example, if they are inadequately cooked because these chemicals can cause sickness.

If you do not have the time to prepare kidney beans, chickpeas and other pulses, use canned products. The only disadvantage is that canned pulses are often rather salty. To overcome this, drain off all the liquid and wash the pulses in cold fresh water. Canned chickpeas or kidney beans make an excellent accompaniment to salad and are delicious if dressed with a little chopped fresh parsley, olive oil, lemon juice and black pepper. They may also be added to stews, or cooked with rice and onions in a similar way to our recipe for lentils and rice (see page 63). Even better, prepare a large quantity of beans and keep them in small packs in the freezer.

Green peas, fresh broad beans and lima beans are also pulses but they are harvested at a younger stage while still soft. They are excellent sources of starch, protein, micronutrients and fibre. They all freeze very successfully, and if you keep packets of them in the freezer you need never be without a vegetable to serve.

Wheat, barley and oats

Wheat

Wheat in the form of wholemeal or white flour is a good source of starch, protein and many micronutrients. Many people eat as much wheat in the form of biscuits, cakes, pastries and other bakery goods as they do in the form of bread or pasta. These types of foods are almost always made with white flour, which has lost some micronutrients, and contain a substantial quantity of fat and sugar. This makes them relatively high in energy and so rather fattening. Keep biscuits, cakes and pastries to a minimum in your diet.

Cracked wheat, also known as bulgur, burghul and pourgouri, is prepared by lightly milling dried par-boiled wheat to make coarse grains. It is the oldest known processed food. It may be added to soups and stews, served like rice as an accompaniment for meat and vegetables, or served as a salad (see recipe page 97).

Barley

Barley is mostly used for making beer. Pearl barley is milled to remove most of the husk and the germ. Nevertheless it is a useful source of vitamins and fibre, and is most commonly used in stews and soups such as Scotch broth.

Oats

Oats are an excellent source of starch as well as being packed with other nutrients. They are a good source of protein and of polyunsaturated and monounsaturated fats and provide generous amounts of fibre, iron, zinc and certain vitamins. Oats, when part of a low-fat diet, have also been found to lower

Simple flapjack

100g (3½oz) light brown sugar
75g (2½oz) soft margarine
50g (2oz) clear honey
150g (5½oz) rolled oats
75g (2½oz) raisins
50g (2oz) dried apricots, chopped
50g (2oz) pitted prunes, chopped

Heat the sugar, margarine and honey gently until melted. Add all the other ingredients and mix well. Press mixture firmly into a 18cm (7in) tin and bake at 90°C/375°F/Gas 5 for 20 minutes.

blood cholesterol and so are commended for the heart. Oats are such an excellent source of nutrients, energy and fibre that they are specially recommended here as a breakfast food (see the recipe for muesli on page 71).

Oats are most commonly eaten as porridge, in muesli, or as various types of flapjack or oatcakes, but may also be incorporated into crumble toppings (see page 126) or baked foods. Oatcakes contain some fat and are rather salty, but low-salt types can be obtained in health-food shops. A special healthy version of flapjack can be made at home (see recipe above).

Porridge was originally made from oatmeal (which is made by grinding the whole oat grain), but oatmeal requires soaking overnight. Nowadays rolled, or porridge, oats are used. Porridge oats are pre-cooked and rolled to make them easily digestible without the need for further cooking. To make porridge, they simply need to be mixed with water, brought to the boil and stirred for about 2 minutes until the mixture thickens – if it is too thin simply add more oats, if too thick add more water. You can also make porridge with milk instead of water.

Meat and poultry

Most people on traditional diets eat much less meat than we do today in Britain, northern Europe and North America. In Chinese, Japanese and Indian dishes, the meat is generally cut up into small portions and mixed in various ways with rice and vegetables. Until recently, ordinary people in the Mediterranean region ate a substantial meat dish only about twice a week, although they might have used small amounts of sausage or meat as flavouring in sauces and vegetable dishes on other days. This tradition has remained in rural areas, and is still usual in large parts of the Middle East. Nowadays, in the cities of Mediterranean Europe, people generally eat meat most days and poultry or fish on other days.

If you are used to eating meat every day you may believe that a meal is not complete without meat, fish or at least eggs. The misleading way in which nutritional information is often presented has led many of us to think of bread and pasta as carbohydrate foods lacking in protein. In fact wheat products such as bread or pasta contain 12–15 per cent protein, whereas meat contains about 20 per cent protein – only a little more than wheat, the rest of the meat being mostly fat. A wholly vegetarian diet, or even a vegan diet (which contains no animal produce at all), can easily provide all the protein anybody needs – and that includes pregnant women and growing children.

However, meat is a good source of iron (in a form that is readily absorbed), zinc, selenium and B vitamins. Eating some meat adds to the variety of the diet and may provide micronutrients that are otherwise in relatively short supply. In pregnancy, when anaemia is a common and a potentially serious complication, meat is a useful source of iron.

In Mediterranean and Eastern cooking, meat is often used in a rather different way from what we are used to. Greek, Italian and Spanish cooks often use meat as a flavouring for vegetable or pasta dishes. From a solely culinary point of view, this is a successful way to use meat. The special flavours of meat combine with the individual qualities of vegetables and the aroma of herbs to provide a much greater variety of tastes than can be obtained by the simple roasting, frying or grilling of various meat joints.

Our recommendation is to eat no more than 80 grams (3 ounces) cooked weight (115 grams or 4 ounces uncooked weight without bone) of meat daily. For many people this might seem a small portion of meat, and if served as a steak many would think it inadequate. However, many delicious and nutritious dishes have only this much meat in them. Try some of these recipes:

● A hearty meat and vegetable stew such as a Greek stifado.
● Baked dishes such as moussaka where meat is combined with vegetables.
● Stuffed tomatoes which include some minced meat mixed with rice.
● Our healthy shepherd's pie.
● Meat used in sauces for pasta where it is combined with other ingredients.
● Meat used in a macaronade where it is combined with pasta and baked in the oven.
● Meat in risotto or in paella dishes.

Many Mediterranean and Eastern dishes include chicken. Chicken is less fatty, and the fat is much less saturated, making it a healthier option than red meat. Many cooks will buy a whole bird, use most of it for one meal, and then use the leftovers and giblets as stock for soup, for a risotto, or to flavour some other dish.

Fish
Fish is important in the Japanese and Spanish diets. The Mediterranean sea has a great variety of all types of fish and seafood which are prized by those who live on its borders. However, much of the fish eaten in Spain, Greece and Italy is salt cod which comes from the North Atlantic. An elaborate process of washing is needed to remove the salt from these fish before they can be eaten. There are many delicious recipes for salt cod but all these dishes tend to remain rather salty even if the fish has been washed. Salt fish dishes should be eaten only occasionally.

Mediterranean and Japanese cooking use many species of fish that we do not commonly see for sale in Britain. Fresh octopus and squid, which are commonly eaten in Mediterranean countries and Japan, are caught in British waters and could be available here if there was a market for them. Even so, supermarkets sell a sufficient variety of fish to enable many different fish and seafood dishes to be easily cooked here.

Quick fish
Fish, unlike meat, can be cooked straight from the freezer without any loss of culinary quality. Many fish dishes can be produced within 40 minutes, or at most an hour (see page 121 for fish with tomatoes and onions). Extra tomato sauce made for pasta (see the recipe on page 94) can also be used to make a delicious quick fish dish. Put the tomato sauce in an ovenproof dish. Separate out the frozen fillets of white fish and place in the sauce. If you like, scatter a few olives or capers over the top. Cover the dish with a lid or foil and put in a moderate oven (180°C/350°F/Gas 4).

Cooking time varies with the size of the fish pieces, but it will generally be about 30 minutes. Carefully cut into the thickest part of the fish; when it has turned opaque it is fully cooked. Serve with pasta, rice or boiled potatoes and a couple of vegetables such as carrots or broccoli.

Fish is an excellent source of protein in a low-fat package. Even oily fish contains only 5–15 per cent fat while white fish contains only 1–2 per cent fat – a fraction of the fat contained in meat. The fat in fish is highly polyunsaturated which is generally believed to be good for the heart and preferable to saturated fat in reducing the risk of cancer.

Milk, yoghurt, cheese and butter

Milk has a traditional place in our diet because the grass which feeds dairy cattle grows better in our northern climate than vegetables and fruits. Britain was the traditional home of pastoralists who depended upon their herds for sustenance, especially in wintertime. This historical background distinguishes us from other countries with a different agricultural development. Milk and milk products have little or no place in the Chinese and Japanese diets. Nor does milk have the same important place in the Mediterranean diet that it has in northern European diets. Milk is seldom drunk in the Mediterranean, and butter is not part of the traditional diet. In India, on the other hand, milk and butter fat, in the form of ghee, are central to their diet.

Milk is a useful source of vitamins B_2 and B_{12}, calcium, zinc and copper, as well as providing some protein. Because we drink a lot of milk, it contributes a high proportion of fat to our diets. Reduce your intake of saturated fat and calories by drinking semi-skimmed milk. It tastes much the same as full cream milk in tea or on breakfast cereal.

Cheese is a good source of protein, vitamins B_2 and B_{12}, calcium, iodine and selenium, but 40–50 per cent of cheese is fat which is mostly saturated. Some cheese is also salty. For health reasons we should eat both less salt and less saturated fat, so eat only moderate amounts of cheese. Use cheese sparingly as a seasoning sprinkled on dishes, tossed with salads, or eat grated with bread or biscuits (but without butter).

Use butter and cream, which also consist mostly of saturated fat, only on special occasions. Choose soft margarine or a low-fat spread for making cakes and spreading on bread. When you cook, use olive oil or rapeseed oil rather than butter, lard or suet.

Yoghurt is a well-established part of the Greek, Middle Eastern and Indian diets because milk itself does not keep long in a warm climate. Yoghurt may be eaten as a dessert, added to stews, or used as a dressing for salads with some vinegar, lemon juice and perhaps mustard. Greek yoghurt is traditionally made from sheep's milk but today is just as commonly made from cow's milk. Much commercial Greek yoghurt is made with whole milk, and is often enriched with added cream. This makes a high-fat food that should be eaten only occasionally. Choose one of the low-fat varieties now available. Many different types of commercial yoghurt are available, and some custard types are thickened with modified starch and/or cream. Whenever possible choose low-fat varieties.

How to make a thick yoghurt for use with salads

Greek yoghurt is traditionally thickened by straining it through muslin. This type of strained yoghurt is much better for making tzatziki (a cucumber and yoghurt dip) which is too watery if made with an ordinary yoghurt. Strain and thicken ordinary yoghurt by putting it in a muslin square, gathering the edges together and squeezing out the excess liquid, or by hanging it up to allow excess liquid to drip out. If you make yoghurt yourself, and want an extra thick variety, add dry skimmed milk powder to the warm milk before adding the yoghurt culture.

Olive oil and other fats

In country areas of Greece, southern Italy and Spain, butter was almost unknown until recently, and cow's milk was rare. Olive oil is the only cooking fat used traditionally in the Mediterranean and large parts of the Middle East, although cheaper alternatives have now found a place. Olive oil is not only used for cooking but, in olive-growing areas, is often dribbled and poured on food in the same way that we might spread bread with butter or dot butter on potatoes or vegetables.

Olive oil is high in monounsaturated fatty acids which are now thought to be beneficial in reducing the risk of heart disease, and so olive oil is recommended here. Rapeseed oil is also high in monounsaturates and may be used as well as, or instead of, olive oil. Rapeseed oil has a neutral flavour and so is particularly useful for dishes which taste better without the flavour of olive oil.

Here are ways of using olive oil, but always remember the need to reduce the amount of fat in our diets.

● Use a low-fat spread made from olive oil.
● Use olive or rapeseed oil instead of butter or other fats for cooking.
● Have a small bottle of olive oil on the table so it can be dribbled on bread as an alternative to butter or margarine.

Olive oil varies a great deal in flavour. Some types are much stronger than others. Extra virgin, which originally was the first pressing of the olive but now is defined by its acidity, generally has most flavour. Its taste may be too strong for some people. Buy small quantities at first and experiment until you find a brand that you like. French and Italian olive oils tend to be blander than Spanish and Greek oils. Olive oil may be diluted with other seed oils to modify the flavour.

Olives may be made into a delicious dip,

A simple salad meal with bread and olive oil

You can make a complete meal of bread and salad with olive oil and perhaps a little cheese. There is no need to put butter or margarine on the table. Use French dressing or just sprinkle oil and vinegar over your salad. Choose a crusty loaf, break pieces off, dunk it into the dressing or oil and eat it with the salad. Finish off with fruit and you have the simplest and healthiest of meals. It is only slightly more complicated to put some feta cheese into the salad itself, with perhaps some green beans and olives to make a Greek salad, or to add anchovies and hard-boiled eggs, or tuna fish, to make a Salade Niçoise (see pages 82 and 83).

---

tapenade (see page 80), which can be served with bread as a starter, with other dips and spreads (see pages 78–80), or as part of a main salad meal.

Wines and spirits

Drinking alcohol is not recommended. There is no evidence that drinking alcohol helps prevent any cancer, and it increases the risk of several cancers. Drinking small amounts of alcohol has, however, been recommended for reducing the risk of heart disease. So, if you do drink alcohol, limit it to one drink a day if you are a woman, two if you are a man.

Many people in France, Spain and Italy drink large amounts of wine, yet their diets seem to be healthy. So, are there differences in drinking habits between northern and southern Europe which are important?

Of course, Mediterranean people might be even healthier if they did not drink any wine. On the other hand, in Mediterranean countries wine is generally not drunk before a meal or on its own as we tend to do in northern Europe. Wine is usually drunk with the meal itself, and when alcohol is drunk with a meal it is absorbed into the blood much more slowly and does not produce the same high peak of alcohol in the blood. It is well known that the intoxicating effect of alcohol is diminished when it is taken with meals. It may be that the ill-effects of alcohol on the body are also diminished when it is taken with food. Further research is needed before this question can be answered. In the meantime it makes sense to eat something when drinking and, if you wish to drink, take your drink with a meal whenever possible.

Wine or spirits may of course be used in cooking without any need to worry about the possible ill-effects of alcohol. Alcohol evaporates very quickly when heated and so none is left within a few minutes of adding it to a dish that is cooking. However, it is the subtle flavours preserved in wine and spirits which add to the culinary success of a dish.

Chilled, frozen and canned food

Good cooks quite rightly emphasise the value of fresh ingredients. Fresh food, provided it is really fresh, generally has more flavour and contains more vitamins and other micro-nutrients, because many micronutrients are slowly lost during storage. However, chilling and freezing of foods has brought about a revolution enabling food to be kept fresh for much longer.

Chilled food

We can buy prepared foods such as soups and ready meals from the chill cabinet and keep them at home at room temperature for eating at our convenience. Avoid ready-prepared foods such as soups made with cream or butter, and foods which are high in salt. Choose the healthier, lower fat, lower salt meals now available.

Healthy food without cooking

It is not necessary to cook meals for yourself in order to eat a healthy diet. But if you want to buy convenient healthy meals from the supermarket it helps greatly if you have a taste for Italian or Greek food. Pasta is an amazingly convenient food which can be cooked or reheated in minutes – and the Greeks have worked out better than anyone else how to produce tasty dips and spreads. It should be possible to eat healthily for at least a week from the chilled and frozen sections of a supermarket without having to repeat a meal. Here's how:

● Wholemeal bread with spreads and a lot of salad (lettuce, tomato cucumber and raw carrot) provide the simplest healthy meal that can be made without cooking. Spreads such as hummus or tahini can be bought in most supermarkets. Alternatively, eat your bread and salad with a little cheese, canned tuna or sardines. The bread can be sprinkled with a little olive oil, spread with a little low-fat spread, or eaten just by itself.

● If you want a hot meal buy one of the chilled fresh soups – some low-salt soups are also available – to eat with wholemeal bread.

● Large supermarkets now do a special range of ready-to-eat healthy dishes which have reduced salt and fat. These include dishes such as lasagne and seafood linguine.

● Many types of pasta, including stuffed varieties, are broadly healthy. They may be combined with a freshly made sauce from the same chilled cabinet in the supermarket and a fresh salad.

● Ready-prepared meals should be eaten with a vegetable or salad. If minimum trouble and preparation time are most important, use ready-washed salad or a frozen vegetable such as frozen broad beans or peas which simply have to be shaken into boiling water. Frozen broad beans make an excellent salad with olive oil, lemon juice and black pepper.

Frozen food

Freezing is a good way of preserving some foods, particularly fish, peas and broad beans, but the flavour and particularly the texture of many fruits and vegetables are affected by freezing. Even so, freezing is convenient and helps preserve micronutrients in foods. Indeed, frozen vegetables may contain more vitamin C than vegetables bought 'fresh' in shops because the frozen vegetables are harvested at the optimum time and quickly frozen within a short time of harvesting. Fish can be cooked straight from the freezer without being defrosted (see page 66), but this is not advised for meat which becomes tough if cooked without defrosting.

Canned food

Serious cooks sometimes dismiss canned food as unworthy of consideration. However, canning food is essentially the same process as bottling which was an important means of preserving fruits and some vegetables for the winter before the days of freezing and improved distribution. The Italian housewife would be lost without canned or bottled tomatoes in the winter months. Canned tomatoes may be used very successfully to make tomato sauce.

The process of canning involves maintaining the temperature of the food at a high level for some time to give a safe and stable product. Some vitamins and other micronutrients are lost in canning, much as they would be as a result of cooking, but many others are preserved. The loss of vitamins in canned food need not be of concern to those who are also eating plenty of fresh vegetables and fruits as recommended here. It is also practical to use canned foods from time to time. The most obvious use is canned tomatoes for pasta sauce and other Italian recipes, and canned pulses (peas and beans) of various kinds, because some types of pulses, for example

> ### The simplest healthy meal ever
> Many fresh pastas available from supermarket cold cabinets are now made with added spinach (green colour) or added tomato paste (red colour). Put fresh pasta into boiling water for 2–3 minutes. Drain and serve with a good dribble of olive oil and a sprinkling of grated cheese (any cheese will do but Pecorino or Parmesan are particularly good as well as being authentic). Serve with a side salad (perhaps with Italian dressing), and follow with fresh fruit for the simplest healthy meal ever. Children love it. For convenience you can buy the fresh pasta and store in the freezer for at least a month. Cook the pasta straight from the freezer – it takes only a couple of minutes longer.

chickpeas, require simmering for hours before they are cooked. If you use canned fruit, choose fruit canned in juice rather than in heavy syrup.

Good cooking

Foods such as salads and some fruits and vegetables are delicious eaten raw, but much of our food is cooked in some way before we eat it.

Cooking has several beneficial effects. It kills bacteria which may contaminate food and which might otherwise cause serious illness. It makes food easier to chew, and makes certain starches and sugars easier to digest. Cooking also releases certain vitamins and micronutrients, enabling them to be more readily absorbed into the body. Cooking destroys certain chemicals, in pulses for example, that have evolved in the plant to poison animals, including man, and prevent the seeds being eaten.

Perhaps most importantly, cooking makes

food more enjoyable by altering flavour and texture, and by combining ingredients in innumerable ways.

To taste its best, food should not be burnt, or overcooked or cooked so long that it loses many of its nutrients. Our recommendation is not to eat food cooked over a direct flame. This is because chemicals known to cause cancer are formed when hot fat or meat juices come into contact with a flame or the hot embers in a barbecue and then stick to the surface of the food. Eating a lot of food cooked in this way – by grilling, frying or barbecuing – may increase the risk of some cancers. For similar reasons, don't eat food that is burnt or charred.

If we also follow the recommendation about reducing the amount of fat in our diets, it is best to avoid ways of cooking that allow the food to absorb a lot of fat.

So what are the best ways of cooking our food?

● Use low-temperature methods such as steaming, boiling, poaching and stewing.
● Grill food only lightly under an electric grill or indirect gas grill – this gets rid of unwanted fat without the risk of burning.
● Fry food lightly. Minimise the need to add oil by using a non-stick pan. Alternatively use a 'spray-on' oil.
● Wrap food in foil before you put it on the barbecue.
● Braise, bake or roast meat.
● Steam vegetables rather than boiling them – less of the micronutrients are lost.
● Pre-cook meat by microwaving (this saves time as well), then finish off with light grilling.
● Use a wok to stir-fry vegetables.
● When oven-roasting, use relatively low temperatures, and cook for a longer time.

Start at the beginning . . . of the day

A simple healthy breakfast may consist of a wholemeal cereal or muesli, or wholemeal bread, and fruit, or you can have a healthy cooked breakfast if you want.

Choose a wholemeal cereal which provides a full complement of vitamins. Avoid those high in sugar or salt. Avoid eating croissants or Danish pastries for breakfast because they are very high in fat and sugar and are made with white flour.

You can make your own individual 'muesli' at the breakfast table from porridge oats, sultanas and nuts (almonds, hazelnuts, walnuts) put out on the table. The dried fruit

Simple muesli made at the table

2 handfuls porridge oats
1 handful sultanas
a few nuts e.g. almonds, hazelnuts

Porridge oats are already cooked, so just put them in a bowl with the other ingredients and add semi-skimmed or skimmed milk to taste. Nothing could be simpler. The sultanas provide sweetness – add more if it is not sweet enough.

Pitted prunes (ready-to-eat) and dried apricots may be included as well as, or instead of, the sultanas. Chopped dates, sunflower seeds or any other muesli ingredient may also be added at the table.

By making your own, you can eat a subtly different mix every day.

Use semi-skimmed milk to reduce the fat in your diet. Most of us find it difficult to tell the difference between ordinary milk and semi-skimmed milk. Use skimmed if you need to reduce weight.

Stewed fruit

Add boiling water to dried fruit such as prunes, boil for a minute, and then leave for a couple of hours or overnight. Do not add any sugar when stewing the prunes or apricots. You may want to add a little sugar to stewed fresh plums and apples. You can use canned prunes, canned apricots, or canned orange or grapefruit segments, but choose fruit that has been canned in juice, not in syrup, which has added sugar.

---

in a muesli which is freshly made at the table is soft and chewy, much better than in commercial pre-packed mueslis in which the raisins and sultanas may turn into hard dry pellets that are difficult to chew.

Stewed fruit, which may be eaten with yoghurt or cereal, is another way to start the day. Dried apricots, prunes and pears are available all year round and are easily stewed (see above), while fresh plums, rhubarb or apples may also be stewed in season. If you add yoghurt, make the portion of yoghurt about half as big as the portion of fruit. This is quite different from starting the day with a carton of fruit yoghurt which provides too much yoghurt in proportion to fruit and contains a great deal of sugar.

Wholemeal toast and marmalade provides a healthy alternative to cereal or stewed fruit. Spread the marmalade directly on to the toast, or use just a little low-fat spread.

Breakfast is a good opportunity to drink fruit juice or eat fresh fruit such as an orange, an apple, a pear, some grapes, cherries or plums. A handful of dried fruit in muesli counts as one helping of fruit, and if you also eat a portion of fresh fruit you will have eaten two of your five daily portions of vegetables and fruits.

For a hot breakfast, try porridge (see page 65) particularly welcome on cold days. It can be flavoured with a blob of jam or a sprinkling

of sugar. It is better not to eat it with salt, as the Scots recommend. Although we suggest you reduce the amount of added sugar in your diet you do not have to totally avoid using sugar to make a wholemeal product such as oats more palatable. Eating sweetened porridge is completely different from eating large quantities of highly sweetened biscuits, sweets and soft drinks, which contain a lot of fat and are not made with whole grains.

A cooked breakfast can also meet with our recommendations for healthy eating. You could have grilled tomatoes on toast, a poached egg with baked beans, or sardines on toast. Kippers should not be eaten regularly because they are smoked and salted. Avoid fried bread which is extremely energy-dense and high in calories.

Why should I eat breakfast?

Some people are happy to go without breakfast in the morning. However, our blood sugar is lowest in the morning, and so it makes sense to eat something within an hour or so of getting up. You may not like eating before leaving the house in the morning, but by the time you reach work you will have been up for at least an hour and should eat something even if, in true continental style, it is just a piece of plain bread with a cup of coffee.

● People who do not have breakfast have been found to be less alert, less able to learn, and more likely to have an accident of some kind.
● If you skip breakfast altogether you will be hungrier at lunchtime, so you may eat more than if you had a simple snack earlier on.
● Regular meals train your body to expect regular food and reduce the urge to binge.
● People who avoid eating breakfast and lunch are likely to binge in the evening, and are more likely to have or to develop weight problems.

A perfect snack

Hallo, LTB – the lettuce, tomato, and bacon sandwich – sister to the BLT, one of the most popular sandwiches sold. Unfortunately, the BLT generally contains too little lettuce and tomato and is often made with rather soggy white factory bread. Make the LTB yourself, or go to one of those sandwich shops where they make the sandwich the way you want.

Here's how. Take two slices of wholemeal bread and spread one slice only with a little low-fat spread. Put in as much lettuce and tomato as you can (at least double the normal amount). Add just a little bacon, or other tasty alternatives such as cheese, chicken or tuna. Whatever you add, it should be just a flavouring – make sure you get the double salad of lettuce and tomato. Try other fish fillings: sardine or salmon. It is best to vary your diet, so you try a different combination of fillings each day.

Any kind of wholemeal sandwich provides healthier fare than snacking on sugary fruit yoghurts and biscuits. Bread with jam should not be dismissed as unhealthy. If the bread is wholemeal, and you use a low-fat spread, bread and jam is a much better snack than biscuits.

If you make your own sandwich lunch, include raw carrot, lettuce, tomato and cucumber in a lunch box: there is no need to squeeze all the salad into a sandwich – eat it separately. By making your own sandwiches, you can get the filling exactly right and ensure that they are not too salty.

Better snacks

The best quick snack is fruit: an apple, pear, orange, or a banana. Almost all the most easily available snacks – sweets, chocolate, crisps and so on – are too sweet, too salt and often too fatty for good health. Fruit bars made from compressed dates, figs, or other dried fruit are good snacks, but don't eat too many of them. They make a sustaining snack because the fruit sugars are released more slowly than the processed sugar in confectionery.

Bread, particularly wholemeal, makes a perfect snack because it gives us the calories we need without unnecessary sugar or fat. If the bread is really freshly baked with a good crust it is good to pull a chunk off the loaf and eat it without anything on it. England has given the sandwich to the world, but too often people think they are not eating properly if they make a meal of sandwiches. In fact, sandwiches provide a substantial quantity of starchy staple which is lacking in a lot of meals.

6 Recipes for health

All these recipes serve 4–6 people, unless otherwise stated.

Soups

Soup is too often relegated to the place of starter or forgotten about entirely. Its proper place is as the central dish of an informal family meal. Soup is a delicious way of eating vegetables and bread, and an increased consumption of these two items is one of our basic recommendations. Good soups are now available in supermarkets, but they are a lot more expensive than home-made soup. The best soup will always be the one you make yourself, when you can monitor fat levels.

Mediterranean

MINESTRONE

There are many minestrones, and every cook in Italy can give you several different recipes. Beans, potatoes, fresh vegetables and herbs are the essential ingredients, and pasta is often added. Never make minestrone without looking in the fridge to see what leftovers can be utilised as the mystery ingredient to give the soup extra flavour.

2 onions
3 celery stalks
2 large potatoes
2 medium carrots
2 tablespoons olive oil
1.5 litres ($2^3/_4$ pints) water or stock
350g (12oz) peas (fresh or frozen)
$^1/_2$ medium cauliflower
1 tablespoon chopped parsley
freshly ground black pepper
Parmesan, Pecorino or other cheese, grated

Peel and chop the onion, celery, potatoes and carrots. Cook the onion in the oil until lightly brown. Add the chopped celery, potatoes and carrots and cook until soft. Add the boiling water or stock and simmer for another 10 minutes. Add the peas, the cauliflower chopped into tiny florets, and the parsley, and season with freshly ground pepper. Cook for another 5–10 minutes and serve with cheese to sprinkle on top. To make this soup into even more of a meal, 2 tablespoons of pasta (or rice) may be added. Any kind of pasta will do but the smaller varieties made specially for soups are best. Add a few minutes before serving so that it is cooked *al dente* when it arrives on the table.

Mediterranean

ONION SOUP

French onion soup is the best-known version of a soup which is served throughout the Mediterranean. Chicken soup has been called 'Jewish penicillin' because it is so often prescribed by Jewish mothers for every ailment. In fact onion soup has a better claim to pharmaceutical virtue, and might well be called 'Mediterranean medicine'. There is scientific evidence that onions have antibiotic properties; they may also decrease the risk of certain cancers, reduce cholesterol levels, reduce blood clotting, and so protect against heart disease.

4 large Spanish onions
2 tablespoons olive oil
1 litre (1³/₄ pints) water (or vegetable stock)
1 medium potato, peeled and finely chopped
a squeeze of lemon juice
1 bouquet garni
freshly ground black pepper
slices of French bread, toasted
Cheddar or Gruyère cheese, grated

Peel the onions and cut into quarters then slice them. Sauté in the oil until golden. Add the water or stock, potato, lemon juice and *bouquet garni*. Simmer for 10 minutes. Season with pepper. Serve in the French manner with toasted bread and cheese floating on top. Put the soup in individual heatproof bowls and float a piece of bread, sprinkled with cheese, on top. Put under the preheated grill until the cheese has melted and is golden.

China

CRAB AND SWEETCORN SOUP

This dish is more popular in Chinese restaurants outside China than ever it was inside China. It combines an exotic flavour with an unusual texture of rough with smooth, and meets well with our recommendations for eating food with little fat. For many people one or two bowls of this soup will make a filling meal and they will not want a main course.

300g (10½oz) frozen corn kernels (sweetcorn)
500ml (18fl oz) chicken stock
3 slices fresh root ginger
100g (3½oz) crabmeat
50ml (2fl oz) sherry (optional)
freshly ground black pepper
1½ tablespoons cornflour
1 tablespoon chopped chives or parsley

Cook the frozen corn kernels in the stock with the ginger until they are soft. Shred the crabmeat and add it to the soup, bringing it again to the boil before adding the sherry and some black pepper. Blend the cornflour in a cup with 4 tablespoons water until smooth, and pour into the soup, stirring well. Put into a large serving bowl or individual bowls and scatter the chives or parsley on top.

Japan

MISO SHIRU (SOYA BEAN PASTE SOUP)

This soup has the reputation of giving 100 years of life to those who eat it regularly. Miso soup is a major item in the Japanese diet, and is as likely to be served for breakfast as any other meal. The basic ingredient of miso is fermented soya bean paste which can be bought nowadays in specialist food shops and health-food shops. Kombu (kelp seaweed), tofu (soya bean curd) and other ingredients can also be bought in these shops. However the only essential ingredient is the miso paste - so try it even if you cannot get the bonito (dried fish) shavings and the kombu. Beansprouts or diced aubergine can be used instead of the wakame (another seaweed) and tofu. Miso paste may also be added to a normal soup instead of stock.

1 piece kombu, 5cm (2in) square
1 litre (1³/₄ pints) water
¹/₂ teaspoon wakame
2 teaspoons dried bonito shavings
2 tablespoons aka miso (red soya bean paste)
or 3 tablespoons shiro miso (white soya beans
paste which is milder)
150g (5¹/₂oz) tofu, chopped

Allow the kombu to soak in the water for 2–3 hours or overnight. Put the wakame into the water to soften 10 minutes before using and, when it opens out, cut it into little pieces, then set aside. Put the kombu and its water into a pan to boil, but just before it boils discard the piece of kombu. Add the bonito shavings, boil for 2–3 minutes, and put the pan aside until the bonito shavings have sunk to the bottom. Pour off the clear liquid and add a few tablespoons of it to the soya paste. Stir until smooth and then return the diluted paste to the clear liquid. Bring to the boil, add the wakame and tofu, heat through and serve.

Spreads

These savoury purées can be used as part of a family meal, if served with plenty of hot bread and salad. In Greece these dips would be served with slices of hot pitta bread (toast it in a toaster or under the grill, fine straight from the freezer). But any kind of bread will do. Serve with a plate of cut vegetables (crudités) - sticks of raw carrot, celery and cucumber, pieces of raw cauliflower, slices of red and green peppers, and perhaps chunks of iceberg lettuce.

Mediterranean

AUBERGINE PURÉE

3 aubergines
1 large onion
juice of 1 lemon
1–2 tablespoons olive oil
2 garlic cloves, crushed
freshly ground black pepper
2 tomatoes

Bake the aubergines in the oven preheated to 200°C/400°F/Gas 6, until very soft inside (about 30–40 minutes). Cut them in half and scoop out the pulp. Discard the skins and mash the pulp. Peel and chop the onion into a few pieces and purée in the blender. Press the resulting pulp into a sieve with the back of a spoon to obtain the juice. Add the onion juice to the mashed aubergine. Add the lemon juice, olive oil, crushed garlic and pepper. Chop the tomatoes roughly and add to the aubergine mixture.

Mediterranean

HUMMUS

Hummus should contain a substantial amount of tahini (sesame seed paste) and olive oil as well as chickpeas, which are the principal ingredient. Some of the cheaper commercial varieties economise by putting in too little tahini, giving the hummus a watery texture and poor taste.

350g (12oz) can of chickpeas (or 175g/6oz dried chickpeas)
150ml (5fl oz) water
150g (5¹/₂oz) tahini
juice of 2 lemons
2 garlic cloves, crushed
2 tablespoons olive oil

If you want to start with dried chickpeas they should be soaked overnight in water. In the morning change the water and boil for 2 hours (sometimes more) until soft. The drained chickpeas (boiled or tinned) can then be put through a mouli or blended to a purée. If a blender is used, put all the ingredients together with the chickpeas and blend. Otherwise cream all ingredients in a bowl with the puréed chickpeas. The final result can be varied to taste by adding more or less garlic, tahini, olive oil and lemon juice.

Mediterranean

TAHINI DIP

This is a very simple standby since an unopened jar of tahini paste will keep for a long time at the back of your cupboard (store in the fridge once opened). Take a couple of tablespoons of the oily paste and mix in the blender or using a spoon with the juice of a lemon and enough water (start with a couple of tablespoons) for it to reach a creamy consistency. Season with freshly ground pepper.

Mediterranean

TZATZIKI

A delicious way to eat cucumber. See page 67 for ways of making your own thick or strained yoghurt at home.

1 medium cucumber
300g (10¹/₂oz) 0% fat Greek yoghurt
2 garlic cloves, crushed
freshly ground black pepper

Peel the cucumber and slice as finely as you can. The thinner it can be sliced the better. Place in a bowl, and add the Greek yoghurt. Add the crushed garlic and season with black pepper.

Mediterranean

TAPENADE

This is a delicious spread which may sometimes be bought ready-made but is even better if you make it yourself. The exact flavour will depend on the type of olives you choose. It is particularly delicious made with Kalamata olives, but you can use any kind of black olives. If the olives have stones you will have to stone them yourself, but this is worth it: olives with stones often have a fuller flavour than those bought ready-stoned because they are picked at a different stage. This spread tends to be rather salty so use judiciously.

250g (9oz) black pitted olives
1–2 tablespoons olive oil
juice of ¹/₂ lemon
100g (3¹/₂oz) capers
50g (2oz) anchovy fillets
1 garlic clove, crushed
1 sprig thyme
freshly ground black pepper

The proportions of the ingredients may be varied according to taste and availability. Put everything in a blender and that is it. If you do not have a blender you can do it the old-fashioned way and combine the ingredients in a mouli or with a pestle and mortar. The resulting purée may be served as a dip or spread, or may be put on small portions of bread and baked in a medium to hot oven (190°C/375°F/Gas 5) for a few minutes before serving.

Breads

Bread is an important starch food, and we should all eat more of it. There are a myriad varieties available now from every country of the world. Avoid factory-made sliced white.

Mediterranean

GARLIC BREAD

Peel garlic cloves and crush them in a press on to a plate. You can use almost any kind of bread but a French baguette works particularly well. Make a lot of slices half-way through the baguette and put bits of crushed garlic in each slit (with other types of bread, spread garlic thinly on chunks). Dribble olive oil sparingly over the bread, wrap in foil, and bake in the oven at 180°C/350°F/Gas 4 for 10 minutes or so.

Mediterranean

TOMATO BREAD

Tomato bread is made by rubbing soft ripe tomatoes over and on to pieces of bread, or into slits cut in a French-type loaf, and dribbling it sparingly with olive oil. If the tomatoes are firm they should be peeled and chopped and smeared on to the bread. The bread is then baked in the oven at 180°C/350°F/Gas 4 for 10 minutes or until the tomato is cooked.

Salads

These salads may be served as a main course. If you prefer, you could serve them with cold meat, cheese, sardines or a plate of hard-boiled eggs cut in half lengthways and scattered with freshly ground black pepper. Serve with good crusty bread.

Mediterranean

SALADE NIÇOISE

Too many people think of this dish as being simply a starter. If eaten with plenty of bread it is not difficult to make it into a main course. It usually stars tuna, but is good with or without.

4 medium tomatoes
4 medium cooked potatoes
8 anchovy fillets
2 hard-boiled eggs
250g (9oz) cooked green beans
8 pitted black olives
1 tablespoon chopped parsley or 5 basil leaves, chopped
2 tablespoons olive oil
$^1/_2$ tablespoon white wine vinegar
freshly ground black pepper

Optional ingredients:
peppers, tuna, fennel, capers, onion and lettuce

Slice the tomatoes and quarter the potatoes. Cut the anchovy fillets in half, and quarter the eggs lengthways. Put these with all the other ingredients in a salad bowl, toss with the oil and vinegar, and season with black pepper (no salt because of the anchovies).

Mediterranean

GREEK SALAD

This will make a good meal on its own but may be served with Hummus, Tzatziki or Aubergine Purée to make a more substantial or varied meal (see Spreads). Serve with plenty of hot pitta bread. The feta cheese, lemon juice and Kalamata or other Greek olives give this dish its authentic Greek character.

2 small continental cucumbers or 1 large English cucumber
2 large beef tomatoes or 4 medium ordinary tomatoes
1 onion
1 green pepper
2 tablespoons olive oil
juice of 1 lemon
115g (4oz) feta cheese, cut into cubes
12 black olives (Kalamata if possible)
freshly ground black pepper

Greeks generally cut the cucumber and tomatoes in pieces rather than slices for their salads. Peel the cucumber, cut it in quarters lengthways almost to the end to make four long pieces and then cut off chunks about 2cm (³/₄in) long. Cut the tomatoes in half and then cut off small bite-sized pieces. Peel and chop the onion coarsely, and cut the seeded pepper into strips. Place all the ingredients, except the cheese and olives, into a bowl and dress with oil and lemon juice. Season with black pepper and garnish with the cheese and olives.

Vegetable dishes

Vegetables are of course at the centre of Mediterranean and Middle Eastern diets, just as rice and vegetable dishes are central to Indian, Chinese and Japanese cooking. These are not vegetarian dishes which try to substitute for or simulate meat products, but dishes which stand proudly for what they are, and nothing else. Most may be eaten by themselves or with another vegetable dish and pasta, rice or bread. Or they may be served as an accompaniment to meat.

If you are not sure where to start, begin with ratatouille because it is so versatile; try different versions and you will be sure to develop favourites. Serve green beans and tomatoes or roast vegetables as a vegetarian main course, or eat with some of your favourite meat dishes.

Japan

AUBERGINE WITH SESAME

The flavour of sesame permeates this dish. It can be served with rice as an accompaniment for simply grilled fish.

2 tablespoons sesame seeds
2 tablespoons sesame oil
2 aubergines, cut into 2.5cm (1in) cubes
a little chopped fresh chilli, seeded (optional)
2 tablespoons miso (soya bean paste)

Toast the sesame seeds in a hot, dry frying pan until they are light brown. Heat the oil and fry the aubergine cubes until brown. Add the chilli if you like. Dilute the miso with a little water and stir into the aubergine until well coated. Sprinkle with the sesame seeds.

Afghanistan

AUBERGINES IN YOGHURT

This delicious Afghan way of cooking aubergines was found by Pat Chapman, an inveterate collector of curry recipes. This dish may be served on its own with rice and/or chapatis, or with a meat dish such as Bombay Chicken (see page 120).

2 aubergines
2 tablespoons vegetable oil
1 teaspoon ground coriander
1 teaspoon ground cumin
¹/₂ teaspoon powdered cinnamon
250g (9oz) onions, peeled and chopped
150g (5oz) low-fat plain yoghurt
1 teaspoon garam masala

Wash the aubergines and cut off the stalks. Cut into pieces about 2.5cm (1in) in size. Heat half the oil in a large frying pan (or wok), and stir-fry the spices for a minute, then add the onion and fry for 5 minutes. Add half the aubergine pieces and stir-fry for 2–3 minutes. Set the aubergine aside and add the remaining oil to the pan. When the oil is hot, add the remainder of the aubergine pieces and stir-fry for 2–3 minutes. Replace the first batch of aubergine and reheat both batches together. When the pieces show signs of softening, reduce the heat and add the yoghurt. (If the pan is too hot the yoghurt will curdle.) Simmer for about 15 minutes or until the aubergine is fully cooked. If the mixture is becoming a little dry carefully add some low-fat milk or water. Place in a serving dish and garnish with the garam masala (bought or home-made).

India

CELERY AND CAULIFLOWER DRY CURRY

This is another dish inspired by the indefatigable Pat Chapman, who found this recipe in eastern India. Celery and cauliflower complement each other in both flavour and texture, but other vegetables might equally well be included. Chilli powder has been omitted from the recipe. Serve with rice and/or chapatis. Recommended with Fish Balls or Koftas (see page 122).

250g (9oz) celery
500g (18oz) cauliflower
5 medium tomatoes
1–2 tablespoons vegetable oil
2 teaspoons cumin seeds
1 teaspoon black mustard seeds
2 teaspoons ground turmeric
3 garlic cloves, crushed
3 slices fresh root ginger

Wash the celery and cut into 2.5cm (1in) pieces. Wash the cauliflower and divide into small florets. Steam the cauliflower until it is cooked but still very crisp; do the same with the celery. (Or boil them.) Seed the tomatoes and remove the woody core. Quarter them. Heat the oil in a large frying pan or wok, and stir-fry the spices for about 1 minute. Stir-fry the garlic and ginger with the spices for another minute. Add the tomato quarters, and when they have softened, add the celery and cauliflower. Mix well and stir-fry for a minute or two. If the mixture becomes too dry, add a little water.

China

FRIED VEGETABLES

This dish is an attractive way of presenting several vegetables in one dish. It may be used to accompany any Chinese meal or can serve as a main dish with boiled rice. The method of cooking ensures that the vegetables have a crisp fresh flavour, while the sesame oil, together with the ginger and garlic, gives the dish its authentic Chinese flavour.

about 3 tablespoons vegetable oil
100g (3^1/$_2$oz) cauliflower
100 g (3^1/$_2$oz) spring greens
100 g (3^1/$_2$oz) carrots
100 g (3^1/$_2$oz) green beans
1 garlic clove
2 slices fresh root ginger
3 teaspoons soy sauce
7 tablespoons chicken or vegetable stock
1 teaspoon sesame oil
2 teaspoons rice vinegar
150g (5^1/$_2$oz) bean sprouts
freshly ground black pepper

Break the cauliflower up into small florets. Cut the greens into pieces about 3cm (1^1/$_4$in) across. Thinly slice the carrots. Trim the beans. Finely chop the garlic. Heat a little of the oil in a wok or large frying pan. Add the ginger and half the garlic and cook for 20 seconds before adding the green beans and carrot, and stir-frying for 3 minutes. Put the beans and carrots to the side of the pan, add a little more oil to the centre of the pan, and stir-fry the rest of the garlic and the cauliflower for 2 minutes. Put the cauliflower to the side of the pan. Add yet more oil, and stir-fry the greens. Sprinkle the soy sauce over the greens and turn. Push all the ingredients into the centre of the pan while keeping each type of vegetable grouped together. Add 3 tablespoons of the stock, cover the pan and let the vegetables simmer for 3–4 minutes. Then sprinkle a few drops of sesame oil over the vegetables and pour another 3 tablespoons of the stock on top. In a separate small frying pan, heat a little vegetable oil and stir-fry the beansprouts for 1^1/$_2$ minutes. Add the remaining stock, the vinegar, the sesame oil and black pepper, to taste, and continue to cook for another 30 seconds. Finally arrange the vegetables in rings of contrasting colour with the cauliflower at the centre surrounded by the green beans, then the carrots, followed by the spring greens and fringed with the beansprouts.

Mediterranean

RATATOUILLE

This is a mainstay of the Mediterranean diet, a delightful way of eating vegetables, usually accompanied by freshly baked bread. There are many versions of this dish: you can use twice as much onion, another pepper, or leave out the garlic if you like, it will still be ratatouille. The essential ingredients are olive oil, onion, some Mediterranean vegetables such as aubergine and courgette, and tomatoes.

1 aubergine
2 courgettes
1 onion
2 red or green peppers
250g (9oz) ripe tomatoes
2 garlic cloves, crushed
4 tablespoons olive oil
2 tablespoons tomto purée
1 tablespoon chopped fresh basil
1 tablespoon chopped fresh thyme
freshly ground black pepper

Chop the aubergine and courgettes; peel the onion and chop; seed and chop the peppers and tomatoes. Fry the onion, the crushed or diced garlic, and the peppers in the oil. When they are beginning to soften add the courgettes and aubergine, cooking them until they are nearly soft. Finally add the chopped tomatoes. When these have slightly softened, add tomato purée and the herbs and some freshly ground black pepper. (If you have no fresh basil to hand use 2 teaspoons pesto or a teaspoon of dried basil.) Serve warm, at room temperature or cold.

Britain

BRAISED GREEN PEAS

Serve this dish as a main course with bread, or as a side dish.

1kg (2¼lb) peas in the pod
1 lettuce
1 onion
1 tablespoon vegetable oil
freshly ground black pepper
1 egg

Peel the onion and cut it and the lettuce into slices. Put into a pan with the podded peas, the oil and pepper, and a tiny amount of water. Stew very gently for half an hour (less if the peas were frozen). Remove from the heat and add the well-beaten egg. Stir to cook the egg in the residual heat from the vegetables. Do not allow the peas to boil after the egg has been added.

Mediterranean

GREEK ROAST VEGETABLES

In small Greek villages women take this dish into the baker to be cooked in his oven while it is still hot after the bread has been baked. With a sprinkling of cheese it can be made into a meal in itself, or it could be served with a French omelette or as an accompaniment to almost any meat or fish dish. Try to include the potatoes, which are a starch.
Choose the quantity and type of vegetables according to the number of people that are to be fed and to what is available: they could include potatoes, peppers, aubergine, courgettes, fennel, onions (particularly red), and tomatoes. Cut medium scrubbed potatoes in half lengthways; larger potatoes may be cut in three lengthways. Cut fennel into four or six lengthways. Cut aubergine in quarters lengthways. Small courgettes may be left whole; larger courgettes should be halved lengthways. Cut large tomatoes in half. Peel and halve onions, and halve and seed peppers. Put a little olive oil in a baking dish and arrange the vegetables at random. Scatter with freshly ground black pepper, chopped basil and oregano. Place in a medium oven preheated to 200°C/400°F/Gas 6. Turn and baste vegetables after 20 minutes and again 15–20 minutes later. Serve when the potatoes are cooked so that the insides are soft and the outsides are crispy and slightly brown.

Middle East

SPINACH WITH BLACK-EYED BEANS

Spinach is a vegetable that is sadly neglected by many people living in northern countries. It is an excellent source of many vitamins, minerals and fibre. Combined with beans, spinach makes a sustaining and highly nourishing dish.

150g (5¹/₂oz) black-eyed beans, soaked overnight
500g (18oz) spinach
1 large onion
2 tablespoons olive or vegetable oil
freshly ground black pepper

Drain and simmer the black-eyed beans for about 20 minutes in a little water until they are soft. Be careful not to overcook or they will become mushy. Wash the spinach and cut up into pieces. Peel and chop the onion, then fry in the oil until soft. Add the spinach and stir until the spinach has wilted, a few minutes only. Add the drained beans and reheat. Season with pepper and serve hot as a side dish, or cold with bread as a starter.

Middle East

LEEK (OR SPINACH) OMELETTE

This is an excellent way to serve eggs. The vegetables add a flavour and texture to the omelette which may be eaten hot or cold.

500g (18oz) leeks (or spinach)
1 tablespoon olive or vegetable oil
lemon juice
freshly ground black pepper
4 eggs

Wash the leeks and remove the tough tops and outer leaves. Slice thinly and fry in half the oil for a few minutes until softened. Season with a squeeze of lemon juice and black pepper, and cook on in the juice until soft and lightly coloured. Beat the eggs, and add the leek mixture. Adjust the seasoning. Heat the remaining oil in a heavy pan until sizzling hot. Put the egg mixture in the pan then turn the heat down and cook gently until the eggs are set. Brown under a grill or turn the omelette to cook on the other side as in the recipe for Spanish Omelette (page 102). If using spinach, wash and cook it without water, then drain and chop it before mixing with the eggs.

Mediterranean

GREEN BEANS AND TOMATOES PROVENÇALE

Cooking tomatoes brings out all their sweetness and flavour.

400g (15oz) green beans
2 shallots or 1 small onion
2 garlic cloves
6 tomatoes
1–2 tablespoons olive oil
freshly ground black pepper
2 tablespoons chopped fresh parsley
1 tablespoon chopped fresh thyme
55g (2oz) fresh breadcrumbs

Top and tail the green beans; peel and chop the shallots and garlic; halve the tomaotes. Steam the beans for 2 minutes. Place them in the bottom of a shallow casserole, and dribble with a little of the oil. Sprinkle the garlic over the beans and season with freshly ground pepper. Fry the onion or shallots in a little oil for 3 minutes, then add half the tomatoes, turning to cook both sides until nearly soft. Put the onions or shallots and tomatoes on top of the beans, and season with pepper. Stir the fresh herbs into the breadcrumbs and sprinkle on top of the tomatoes. Dribble again with a little oil. Bake in the pre-heated oven at 200°C/400°F/Gas 6 for about 15 minutes.

Britain

BAKED TOMATOES

These tomatoes make a nice accompaniment to all kinds of roast meats. If you were to put on a cheese topping, they might equally well be served as a main dish with boiled potatoes and a green vegetable.

8–10 tomatoes
freshly ground black pepper
4 tablespoons fresh breadcrumbs
1 tablespoon vegetable oil

Cut the tomatoes into thick slices and place in a deep baking dish. Season with pepper, and cover with breadcrumbs. Dribble the oil over the breadcrumbs. Bake in the preheated oven at 180°C/350°F/Gas 4 for 15–20 minutes.

Britain

MASHED SWEDE OR TURNIP

Mashed buttered swede or turnip is a traditional British dish that is seen much less today than it used to be, except in Scotland, where 'neeps' is a necessary accompaniment to the Scottish haggis. This is the yellow-fleshed vegetable which is called swede in southern England but turnip in northern England and Scotland. The flavour of swede is sweeter and less pungent than that of the white-fleshed turnip, and its yellow flesh contains a high content of the important nutrient, beta-carotene.
Peel your swede and cut it into pieces of about 3cm (1¼in) across. Cover with water and boil until tender, about 15 minutes (or alternatively steam). Drain the swede and mash it with a tablespoon of low-fat milk or yoghurt. Season with black pepper. If a bit stiff, add a little of the turnip water. Serve mashed swede with lean grilled meat or oily fish and mashed potato.

Pasta and noodle dishes

Every sauce can be combined with 20 or more different types of pasta, making many different dishes. Here are just two pasta dishes, chosen because they are basic and show that little effort is required to produce a meal that is both nutritionally balanced, and satisfying and enjoyable. There is also a basic tomato sauce, for serving with pasta and grated cheese.

Mediterranean

TOMATO SAUCE

For the most authentic flavour, Italian plum tomatoes should be used. However any variety of fresh tomato will make a good sauce, and remember that in winter even Italians use canned tomatoes. This sauce can be used with any kind of pasta. Sprinkle with a little grated Parmesan to complete the meal. Other lighter cheeses such as Pecorino or Emmental may be used instead.

1kg (2¼lb) ripe tomatoes (canned may be used)
2 large garlic cloves
1 tablespoon olive oil
2 tablespoons chopped flat-leaf parsley
10 fresh basil leaves, chopped, or 2 teaspoons
pesto, or 1 teaspoon dried oregano.

Halve the fresh tomatoes and squeeze to remove the seeds if you like. Chop the flesh coarsely. Peel and crush the garlic and fry in the oil in a saucepan. Discard the garlic when it goes brown. Place the tomato and parsley into the pan and simmer for 20 minutes. (Sieve if you like.) Add the basil, pesto or oregano, and cook for a minute before serving.

Mediterranean

PASTA E FAGIOLI

This traditional dish would originally have been made in a large pot simmering beside or over a fire. You can start with 500g (18oz) of dry white haricot beans, soaking them overnight then simmering them for 2 hours, but there is no reason not to cheat and start with two cans of canned beans. Almost any kind of canned beans (other than baked beans) will do; drain and rinse them well.

500g (18oz) dry white beans, soaked and cooked,
or 2 x 400g (14oz) cans white beans
1.5 litres (2³/₄ pints) water
freshly ground black pepper
2–3 celery stalks, chopped
1 garlic clove, crushed
1 carrot, chopped
250g (9oz) tomatoes (or the equivalent canned), chopped
1 teaspoon rosemary leaves
2 tablespoons olive oil
250g (9oz) small pasta shapes

Put the cooked or canned rinsed beans in a pan with the water, and bring to the boil. Season with pepper, then add the celery, garlic, chopped carrot, tomatoes, rosemary and oil. Simmer for at least 15 minutes until the carrot and celery are thoroughly cooked. Add the pasta to the liquid, and cook until *al dente*, a few minutes only. Serve in soup dishes.

China

CHOW MEIN

Chow mein, or fried noodles, is a staple food served all over China. It uses a modest amount of meat in proportion to the starchy staple, proportions which we recommend, yet the method of preparation ensures that the full flavour of the meat and vegetables is absorbed into the noodles. Here is a simple basic recipe which can easily be varied - for example, by using bacon (unsmoked) instead of pork, shredded carrot or cabbage instead of celery. This dish is complete in itself but if you are serving more than four people, Fried Vegetables (see page 87) may be served as well.

550g (1¹/₂lb) Chinese noodles
300g (10¹/₂oz) lean pork
250g (9oz) mushrooms
1 garlic clove
5 spring onions
125 g (4¹/₂oz) celery
2 tablespoons vegetable oil
55g (2oz) bamboo shoots
2 tablespoons rice wine (optional)
2¹/₂ tablespoons soy sauce
100g (3¹/₂oz) shelled shrimps

Cook the noodles in boiling water until nearly soft. Then drain and rinse in a colander under the cold tap to prevent them sticking when fried. Slice the meat into the thinnest possible strips and cut up the mushrooms; peel and chop the garlic, chop the spring onion and shred the celery. Heat the oil in a wok or large frying pan, and fry the pork for 5 minutes. Add the chopped garlic, spring onion, celery, bamboo shoots and mushrooms, and stir-fry for 2–3 minutes. The oil should be hot enough so the food sizzles a little. Add the noodles, wine, soy sauce and shrimps. Mix all the ingredients together and cook for 5 minutes or until all is heated through.

Cracked wheat and chapatis

One recommended way of persuading people to eat more of the starchy staple foods is to try out new staples. Cracked wheat deserves to be better known, and chapatis are not difficult to make. Cracked wheat may be used in many recipes in a way similar to rice, and makes an interesting alternative. Frequent eaters of rice will find that it fits in with many of their recipes.

Mediterranean

CRACKED WHEAT (BULGUR OR BURGHUL) SALAD

This salad is an everyday dish in Cyprus, and is popular in other parts of Greece. It is a national dish in Syria and the Lebanon. Bulgur (called pourgouri in Cyprus) may also be used instead of rice in pilaf- and risotto-type dishes.

100g (3¹/₂oz) medium burghul
150g (5¹/₂oz) spring onions or Spanish onion, peeled
3 tomatoes
100g (3¹/₂oz) flat-leaf parsley, chopped
25g (1oz) fresh mint, chopped
freshly ground black pepper
3 tablespoons olive oil
juice of 1–2 lemons
pitted black olives
fresh lettuce leaves

Soak the burghul for 20 minutes in enough warm water to cover it. Drain well and put in a large bowl. Finely chop the onion and tomatoes, and add with the herbs and pepper to the burghul. Stir in the oil and lemon juice. Allow to stand for at least an hour before serving to allow the oil and lemon juice to be absorbed. Garnish with black olives and serve with lettuce leaves around the edge of dish. The lettuce leaves may be used to scoop up the delicious mixture. This dish may be served as a starter or as part of a larger salad meal.

India

CHAPATIS

Chapatis can be made from rice flour or wholemeal wheat flour. Indians use atta wholemeal flour, available from Indian or specialist shops, but ordinary wholemeal flour will serve well if it is sifted to remove any coarse particles.

Makes 10 chapatis

300g (10¹/₂oz) wholemeal flour
250–300ml (9–10fl oz) water

Mix the flour and water to a soft dough, and set aside for 30 minutes. Divide into 10 pieces and roll into thin pancakes on a floured surface, using plenty of extra flour with the rolling pin. Heat a heavy pan (cast-iron if you have one) or griddle over a low to medium flame for 10 minutes. Do not put any oil on the pan. Shake any loose flour off the dough cake and put it on the pan to cook for a minute or so, first on one side then on the other. Afterwards briefly grill the chapatis to puff them up. Stack one on top of another and keep warm.

Rice dishes

Here we give just three simple rice dishes in which the ingredients are cooked with the rice. Many other dishes given here will be served with rice, and we recommend that this should be cooked by the absorption method (see page 62) for maximum conservation of micronutrients.

Mediterranean

RAISIN PILAFF

This Albanian national dish may be served as a main course or as an accompaniment to meat. It is a good meal to make when you have a cooked chicken carcass left over to make the stock. Some pieces of cooked chicken may also be added after the rice is cooked to make it a more substantial meal. We are indebted to Robin Howe for the basic recipe.

2 tablespoons olive oil
200g (7oz) long-grain rice
600ml (1 pint) chicken or vegetable stock or water
100g (3¹/₂oz) raisins
a pinch of powdered cinnamon

Heat the oil in a sucepan and fry the rice, stirring well until it is translucent. Slowly stir in the stock or water, and simmer for 10 minutes. Add the raisins, put a lid on the pan and simmer for another 15 minutes until all the liquid is absorbed and the rice is tender. Stir the cinnamon into the rice.

Mediterranean

RISOTTO

This is a basic recipe for a very versatile dish. Small quantities of meat, poultry or vegetables may be added to the rice base to enrich its flavour and nutritive qualities.

1 onion
1 tablespoon olive oil
4–5 mushrooms
300g (10^1/$_2$oz) risotto rice
1 litre (1^3/$_4$ pints) stock or water
freshly ground black pepper
55g (2oz) almonds or pine kernels, chopped (optional)
Parmesan cheese, grated

Peel and chop the onion and fry in the oil with the chopped mushrooms for 5 minutes. Add the rice and fry for about another 3 minutes, stirring from time to time until translucent. Add about one-third of the stock and cook, stirring, until the liquid is absorbed. Add more liquid, and cook until the rice is *al dente*. Season with pepper, add the nuts, and serve with grated Parmesan.

Mediterranean

SIMPLE PAELLA

The seafood paella is best known but paella, like risotto, is a very versatile dish, and this version makes use of chicken and shrimps.

300g (10¹/₂oz) chicken breasts, without skin and bone
2 tablespoons olive oil
1 medium onion, peeled and chopped
1 green pepper, seeded and chopped
1 garlic clove, crushed
300g (10¹/₂oz) risotto rice
4 tomatoes, chopped
100g (4¹/₂oz) frozen peas
1–2 pinches saffron
600ml (1 pint) chicken stock or water
freshly ground black pepper
100g (3¹/₂oz) cooked peeled shrimps or prawns
freshly chopped parsley

Cut the chicken breasts into two or three pieces and fry in the olive oil until golden. Remove from the pan to a warm place. Sauté the onion, pepper and garlic for 3–4 minutes. Stir in the rice and cook for a few minutes until translucent. Add the tomatoes, peas, saffron and about one-third of the stock. Bring the mixture to the boil, making sure that it does not stick to the bottom of the pan, and return the chicken pieces to the pan. When the liquid has been absorbed, add another third of the stock and cook for a few minutes. When this too is absorbed add the remaining stock, cover the pot and cook until the rice is tender and has absorbed the liquid. Add the freshly ground pepper and prawns and heat through for 5 minutes. Garnish with parsley before serving.
Most paellas are more elaborate than this one, often containing shellfish such as mussels. These can be washed, steamed for 5 minutes (discarding any that do not open) and added for the last 5 minutes of cooking.

Potato dishes

Potatoes are a greatly underrated food. They have the potential to be combined in many exciting ways with other foods, but too often are served either plain boiled or plain fried. Here are two Mediterranean recipes which do something different with the potato.

Mediterranean

SPANISH OMELETTE

The contrasting textures and flavours of egg, potato and onion complement each other very successfully in this dish. It is good served hot with salad and bread, but can be served cold. A true Spanish omelette contains only onions and potatoes but you can vary it by frying chopped green and red peppers with the onion, or warming up cold leftover green beans or peas with the potato just before adding the egg.

1kg (2¼lb) potatoes (waxy are best), peeled and diced
2 large onions, peeled and diced
2 tablespoons olive oil
6 large eggs
2 tablespoons skimmed or semi-skimmed milk
freshly ground black pepper

Fry the potato and onion dice very slowly in the oil until softened; they should not brown. Beat the eggs with a fork and combine with the milk and black pepper. Turn up the heat under the onion and potato until the oil begins to smoke a little. Add the egg mixture to the potatoes and onions in the frying pan and mix well. Turn the heat down, and continue to fry gently, shaking the pan to make sure the liquid egg reaches the heat and sets. When the omelette is well cooked on the bottom the top will still be slightly runny. Loosen the omelette with a fish slice or palette knife. Place a plate over the top of the frying pan. Then, with a hand on top of the plate, turn pan and plate over together. Put the pan back on the heat adding a little more oil if necessary, and slide the omelette back into the pan. Cook for 2–3 minutes until done.

Mediterranean

GARLIC POTATOES

This dish might be seen as the epitome of Mediterranean fare, being a combination of two staples – the potato and garlic – blended with olive oil and mellowed by parsley, chives and lemon juice. This is simple but healthy food.

1kg (2¼lb) maincrop (not new) potatoes
3 tablespoons olive oil
6 garlic cloves
2 tablespoons each chopped parsley and chives
juice of 1–2 lemons

Peel and cut the potatoes into oblong pieces 2.5cm (1in) across and not more than about 4cm (1½in) long. Dry with kitchen paper. Heat the oil in a large pan, add the potatoes, and cook until light brown (about 7 minutes), turning as necessary. Add the unpeeled garlic cloves and cook for another 15 minutes, still turning the potatoes from time to time. When the potatoes are soft inside, remove the garlic cloves and peel them. Crush the garlic, then mix with the lemon juice and stir into the potatoes. Heat for a minute or two. Put into a hot serving dish and sprinkle with the parsley and chives.

Pulse dishes

Beans and peas were once important items in the British diet (although pease pudding, a staple dish of the poor, is probably best forgotten). In other cuisines, however, they have maintained their place because they are widely enjoyed, not simply because they are highly nutritious. Here are a few interesting ways of serving them.

Mediterranean

CHICKPEA SALAD

This is a favourite Spanish dish and not difficult to make with the help of canned chickpeas (garbanzos). Any hesitation about using canned food will be overcome when you consider the other fresh ingredients that are used to dress the chickpeas. Alternatively, prepare your own chickpeas (see below). Serve with bread, and a tomato and cucumber salad.

450g (1lb) cooked chickpeas (or 2 cans)
3 medium onions (or 3 bunches spring onions), peeled
2 peppers (red look best), seeded
juice of 2 lemons
1 tablespoon olive oil
1 tablespoons chopped parsley
a pinch of cayenne pepper (optional)

Chop the onions and peppers up small and mix with the chickpeas, lemon juice, oil, parsley and cayenne, if using. Allow to stand for at least half an hour so that the beans are well marinated.
To cook dry chickpeas, soak them overnight in plenty of water. Discard water in the morning, wash the chickpeas and cover with fresh water. Simmer until tender. Cooking time will depend on the age of the peas and how dry they were when you started, but will take at least an hour or two.

India

DHAL

The word 'dhal' is used to describe a wide variety of pulses (dried peas and beans), and the basic dishes made from them. Poor Indians eat dhal with rice, a small amount of vegetable and little else for most meals. For the better off, dhal is served as a sort of gravy that is spooned over dry dishes and rice to moisten them and make them more interesting. It is an excellent accompaniment to most meat or vegetable dishes.

400g (14oz) moong dhal, yellow lentils, green lentils or other dhal
I litre (1³/₄ pints) water
2 garlic cloves, chopped
4 cardamom pods, crushed or I teaspoon ground cardamom
I tablespoon cumin seeds or 2 teaspoons ground cumin
I tablespoon vegetable oil
juice of I lime

Simmer the dhal (lentils) in the water for an hour. Fry the chopped garlic, cardamom and cumin for 5 minutes in the oil, then mix with the dhal. Sprinkle with lime juice.

Mediterranean

BROAD BEANS WITH FRESH CHEESE

For this recipe, we are indebted to Ursula Ferrigno, who is an inspiration to those interested in new ways of cooking vegetables.

Ikg (2¹/₄lb) broad beans, podded
2 large red onions
I tablespoon of olive oil
250g (9oz) soft, barely salted sheep or goats' cheese
freshly ground black pepper

The beans are best fresh, but frozen will do. Peel and chop the onions, and fry gently in the oil until golden. Add the beans, season with pepper and barely cover with water. Simmer for 5–7 minutes, or until the beans are cooked. Cut the cheese into slices and warm briefly under the grill. Serve with the hot beans and hot ciabatta bread.

Meat dishes

The recipes which follow, many of them adaptations of classic British dishes, show how meat can be used in a more economical way to provide a well-balanced meal which is not lacking in vegetables or starchy food. Meat may still have a central place in the meal because of its strong flavour, but in these dishes, as in the Mediterranean, Middle Eastern or Chinese cuisines, it does not dominate. Meat has a different place in these diets, and tends to be used as one ingredient among others, as a flavouring and a garnish.

Mediterranean

LAMB CUTLETS AND SPINACH

Lamb cutlets are very British, but try them this way, inspired by Greek cooking. The herbs give the lamb a fresh smell that may remind you of evenings spent in Greek tavernas.

Serves 6

6 lamb cutlets
2 tablespoons fresh oregano
1.5kg (3lb 5oz) spinach
1 tablespoon olive oil
juice of $^1/_2$ lemon

Trim visible fat from the cutlets, and place them on a baking tray. Sprinkle with oregano, and bake in the oven preheated to 180°C/350°F/Gas 4 for about 20–30 minutes. Wash the spinach, shake it dry, and tear into smallish pieces. Cook in a pan without water with the lemon juice and olive oil. Season with black pepper. Arrange the cutlets on a plate with the spinach at the centre. Serve with boiled potatoes and an additional vegetable.

Britain

NEW SHEPHERD'S PIE

Shepherd's pie should, of course, be made with lamb but the name is often used for any meat pie topped with mashed potato and, contrary to all logic, the meat is often beef. There could scarcely be any dish which is more British than this, the staple fare of canteens and homes up and down the country. Although simple, it is still delicious when made with good-quality fresh ingredients.

Serves 5

1 medium onion
2 medium carrots
1 tablespoon vegetable oil
400g (14oz) extra lean beef mince (or lamb)
freshly ground black pepper
150g (5¹/₂oz) mushrooms
250g (9oz) frozen peas
750g (1lb 10oz) potatoes, boiled and mashed

Peel and chop the onion and carrot, and fry in the oil for a few minutes. Add the mince and cook, stirring, until brown. Season to taste with pepper, then add the mushrooms and frozen peas, and cook just until the peas are defrosted. Put in an ovenproof dish and pile on the mashed potato, texturing the top with a fork. Bake for 30–45 minutes or until brown in a preheated oven at 200°C/400°F/Gas 6. Serve with green vegetables such as cabbage or broccoli, lightly boiled or steamed.

Britain

NEW LANCASHIRE HOTPOT
....

This dish has been eaten by generations of Britons. Long slow cooking, originally beside or over an open fire, produces a delicious melding of flavours. The dish is complete in itself so all you need is the time to cook it – about 2¹/₂ hours.

Serves 6

500g (18oz) extra-lean middle or best end neck of lamb
4 carrots
1 small turnip
2 onions
1 leek
2 tablespoons vegetable oil
freshly ground black pepper
2 tablespoons chopped parsley
750g (1lb 10oz) potatoes
300ml (¹/₂ pint) stock or water

Peel and chop the vegetables as appropriate. Put enough of the carrot, turnip, onion and leek into a casserole to cover the bottom. Sprinkle with half the oil. Remove any large pieces of fat from the meat, then place the meat on top of the layer of vegetables and cover with the rest of the vegetables. Season with black pepper and chopped parsley. Slice the potatoes thickly and place overlapping in several layers on top of the vegetables and meat. Add the stock or water, and dribble the rest of the oil over the potato slices. Cover the casserole with a lid or foil and put into the oven preheated to 150°C/300°F/Gas 3 for 2 hours. For the last half hour uncover the casserole and increase the temperature of the oven to 200°C/400°F/Gas 6 to brown the top of the potato. Serve with additional green vegetables such as cabbage and broccoli, lightly boiled or steamed.

Britain

NEW CORNISH PASTY

Use Greek filo pastry which is made with only flour and water, for a low-fat alternative to the traditional shortcrust pastry. Filo pastry is brushed with oil during preparation, but the amount used can be kept to a minimum.

Serves 6

500g (18oz) extra-lean minced steak
1 large onion
1 large turnip
4 medium potatoes
2 tablespoons mixed chopped fresh herbs
freshly ground black pepper
500g (18oz) filo pastry
vegetable oil
1 small egg

Peel and finely chop the potato, onion and turnip, mix with the meat and herbs and season with pepper. Take 8–10 sheets of filo pastry, brush each sheet lightly with oil and place on top of each other. Cut through the 10 sheets dividing them into 4 smaller sheets. Place a quarter of the meat mixture into each of these. Dampen the edges with beaten egg, working it slightly between the sheets. Pull the sheets up to meet at the centre and seal by doubling over and pressing. Brush the pasties with beaten egg. Put on a greased baking tray and bake in the preheated oven at 200°C/400°F/Gas 6 for 20 minutes. Turn the heat down to 180°C/350°F/Gas 4, and cook for a further 20 minutes. Serve hot or cold with a good salad.

Britain

NEW STEAK AND KIDNEY PIE

This is a classic English dish. However, this recipe has no suet pastry, no dripping and no melted butter, adding up to a lower-fat version. Fortunately, it still has that thick meaty gravy and the Worcestershire sauce, which provides a special English flavour, enhanced by extra carrots and peas. The parsnip, a vegetable underrated in other countries, can add another dimension of Englishness to this dish.

Serves 6

2 medium onions
2 medium carrots
1 tablespoon vegetable oil
300g (10¹/₂oz) chuck steak
200g (7oz) ox kidney
1 tablespoon plain flour
1 teaspoon Worcestershire sauce
50ml (2fl oz) low-fat milk
100g (3¹/₂oz) frozen peas
freshly ground black pepper
1kg (2¹/₄lb) potatoes
150ml (5fl oz) beef stock or water
1 large parsnip (optional)

Peel and chop up the onion and carrot and fry in the oil for a few minutes. Chop the steak and kidney into small pieces. Turn up the heat under the pan and add the meat, cooking it until well browned. Sprinkle in the flour and stir well so that fat and juices are absorbed. Add the Worcestershire sauce and slowly stir in the stock or water. Allow to simmer for a minute and then add the peas and pepper and bring back to the boil. Meanwhile peel the potatoes and parsnip and boil until soft. Mash together with a little low-fat milk. Pour the meat and vegetable mixture into a casserole dish and top off with the mixture of mashed potato and parsnip. Texture the top with a fork, then cover with a lid or foil and bake for 1 hour in the oven preheated to 200°C/400°F/Gas 6. Remove the lid for the last 20 minutes to allow the top to brown. Serve with green vegetables such as cabbage and broccoli, lightly boiled or steamed.

Mediterranean

STIFADO

The value of the Mediterranean diet in preventing heart disease was shown by Ancel Keys' famous Seven Countries Study many years before others understood and appreciated it. He and his wife Margaret grew olives on their own land near Naples and collected recipes from all over the Mediterranean. We are indebted to them for this recipe for stifado which they emphasise should have at least as much onion as meat.

Serves 6

500g (18oz) lamb, cut into 2.5cm (1in) cubes
2 tablespoons olive oil
70g (2¹/₂oz) tomato paste
1–2 garlic cloves, peeled and chopped
1 bay leaf
1 tablespoon red wine vinegar
freshly ground black pepper
700g (1lb 9oz) small white onions, peeled

Trim the meat of all visible fat, then brown in the oil in a casserole. Add all the other ingredients apart from the onions, and cover with water. Simmer for about an hour. Skim off any excess fat. Add the whole onions to the casserole and simmer for about another hour until they are soft and the meat is meltingly tender.

Mediterranean

MOUSSAKA

This dish might be called Greek shepherd's pie and should be cooked with lamb.
But it is too often adapted to English tastes, using beef instead of lamb (and *more* than
necessary), and butter rather than olive oil. Eat with a salad or a vegetable side dish
such as green beans.

Serves 6

1 kg (2¼lb) aubergines
olive oil
2 onions
500g (18oz) tomatoes
500g (18oz) extra lean minced lamb
1 tablespoon chopped parsley
freshly ground black pepper
300g (10½oz) breadcrumbs
25g (1oz) butter or low-fat soft margarine
40g (1½oz) plain flour
600ml (1pt) skimmed or semi-skimmed milk
2 eggs, beaten
3 tablespoons grated cheese (use reduced-fat Cheddar)
freshly grated nutmeg

Slice the aubergine and fry in a little oil on both sides until brown. Peel and chop the
onion; chop the tomatoes. Fry the meat and onion in a little oil until brown, then add
the tomato, parsley and black pepper. Remove from the heat and stir in half the
breadcrumbs. Make a white sauce with the butter, flour and milk. Beat in the eggs and
the nutmeg.
Then assemble the moussaka in an oiled baking dish which is traditionally square or
rectangular so the moussaka can be cut into equal oblong portions. Sprinkle the bottom
of the dish with some of the remaining breadcrumbs, add a layer of aubergine (using half
of the slices), and a layer of lamb mixture, then another layer of each, using up the
aubergine and meat. Pour the white sauce over the top and sprinkle the rest of the
breadcrumbs. Add the cheese on top. Bake in the preheated oven at
190°C/375°F/Gas 5 for 40 minutes until crusty on top.

Mediterranean

MACARONADE

This is a thrifty recipe which combines a small amount of meat with a larger ratio of starch, here pasta. A macaronade may make use of gravy and pieces of meat that are left over from a previous meal, or it may be made with a small amount of fresh minced meat. Any kind of meat may be used: beef, lamb, pork or chicken. Serve with vegetables, or a special vegetable dish such as Baked Tomatoes (see page 93).

115g (4oz) lean minced meat or small pieces of trimmed leftover roast meat
1 small onion, peeled and chopped
1 tablespoon olive oil
100ml (3¹/₂fl oz) water or stock
175ml (6fl oz) leftover meat gravy
300g (10¹/₂oz) macaroni or similar pasta
25–55g (1–2oz) Parmesan or reduced-fat Cheddar cheese, grated

If starting with fresh meat, fry the onion in the oil until golden, then add the mince, breaking it up into very small bits. When the mince has changed colour, add the water or stock and stir well. Use this mixture instead of the leftover meat and gravy. Cook the pasta in the usual way, drain and put in an ovenproof dish. Remove any congealed fat from the cooked or leftover meat and gravy. Add the meat to the pasta and mix well. Sprinkle the grated cheese on top. Bake in the oven preheated to 170°C/325°F/Gas 3 for about 20–30 minutes.

Mediterranean

LIVER AND ONIONS (FEGATO ALLA VENEZIANA)

Liver is an exceptionally good source of micronutrients. It is rich in vitamins A, B_2, B_6, B_{12}, C, D, niacin, zinc, iron and selenium as well as being a good source of protein. In this recipe the liver is combined with plenty of onions and served with boiled potatoes, pasta or rice, making a particularly nourishing dish.

Serves 4

300g (10^1/$_2$oz) liver (from calf or lamb)
4 large onions, peeled and halved
1 tablespoon olive oil
85ml (3fl oz) white wine

Cut the halved onions into half rings and fry in the oil very gently, until golden brown, about 20–30 minutes. Cut the liver into small pieces, less than bite-sized. Add the liver to the onions and stir-fry for 2–3 minutes only, then add the white wine to make a sauce. Stir well, bubble to heat through, and serve straight away.

Middle East

STUFFED TOMATOES

This dish makes imaginative use of a vegetable which we particularly recommend for its high content of micronutrients and its reputation for reducing the risk of certain cancers. It also makes very effective use of a small amount of meat. Medium to large tomatoes or beef tomatoes are easiest to stuff.

500g (18oz) large tomatoes
1 small onion
1 tablespoon olive oil
100g (3¹/₂oz) sultanas or raisins
100g (3¹/₂oz) extra-lean minced beef or lamb
100 g (2¹/₂oz) cooked rice
1 dessertspoon each of chopped basil and coriander,
or a pinch each of coriander, dried oregano and dried basil
a squeeze of lemon juice
freshly ground black pepper

Cut the tops off the tomatoes and scoop out the centres, reserving the tops, the juice and pulp. Peel and chop the onions, then fry in the oil until tender. Add the sultanas and meat, and fry, stirring, for another 3 or so minutes. Mix the meat and onion with the cooked rice and the chopped pulp and the juice of the tomatoes. Add the herbs and lemon juice, and season to taste with peppers. If necessary, add a little water or wine so that you can easily spoon the mixture into the tomatoes. Put the tomato tops back on, place in an ovenproof dish and bake in the oven preheated to 170°C/325°F/Gas 3 for about 50 minutes.

Middle East

CRACKED WHEAT AND CHICKPEA STEW

This dish can be made with meat or with tomatoes. Serve as a main dish with bread or potatoes and, if you like, some thick 0% fat Greek-style (strained) yoghurt.

1 large onion
2 tablespoons of oil
500g (18oz) extra-lean stewing lamb or beef,
or 500g (18oz) chopped tomatoes
100g (3¹/₂ oz) chickpeas (soaked overnight or from a can)
freshly ground black pepper
1 teaspoon powdered cinnamon
225g (8oz) coarse burghul

Peel and chop the onion then fry in the oil until it is brown. Add the meat, frying and stirring it until it changes colour. If using tomatoes, do not add them yet. Add the drained chickpeas, cover with water and bring to the boil. Season with pepper and half the cinnamon. Simmer gently for at least an hour or until the chickpeas are cooked and the meat is tender. Add the burghul – and the tomatoes, if using them instead of meat – and cook for another 15 minutes when the stew should be thick. Add water if necessary. Adjust seasoning. Put in a shallow dish and sprinkle the remaining cinnamon on top.

Middle East

LAMB STEW

This recipe shows how a small amount of meat, married with vegetables and pulses, can make a delicious dish to serve a family. The garlic, coriander and other spices give it an unmistakable aroma that evokes kitchens all over the Middle East. Serve it with rice.

500g (18oz) vegetables (courgettes,
aubergines, tomatoes, green beans, okra,
cabbage, spinach or artichoke hearts)
1 large onion
1 tablespoon olive oil or other vegetable oil
300g (10¹/₂oz) stewing lamb, well trimmed and chopped
2–3 tablespoons ground allspice, cumin or coriander
freshly ground black pepper
250g (9oz) potatoes
150g (5¹/₂oz) cooked chickpeas, lentils or split peas

Peel, trim and chop the chosen vegetables as appropriate. Peel and chop the onion, then fry in the oil for a minute or so. Add the meat, frying and stirring until it is brown. Add the chopped vegetables and cook for a few minutes, stirring occasionally. Cover with water and stir in the tomato paste, parsley and spice and pepper. Simmer for 1¹/₂ hours adding water if the sauce becomes too thick. Add the potatoes and pulses about 20 minutes before the end of the cooking time.

Chicken dishes

Chicken is perhaps the healthiest meat that is readily available to us on a regular basis. It is also very versatile in the kitchen, lending itself well to dishes which supply generous helpings of vegetables and starch.

Mediterranean

PROVENÇALE FRIED CHICKEN

Any part of the chicken, or a whole chicken divided up, may be used in this recipe, but breast is convenient because it is easily made into small portions.

Serves 6

400g (14oz) chicken breasts without skin and bone
1 tablespoon olive oil
2 garlic cloves
1 tablespoon chopped parsley
1 tablespoon chopped thyme, oregano or basil
1 large onion, peeled and sliced
10 small mushrooms
150ml (5fl oz) white wine or water
juice of $1/2$ lemon

Lightly brown the chicken all over in the oil. Cut the garlic into pieces and add along with half the herbs. Cook for another 2 minutes, turning the chicken to absorb the flavour of the garlic and herbs. Add the onion and continue cooking until it just begins to colour, then add the mushrooms. When the mushrooms are cooked, add the white wine (or water) and pepper and bring to the boil. Cover and simmer for about 20–25 minutes or until the chicken is tender and the sauce has thickened. Put the chicken on a plate and cover with the sauce. Sprinkle the remainder of the herbs and the lemon juice over it. Serve with rice and vegetables.

China

CHICKEN AND MUSHROOMS

This dish should be made with Chinese mushrooms if you want an authentic Cantonese taste. However, it is also delicious made with button mushrooms. Serve this dish with plenty of boiled rice and Fried Vegetables (see page 87).

150g (5¹/₂oz) chicken breast without skin and bone
1 dessertspoon cornflour
2 tablespoons vegetable oil
1 slice fresh ginger root, finely chopped
1 garlic clove, crushed
1 small onion, peeled and finely chopped
150g (5¹/₂oz) mushrooms
3 tablespoons chicken stock
1 dessertspoon soy sauce
1 tablespoon dry sherry

Slice the chicken into pieces about 1cm (¹/₂in) thick and 2cm (1in) long. Dust the chicken with half the cornflour, rub it well in and leave aside for 15 minutes so that the starch can absorb the meat juices and swell. Heat 1 tablespoon oil in a frying pan (or wok), add the ginger, garlic and onion, and stir-fry for 20 seconds. Add the chicken and stir-fry for about 2 minutes. Add the mushrooms and stir-fry for 2 minutes. Mix the remaining cornflour with the chicken stock, soy sauce and sherry. Add to the pan, continuing to stir-fry for about a minute. Put into a warm dish and serve straightaway.

Garam Masala

Garam masala has no standard formula, but varies with the cook and the region. Proprietary versions may easily be bought in supermarkets, but they put in less of the more expensive spices such as cardamom and cloves. Madhur Jaffrey recommends that you make your own garam masala in a clean coffee grinder using: 1 tablespoon cardamom seeds, 5cm (2in) cinnamon stick, 1 teaspoon black cumin seeds (or regular cumin seeds if black are unavailable), 1 teaspoon cloves, 1 teaspoon black peppercorns and 1/4 average nutmeg. Store in an airtight jar.

India

BOMBAY CHICKEN WITH RED SPLIT LENTILS

We are indebted to Madhur Jaffrey, doyenne of Indian cooks, for this recipe which combines in one dish both chicken curry and dhal. The combination enables a relatively small amount of chicken to go a long way. Serve with rice and, if desired, Chapatis (see page 98)

Serves 6

100g (3^{1}/$_{2}$oz) onions
I litre (1^{3}/$_{4}$pt) water
250g (9oz) red split lentils
2 teaspoons ground cumin
I teaspoon ground turmeric
400g (14oz) chicken breasts without skin and bone
I tablespoon vegetable oil
I teaspoon cumin seeds
2 garlic cloves, chopped
I teaspoon finely chopped fresh root ginger
250g (9oz) peas (fresh or frozen)
I tablespoon lemon juice
^{1}/$_{4}$ teaspoon garam masala (bought or home-made) (see above)
2 tablespoons chopped fresh coriander

Peel and chop the onions, and simmer in the water in a heavy pan with the lentils, ground cumin and turmeric. Cook on a low heat for 30 minutes. Add the chicken, bring back to the boil, and simmer again on a low heat for 30 minutes. Heat the oil in a small frying pan and put in the cumin seeds. When they begin to sizzle add the garlic and ginger. When the garlic has turned slightly brown add the mixture to the chicken and lentils in the other pan. Add the peas, lemon juice and garam masala. Cook for 5 minutes, and sprinkle with fresh coriander just before serving.

Fish dishes

Fish is an inherently healthy food, and is very easy to cook. Unlike meat, you do not have to worry about eating too much of it. In fact most people eat too little fish. Keep a supply in your freezer and you can eat it whenever you like within about 40 minutes of a cold start (see the recipe for Fish with Tomatoes and Onions below).

Mediterranean

FISH WITH TOMATOES AND ONIONS

Nothing could be simpler than this delightful Greek method of cooking fish. Almost any fish can be cooked this way, including fillets or pieces of fish straight from the freezer. Use maincrop potatoes rather than new potatoes with this dish so they can be mashed on your plate with the juice from the fish to make a delicious mixture.

2 tablespoons olive oil
4 fish fillets or steaks
4 medium tomatoes
2 large onions
12 black pitted olives
juice of ¹/₂ lemon
150ml (5fl oz) white wine
2 tablespoons chopped parsley

Put half the oil in a suitable baking dish and spread it around. Put the fish pieces on top of the oil. Cut the tomatoes and onions into slices and arrange over and around the fish. Scatter the olives on top. Dribble lemon juice, the remainder of the oil, the wine and parsley over the top. Bake in the oven preheated to 180°C/350°F/Gas 4 for about 40 minutes (or up to an hour if starting with frozen fish). Serve with rice or potatoes.

India

FISH BALLS (KOFTAS)

This dish will be enjoyed alike by those who love fish and those who find simple fish recipes rather bland as the herb and spices give an extremely exotic taste. Combine with rice and a vegetable dish such as Celery and Cauliflower Dry Curry (see page 86).

500g (18oz) white fish
1 medium onion, peeled and finely chopped
2 tablespoons fresh chopped coriander
1 tablespoon ground cumin
3 slices fresh root ginger, finely chopped
1 egg, beaten
breadcrumbs
oil for frying

Mince the fish if you have a mincer, or chop it coarsely and put in a blender for about 20 seconds or long enough to produce a coarse mince. Alternatively chop the fish as finely as you can. Mix with the onion, coriander and ginger and cumin. Add the egg as a binder, and shape the mixture into smallish balls. Roll the balls in breadcrumbs and shallow-fry in oil. Drain very well on kitchen paper.

Mediterranean

MONKFISH WITH RATATOUILLE

Monkfish can be expensive, but it is a good firm fish. This recipe comes from the South of France.

1kg (2¼lb) monkfish tail
4 garlic cloves, peeled and cut into slivers
freshly ground black pepper
Ratatouille (see page 88)

Make slits in the flesh of the fish and insert slivers of garlic. Season with black pepper. Put the ratatouille in a casserole and place the fish on top. Bake in the oven preheated to 180°C/350°F/Gas 4 for 30–45 minutes, turning the fish from time to time.

China

SKEWERED FISH WITH VEGETABLES

Oily fish such as tuna is full of nutrients, but a firm white fish such as monkfish could be used instead.

750g (1lb 10oz) tuna steak, about 4cm (1¹/₂ in) thick
2 red peppers, seeded
2 medium onions, peeled
75ml (2¹/₂ fl oz) dry white wine
2 tablespoons soy sauce
freshly ground black pepper

Cut the tuna into 4cm (1¹/₂ in) cubes. Cut the peppers and onion 'layers' into pieces about the same size. Put the tuna into a dish and pour over the wine and soy, then season with black pepper. Leave to marinate for at least an hour. Impale alternate pieces of fish, pepper and onion on skewers and cook under a preheated grill for about 10 minutes, occasionally turning the skewers. Serve with rice and a green vegetable or salad.

Fruit desserts

Fruit is the usual everyday dessert in the Mediterranean, the Middle East and parts of China. In these places fresh fruit is available for much of the year. On special occasions Italians, for example, may serve quite elaborate desserts such as tiramisu, a creamy pudding, but normally it would be fruit. As well as recipes for cooking fruit, we suggest special ways of serving fresh fruits which make fruits more enticing and easier to eat.

Mediterranean

PRUNES IN RED WINE

This delicious dessert counts as one of your five plus portions of vegetables and fruits daily, and it is very easy to prepare.

500g (18oz) prunes (the pitted, pre-soaked ones)
500 ml (18fl oz) red wine
2 cloves
strips of rind from 1 orange
1/2 cinnamon stick

If starting with pitted prunes, put all the ingredients into a saucepan and simmer for an hour. At the end of that time the prunes should be fully swollen and the alcohol will have partially evaporated, leaving a delicious liquor. Cool and refrigerate then serve with 0% fat Greek yoghurt.
If you start with whole prunes (with stones), cover them with water and bring to the boil. Leave for at least 3–4 hours to swell – overnight is best. Then proceed as above.

Mediterranean

FLAMBÉ BANANAS

This is a very simple dish to prepare, but spectacular, and very flavourful.

5 bananas
2 oranges
2 teaspoons sugar
2 teaspoons powdered cinnamon (optional)
4 tablespoons rum

Peel the bananas and place in a greased baking dish. Squeeze the oranges and pour the juice over the bananas. Sprinkle sugar and cinnamon over the bananas. Pour the rum over the bananas, stand back and ignite. Serve as soon as the flames have gone out.

Middle East

FRUIT SALAD OF APRICOTS, SULTANAS AND NUTS

This dish is eaten in large quantities by Muslims during Ramadan to break their fast. Apricots, sultanas and nuts are the basic ingredients, although prunes may also be added. This dish improves on keeping.

250g (9oz) dried apricots
125g (4¹/₂oz) sultanas and/or prunes
55g (2oz) blanched halved almonds and/or
pine kernels and/or pistachios
1 tablespoon sugar
1 tablespoon rose water or orange-blossom
water

Put the dried fruit in a bowl with the sugar and add enough boiling water to cover. Allow to cool, then add the nuts and rose water. Cover and put in the refrigerator for a day or two before eating.

Britain

FRUIT CRUMBLE

Our recommendations for healthy eating are incorporated in this traditional English pudding, made healthier by adding oats to the crumble topping to give an interesting texture and a slightly nutty flavour. Some ground almonds or hazelnuts may also be added. Wholemeal flour may be used instead of plain flour and a little raising agent may then be added to lighten it.

3–4 large cooking apples,
or 1kg (2¼lb) of other fruit such as rhubarb, plums,
gooseberries or summer fruits
100g (3½oz) soft margarine
150g (5½oz) plain flour
cornflour or arrowroot (optional)
40g (1½oz) brown sugar
200g (7oz) porridge oats

Cut the apples into thin slices; cut the plums in half and remove stones. If the plums are hard, pre-stew for a few minutes with 2 dessertspoons of water and a dessertspoon of brown sugar (or to taste). Unless the gooseberries are very ripe, they will also have to be pre-stewed. Rub the margarine into the flour and oats mixture. Add the sugar and mix with a knife. Put the fruit in a baking dish and cover with the crumble mixture. Bake in a preheated oven at 200°C/400°F/Gas 5 until the fruit is cooked and the top is golden brown. Apples may be mixed very successfully with summer and autumn fruits, particularly blackberries. Serve with English custard, *crème fraîche* or low-fat natural yoghurt, all of which are to be preferred to cream.

Britain

SIMPLE STEWED FRUIT

Cooking apples, plums, gooseberries and rhubarb are particularly delicious simply stewed with the minimum of sugar. Blackcurrants are also delicious stewed, and are very high in vitamin C. Good cooking apples (Bramleys) are available most of the year, although they may be more difficult to get at the end of the summer. Cut up the apples, core and peel. Add about a tablespoon of muscovado (or other) sugar to each 450g (1lb) apples (or to taste), a little water and cook until tender. Serve with some low-fat yoghurt or custard, or with cereal at breakfast.

Britain

SUMMER PUDDING

This is a classic English pudding which at one time could only be made at the height of summer. Now soft fruit such as raspberries, blackberries and blackcurrants can be bought frozen all year round, and there is no reason why it should not be served in the depths of winter. The dish works best if made with factory sliced white bread which turns into a delicious 'gunge' when it absorbs the fruit juices. It can also be made with brown or wholemeal bread; use the factory sliced type. Crusty bread is not suitable.

900g (2lb) mixed raspberries, blackberries
and/or blackcurrants
2 tablespoons sugar
several slices of bread

Stew the berries with the sugar and about a tablespoon of water in a pan over moderate heat, stirring from time to time. The berries should be cooked for only a minute after they have boiled. (Frozen berries can be cooked without defrosting but may require more water.) Cut the crusts off the slices of bread and line a greased pudding basin with it. First pour some of the liquid from the stewed fruit into the lined basin to make sure the bread is soaked through. Then put the remainder of the fruit into the basin, reserving any excess liquid. Place a layer of bread on top and pour some more liquid on to it if necessary. Put a small plate or saucer on the top and a weight on top of that. Leave to cool. When the pudding has cooled, put it into the refrigerator for an hour or two. To serve, turn the pudding out of the basin and pour the reserved liquid over it. Serve with a low-fat plain yoghurt or *fromage frais*.

India

MANGO AND RICE PUDDING

The bouquet of ripe mangoes seldom fails to delight, even when the fruit is canned or dried. The mango purée used in this dish may be bought in cans or made from dried mangoes. Alternatively a delicious purée may be made from dried apricots. This recipe is borrowed from the stalwart scholar Dharamjit Singh.

500g (18oz) sweet mango (or apricot)
100ml (3¹/₂fl oz) skimmed or semi-skimmed milk
100ml (3¹/₂oz) strained plain yoghurt
¹/₂ tablespoon sugar
¹/₄ teaspoon saffron
2 teaspoons rose water
450g (1lb) pudding rice

If using dried mango or dried apricots, prepare the purée by covering the dried fruit with boiling water and simmering for 5 minutes. Leave the fruit overnight or for at least 2–3 hours to swell. Purée in a blender, adding water if necessary.
Boil the milk, and stirring over a medium heat, reduce it by half its volume. Allow to cool a little then add the boiled milk to the purée, together with the yoghurt, sugar, saffron and rose water. Boil the rice in a little water until very soft, then drain. Put a layer of the boiled rice in a deep dish, cover with a layer of mango, then add another layer of rice, and another of mango. Cook in a slow oven preheated to 150°C/300°F/Gas 2 for about 40 minutes or until set. Serve hot or cold.

Fresh fruit desserts

In Britain we are often rather unimaginative in the way we serve fruit, and do not seem to think often enough of what else we might do to make the fruit more inviting.

Mediterranean

MACEDONIA DI FRUTTA (FRUIT SALAD)

A successful fruit salad reflects the fruits that are in season. Nowadays many fruits are available all the year round but there are still times when each fruit is at its best. Careful choice of fresh fruits in the market makes this dish most successful. In Mediterranean countries, fruit salad would generally be eaten without cream or any other such foil to the acidity of the fruit. It may be eaten with two or three spoonfuls of low-fat yoghurt, *fromage frais* or *crème fraîche*, but the fruit should always be the predominant ingredient. The sugar may be omitted to give a fine juice with a clearer note, or chopped compressed dates may be added instead.

3 apples
2 bananas
a bunch of grapes
2 ripe pears
4 apricots or plums, or 2 nectarines or peaches, or 4 kiwi fruit
juice of 2 lemons and 3 oranges
1 tablespoon sugar

Put the citrus juice in a large serving bowl. Wash the fruit, then peel, core, seed or stone as appropriate, and slice into smallish cubes. Add to the juice along with the sugar. Put in a cool place such as the refrigerator for at least 3 hours. Remove from the refrigerator at least an hour before serving.

Mediterranean

GREEK FRUIT PLATE

This is a delightful way of serving fruit ready cut and prepared for eating in portions. It is helpful for those who do not want to eat a whole fruit, and enables others at the table to sample several different fruits. Choose fruit in season. Fresh dates, if they can be obtained, will give this dish a particularly Greek flavour.

1 or 2 apples
1 or 2 pears
1 or 2 oranges
1 or 2 bananas
some grapes, plums, cherries, strawberries or
kiwis, according to season

Wash the fruit. Cut the apple and pear up into six or eight pieces, removing the core. If the skin of the apple is pretty leave it on. Peel the orange, being careful to remove the bitter pith. Divide into segments. Cut the banana into 4cm (1½ in) lengths. Divide the grapes into small bunches. Scatter the pieces on a large platter with some ice cubes, using any more highly coloured fruit to decorate the dish. This dish should be prepared immediately before serving so that the pieces do not go brown.

Japan

JAPANESE FRUIT DESSERT

In Japanese families a meal is often finished with fruit which is cut and sculpted into interesting shapes which are then arranged in patterns on the plate. Cooked or prepared desserts of other kinds are seldom served in Japan.

To present fruit the Japanese way, first take an apple and make a series of stabbing cuts into the centre across the core to produce two halves each with 'teeth'. Place one half in the centre of a small plate (one plate for each person). Peel some satsumas, mandarines or tangerines and arrange the segments in a circle around the apple. Take some of the citrus peel, cut into a small flower shape and place in the centre of the apple. Japanese cooks generally go further and add some twists of peel and pieces of green paper to simulate leaves. If you like, you could sculpt some kiwi fruit into green leaf shapes.

Non-fruit desserts

The old-fashioned rice, semolina and other starchy puddings were excellent sources of lasting energy, unspoiled by excessive fat or sugar. With affluence they went out of fashion, but children love them and they are an excellent way of eating more starch.

Mediterranean

GREEK RICE PUDDING

This delicious Greek rice pudding is commonly seen in tavernas. It is generally served at about room temperature, but may also be kept in the fridge. It can be served to children as an alternative to the ubiquitous cartons of fruit yoghurt. Serve it with Prunes in Red Wine (see page 124) if you like.

2 teaspoons cornflour
55g (2oz) sugar
1 litre (1³/₄pt) skimmed or semi-skimmed milk
140g (5oz) short-grain (pudding) rice
2–3 strips lemon zest
powdered cinnamon

Mix the cornflour and sugar together with a little milk, making sure to get rid of any lumps. Put aside. Cook the rice with the rest of the milk and the lemon zest in a thick-bottomed pan over a gentle flame for 30 minutes, stirring well. Pour the cornflour mixture into the rice, stirring well. Cook for another 20 minutes or so until the pudding is very creamy, stirring well to prevent it from sticking. When the pudding is cool, discard the lemon zest. Put the pudding into individual bowls for serving with a sprinkling of cinnamon on each.

SECTION 3
7 The A–Z of foods

THIS SECTION will help you to understand more about the food you eat and help you to choose the best diet for health. Each entry explains the nature of a food or food constituent, and summarises what we know about how it may alter the risk of cancer and other diseases. Follow the information and advice given in the context of the recommendations in Chapter 3.

Alcohol

Most beers contain 4–7 per cent alcohol, wine contains 10–13 per cent alcohol and distilled drinks (spirits) 30–50 per cent alcohol. Alcoholic drinks may also contain carcinogens, including nitrosamines, polycyclic aromatic hydrocarbons, and fungal toxins, and a wide variety of other chemicals whose action on the body is not known.

Alcohol is not a nutrient and is not needed as part of the diet. Heavy drinkers often eat only small amounts of vegetables and fruits and generally tend to have a poor diet lacking in nutrients. Heavy drinkers also tend to smoke.

The alcohol in drinks is known chemically as ethyl alcohol or ethanol. In the body ethanol is broken down in the liver to acetaldehyde and acetic acid which are themselves broken down further.

Strong and extensive data provides convincing evidence that alcoholic drinks increase the risk of cancers of the mouth, pharynx and oesophagus. The risk is markedly increased for drinkers who also smoke. The risk of cancer of the larynx is probably also increased by drinking. Many studies provide convincing evidence that the risk of liver cancer is increased by alcohol. Liver cancer probably develops following cirrhosis of the liver, a complication of heavy drinking. Heavy drinkers may consume as much as 25 per cent or more of their total energy as alcohol.

Alcohol probably also increases the risk of cancer of the colon, rectum and breast. The risk of breast cancer begins to increase at virtually any level of intake, even less than one drink a day. A woman who takes one alcoholic drink per day has a 10 per cent greater risk of getting breast cancer than a woman who does not drink.

Alcohol has not been shown to be carcinogenic, although acetaldehyde, which is produced from alcohol in the body, can cause damage to DNA. Such damage is often the first stage in inducing cancer. Alcohol may act as a co-carcinogen: that is, it acts as a carcinogen in conjunction with another substance. Or alcohol may act as a promoting agent by, for example, assisting the entry of carcinogens into body tissues. Other ways in which alcohol might promote cancer are by altering the ability of the liver to break down and inactivate carcinogens, or by altering levels of oestrogens (female hormones) in the body.

While in the context of cancer, alcohol is not

recommended, a small but regular consumption of alcohol (no more than one drink a day for a woman, two for a man) may reduce the risk of heart disease.

On the other hand, persistent heavy drinking damages the liver, digestive tract, central nervous system, heart and blood vessels. One in four hospital beds is occupied as a result of diseases or disorders in which alcohol plays a major contributory role.

The social effects of alcohol are also significant. The risk of death by murder, suicide, traffic accident, accidents in the home, at work or elsewhere increases directly with alcohol consumption. Alcohol is a drug of addiction. A substantial proportion of violent crime, including rape and murder, is committed under the influence of alcohol. In France, which has one of the highest levels of alcohol consumption in the world, 40 per cent of accidents of all kinds are related to consumption of alcohol.

Antioxidants

Antioxidants are vitamins and other bioactive compounds found in foods of plant origin which are believed to protect against cancer. Vitamin C, vitamin E, carotenoids (including beta-carotene), and the trace element selenium, have antioxidant properties, as do certain other plant substances.

In the diet, most carotenoids and vitamin C come from vegetables and fruits. Vitamin E comes from vegetables and seeds and most vegetable oils. The mineral selenium is found in plant foods such as grains and seeds in amounts proportional to the selenium content of the soil in which they are grown. It is also found in offal, notably liver and kidney, and in seafood. Antioxidants are also added to manufactured foods as preservatives.

Carotenoids, vitamin C and vitamin E have all been shown to be involved in reducing cancer risk at a number of sites.

Antioxidants help to protect cell membranes, DNA, and other important body constituents from damage caused by reactive oxygen molecules. This reactive oxygen is formed during normal human metabolism and following exposure to carcinogenic substances in tobacco smoke and foods and drinks. Vulnerability to damage by reactive oxygen is increased by infection and chronic inflammation. How much antioxidant activity is required to give maximum protection to the body depends on a person's general health and on their diet and on whether they smoke tobacco.

Antioxidants may also protect against a number of degenerative diseases and against the ageing process in general. Antioxidants have been linked to prevention of heart and blood vessel disease because oxidised blood fats appear to be involved in atherogenesis, the disease process which causes blocking of blood vessels. Reactive oxygen may contribute to diabetes, certain eye and nerve diseases, and to Parkinson's disease. Antioxidants may help to combat these diseases.

Antioxidants may have other properties that protect against cancer.

See also: **Bioactive compounds, Vitamins**

Beta-carotene, see Carotenoids

Bioactive compounds

Plants contain many bioactive compounds that are not conventionally classed, like vitamins and certain minerals, as nutrients. In the past these compounds, which are organic chemicals, were generally assumed to be irrelevant to human health. Until recently minor constituents in the diet were thought to be necessary for health only if, like vitamins, they had been shown to protect against deficiency diseases. It is now thought that certain chronic diseases such as cancer may sometimes be prevented by intakes of vitamins or minerals higher than those that prevent obvious deficiency diseases. This is a relatively new idea which only began to emerge in the 1980s. The idea that some bioactive compounds other than vitamins may be protective against chronic disease is more recent still.

There is as yet little evidence that shows a direct effect of these compounds in the prevention of cancer. But the wealth of evidence showing that vegetables and fruits reduce the risk of cancer also suggests that some of these bioactive compounds, and others not yet identified, may be important in cancer prevention. Often there is evidence of biological activity of the compound and a plausible biological pathway.

Study of these bioactive compounds is not easy because they may not work in isolation. Some bioactive compounds such as beta-carotene and lipotropes act in groups and need to be present with other bioactive compounds for optimal beneficial effect. An excess of a compound taken as a supplement may even have a negative effect. As far as we know at present, the benefits of bioactive compounds may only be obtainable by eating whole vegetables and fruits.

A number of bioactive compounds which have been studied to some degree are listed below. As yet, there is insufficient evidence from human studies on any of these for any scientific judgement to be made about how, in the diet, they may reduce cancer risk. We do, however, have some understanding of the action of some of these compounds at a cellular and genetic level, and some of these functions are described below.

Coumarins

These are found in some vegetables (particularly cassava), citrus fruit and some herbs. They delay blood clotting by interfering with synthesis of vitamin K dependent coagulation factors and have anti-inflammatory properties. A number of coumarin-type compounds are used as drugs to inhibit clotting. In mice, they have been shown to induce detoxification enzymes in the liver and small intestine.

Dithiolthiones and isothiocyanates

Dithiolthiones are sulphur-containing compounds found in cruciferous vegetables (cabbage, broccoli, Brussels sprouts, kale etc.). They block the reaction of certain carcinogens with DNA and other large molecules, and induce detoxifying enzymes. Isothiocyanates and sulforaphane contain sulphur and are found in other vegetables. Isothiocyanates are also found in spices and can be produced synthetically. Isothiocyanates prevent carcinogens reacting with various critical sites and may suppress multiplication of cells that have taken some steps along the road to cancer.

Flavonoids

These are found in fruits, vegetables, coffee, tea, cola and alcoholic drinks. One flavonoid, quercetin, is found abundantly in berries, tomatoes, potatoes, broad beans, broccoli, Italian squash and onions. Another, kaempferol, is abundant in radishes, horseradish, kale and endive. Several others are found in citrus fruits. Over 2,000 different flavonoids have been found in plants. Flavonoids act as antioxidants and react with metals, so controlling the activity of metals in the plant, and they may induce enzymes which inactivate carcinogens. Higher intake of flavonoids has been linked with decreased mortality from heart disease in the Zutphen study in the Netherlands. Flavonoids may act by protecting good cholesterol from oxidation and by reducing the tendency of blood to clot.

Glutathione

Found in vegetables, fruit and meat, this is produced in the human liver from glutamate, glycine and cysteine. It is probably the most important antioxidant within cells and protects them against the toxic effects of oxygen radicals and so against the action of certain carcinogens.

Glucosinolates and indoles

More than 20 glucosinolates and indoles have been isolated from cruciferous vegetables (cabbage, broccoli, Brussels sprouts, kale etc.) and other edible plants. One of them is known to both activate and detoxify various carcinogenic compounds. Indoles also increase the metabolism of the female hormone oestradiol in the liver so reducing female hormone activity in the body.

Goitrogens

These are found in a range of foods, especially in cruciferous vegetables (cabbage and related vegetables), but also in peanuts, cassava and soya beans. They interfere with the synthesis of thyroid hormones or with the uptake of iodine and so can cause goitre, especially when iodine in the diet is marginal.

Limonoids

The bitter component in the white pith of citrus fruit such as the Valencia or navel orange; it may help to stimulate an enzyme, glutathione transferase, which acts against carcinogens.

Other phenolic compounds

Found in freshly harvested vegetables and fruits and in relatively large amounts in teas and wines. Ellagic acid is found in high concentrations in fruits and nuts, specifically in strawberries, raspberries, blackberries, walnuts and pecans. Phenolic compounds act to trap nitrate which might otherwise prove toxic to the plant.

Phytic acid

Found in cereals, nuts, seeds and pulses. It occurs at high levels in sesame seeds, lima beans, peanuts and soya beans. Phytic acid alters the absorption of minerals in the intestine. In experimental studies it has been found to be anti-carcinogenic.

Phytoestrogens

These are compounds, including isoflavones and lignans, which act weakly as female hormones. They are found in grains and pulses, particularly in the part of the grain that is removed when grains are milled. Phytoestrogens may alter the metabolism of steroid hormones in the body and inhibit growth and proliferation of cancer cells that are dependent on hormones.

Plant sterols

These have a structure similar to cholesterol. They mostly pass through the bowel without being absorbed, but they influence absorption and metabolism of cholesterol and possibly also steroid hormone metabolism.

Protease inhibitors

Found in grains such as barley, wheat, oats, and rye. Soya beans, kidney beans, chickpeas and other pulses contain protease inhibitors, some of which survive processing, including that involved in making tofu (soya bean curd). Proteases present in cancer cells probably enhance the ability of cancers to invade surrounding tissues. Under suitable conditions, plant protease inhibitors may inhibit human proteases.

Saponins

Found in various foods of plant origin: soya beans are a rich source. Saponins inhibit the growth of a wide variety of cells and inhibit tumour growth in animals.

Terpenoids

The most studied terpenoid is D-limonene, the major component of citrus fruit peel. It is commonly used as a flavouring agent in drinks, ice-cream, desserts and baked goods. D-limonene induces the action of the enzyme glutathione transferase, which acts against carcinogens.

Butter

Butter, made from milk or cream, is 80 per cent fat. The rest is mostly water. About 60 per cent of the butterfat is saturated fat. Butter, and other fats and oils, are the most energy-dense constituents of diets. Diets high in butter and other fats increase the risk of obesity and hence the risk of cancer.

Diets high in total fat and animal fat possibly increase the risk of lung, colorectal, breast and prostate cancers, and diets high in animal fat possibly increase the risk of endometrial cancer. It is generally agreed that the quantity of saturated fats such as butter in the diet should be reduced in order to reduce the risk of heart and blood vessel disease.

Our recommendation is that fatty foods, particularly those of animal origin, should be limited.

See also: **Fat**

Cabbage family

Vegetables of the botanical family Cruciferae are often called the cabbage family. It includes broccoli, Brussels sprouts, all varieties of cabbage, cauliflower, kale, kohlrabi, mustard, and the root vegetables, swede and turnip. Cruciferous vegetables are a good source of fibre, carotenoids, vitamin C, folate, potassium and other vitamins, minerals and bioactive compounds.

Within the evidence that diets high in vegetables and fruits decrease the risk of cancer at a number of sites, there is specific evidence that diets high in cruciferous vegetables probably decrease the risk of cancers of the colon and rectum and thyroid.

See also: **Vegetables**

Calcium

Calcium is important for nerve and muscle activity in the body, as well as for growth and strength: calcium is the major mineral constituent of bone.

Calcium is found in foods of animal origin, particularly milk, cheese, dairy products and small fish (when eaten whole with their bones). Foods of plant origin, vegetables and fruits, cereals and roots and tubers, are also rich sources of calcium but absorption may be hindered by certain other substances found in plants: oxalates (found in cocoa, rhubarb and spinach) and phytates (found in grains such as wheat).

Diets eaten in Britain contain plenty of calcium. The average intakes, 940mg per day for men and 730mg per day for women, are almost double the World Health Organization's recommendation.

Diets rich in calcium may decrease the risk of cancers of the colon and rectum.

See also: **Vitamins**

Carbohydrate

There are three major types of carbohydrate: starches, sugars, and fibre. The carbohydrate in our diets comes from plant foods – cereals, roots and tubers, pulses, vegetables and fruits. Carbohydrate is the main source of energy in most diets. In Britain 40–50 per cent of dietary energy comes from carbohydrate, and much of that from refined sugar.

Starches and sugars in the diet vary greatly in the degree to which they are processed. They may be minimally processed and eaten as wholemeal bread, breakfast cereals, pulses, potatoes, roots and fruits. Or they may be eaten in forms which have been refined or milled such as white rice and pasta, and flour and sugar. Even crude molasses sugar (dark brown in colour) is a highly refined product that differs little from white sugar from the nutritional point of view.

Different types of carbohydrates differ greatly in the way they are absorbed by the bowel. The less processed carbohydrates and fibre are digested largely by the action of bacteria in the large intestine. By contrast, sugars are absorbed in the small intestine and result in the release of glucose into the bloodstream relatively quickly. This provides the body with energy. In general, carbohydrates from foods that are eaten whole (whole foods) are digested much more slowly. Whole foods provide energy over a longer period and sustain a steadier level of blood glucose, so a feeling of hunger will return less quickly when whole foods are eaten.

Some highly processed starches and cooked starches such as white flour are absorbed almost as rapidly as sugar. The human digestive system is not adapted to the large quantities of sugar and processed starch eaten in some diets. This excessive load of sugar has been identified as an important contributory cause of being overweight and the major cause of tooth decay. Diets rich in wholemeal and wholegrain cereals and fibre are recommended to keep the intestinal tract healthy, and, among other benefits, to prevent constipation.

Expert reports on diet and heart disease or other chronic disease almost invariably have recommended an increase in the proportion of starch or complex carbohydrates in the diet and a reduction in the consumption of refined sugar.

In third world countries, poverty diets often consist mainly of one starchy food which may be relatively highly refined or may be lacking in certain micronutrients. Evidence which links such very high-starch, high-bulk diets with an increase in the risk of oesophageal cancer and stomach cancer are most likely the result of gross deficiency of certain essential micro-nutrients. Wholegrain/wholemeal cereals, which are comparatively high in fibre, vitamins and minerals, are, if anything, protective against cancer at some sites. Traditional diets eaten in many parts of the developing world are made up mostly of starchy staples. These diets are not associated with an increase in the risk of cancer so long as they include a variety of other foods such as vegetables and fruits, pulses, nuts and seeds, with or without meat, fish and dairy produce.

See also: **Fibre, Starch, Sugars**

Carotenoids

Beta-carotene and other carotenoids are pigments found in foods of plant origin. They are particularly abundant in orange-coloured and dark green leafy vegetables and fruit. Beta-carotene and probably other carote-noids are active as vitamins but are also important as biochemical precursors of vitamin A.

Carotenoids are soluble in fat and so their absorption in the body is dependent on fat intake as well as on intakes of the vegetables and fruits that contain them. Carotenoids can be stored for considerable lengths of time in the body in fatty tissue.

Abundant evidence suggests that carotenoids decrease the risk of several types of cancer. Diets high in carotenoids probably reduce the risk of lung cancer and possibly reduce the risk of cancers of the oesophagus, stomach, colon, rectum, breast and cervix. Evidence for other sites is not as clear, although it generally shows that carotenoids reduce cancer risk. Carotenoids have also been associated with a decrease in the risk of heart disease.

Several ways have been suggested in which carotenoids may protect against cancer. The most important may be their antioxidant properties. Carotenoids may be converted in the body into vitamin A which is essential for the normal development and differentiation of epithelial cells, the cells that cover the surface of the body and line most of the hollow organs within it. In addition carotenoids improve communication between cells, inhibit proliferation of cells, and enhance aspects of immunological function.

Because of the evidence on carotenoids and lung cancer, it was thought that giving smokers carotenoid supplements in the form of pills might reduce their lung cancer risk. However, two large trials which followed people taking such supplements over a number of years found that the risk of lung cancer increased. The reason why supplementation with carotenoids might increase the risk while diets high in carotenoids reduce the risk is not properly understood, but taking supplements is not recommended. The trials are discussed in the section on lung cancer, page 173.

Eating diets with more vegetables and fruits will increase intakes of carotenoids.

See also: **Antioxidants**

Carrots

Carrots are a rich source of carotene, one of the carotenoids, and also provide useful fibre. Within the evidence that diets high in vegetables and fruits decrease the risk of cancer at a number of sites, there is specific evidence that diets high in carrots probably

---

Types of carotenoids

There are many types of carotenoids. Most are orange coloured but xanthophyll is a dark green colour. Sources of some of the more common types are given here:

beta-carotene	carrots, sweet potatoes, pumpkin, winter squash, cantaloupe melon, apricots, mangoes, kale, spinach, collard greens, chicory
alpha-carotene	carrots, avocado, pumpkin
xanthophyll	dark green leafy vegetables
lycopene	tomatoes, watermelon, pink grapefruit, guava
cryptoxanthin	mangoes, pawpaw, red peppers, pumpkin, oranges

decrease the risk of cancers of the lung, stomach and bladder, and may reduce the risk of cancers of the mouth and pharynx and rectum.

See also: **Fruits, Vegetables**

Cereals

Cereals, meaning all types of grains and not just breakfast cereals, are the most important foodstuff in most diets, and are the major source of starch and fibre. The major cereals in countries like Britain are wheat, rice, maize (corn), barley, oats and rye. In the developing world, cereals constitute most of the bulk of the diet while in more industrialised societies, where less bulky and more energy-dense foods are preferred, cereals tend to be eaten in smaller quantities and in more refined forms. In Britain between 25 and 30 per cent of the energy in our diets comes from bread and flour.

Grains are milled, ground and processed into a great variety of foods including breads, unleavened breads (chapati, tortilla, pitta), noodles, pasta, dumplings, gruels and porridges. Rice is most commonly eaten as boiled grains but can be milled to make flour.

Baked goods such as biscuits and cakes, which are mostly made from refined flour, also contain substantial amounts of fat and sugar and so have a relatively high calorie content for their weight.

Unprocessed cereals contain approximately 70 per cent starch by weight and varying amounts of fibre, protein, water-soluble B vitamins, vitamin E, iron, and other bioactive compounds. Most of the non-starch nutrients of cereals are concentrated in the outer part of the grain, and this is removed or partially removed during processing. The amount of various dietary constituents in cereal foods therefore depends very much on the extent of processing. For example, wholemeal bread is made from wholemeal flour which is produced by milling the whole grain (100 per cent extraction flour), whereas white bread is made with flour which contains only 72 per cent of the grain. Most of the germ, which is rich in vitamins and fat, and the bran, which is largely fibre, is lost from white flour.

Wholegrain foods are foods which have not been refined, although they may have been milled into a wholemeal flour. Wholegrain foods include wholemeal flour, wholegrain pasta, porridge oats, whole maize and brown rice. Evidence suggests that diets high in wholegrain cereals possibly decrease the risk of stomach cancer. In addition, diets high in fibre probably reduce the risk of colorectal cancer.

Evidence that diets high in refined cereals possibly increase the risk of cancer of the oesophagus is thought to be due to deficiencies of micronutrients in monotonous diets that are dominated by one starchy staple, rather than to the refined cereals themselves.

Our recommendation is that diets should contain 45–65 per cent of energy in the form of starchy staple foods – amounting to at least seven servings (600–800 grams or 20–30 ounces a day). The World Health Organization has recommended that diets should contain between 50 and 70 per cent of energy in the form of complex carbohydrate and should contain 16–24 grams ($^3/_4$–1 ounce) of fibre. It has been widely recommended in reports on diet and health that intake of grains, and particularly wholegrains, should be increased as a means of preventing heart disease and other chronic diseases.

Cheese

Cheese is a fatty food and very energy dense. Different cheeses differ greatly in their fat, salt and water content, depending on how they are manufactured. A hard cheese such as Cheddar traditionally contains not less than 40 per cent fat (although low-fat versions are now made) and the fat in cheese is 65–70 per cent saturated. Cheese is a good source of protein, vitamin B$_{12}$, and calcium. Some cheeses may be very salty.

Diets high in milk and dairy products possibly increase the risk of prostate and kidney cancer. Diets high in fat or high in animal fat possibly increase the risk of lung, colorectal, breast, womb and prostate cancers. So the amount of cheese eaten, and of other fatty foods in the diet, should be limited. A high-fat diet also increases the risk of obesity which in turn increases the risk of womb and kidney cancers and postmenopausal breast cancer.

See also: **Milk and dairy products**

Chilli peppers

Chillies (chilli peppers) are the aromatic fruit of the pepper plant *Capsicum frutescens* (not to be confused with the pepper vegetable, *Capsicum annuum*). Chillies are used fresh or as a powder made from the dried fruit which is known as chilli powder, red chilli powder, or cayenne pepper. Their flavour varies in intensity from mild to very hot, depending on the type of pepper. Chilli is an ingredient of curry, pickles and Tabasco sauce, which is prepared by fermentation of chillies.

There is some hint in the scientific literature that regular consumption of red chilli powder might increase the risk of some cancers, but the evidence is conflicting. Chillies have been associated with a decreased risk of stomach cancer in Italy and an increased risk with high consumption in Mexico. Capsaicin, the pungent component of chilli peppers, has been shown in experimental studies to be both mutagenic and carcinogenic.

It may be wise to avoid eating chilli and the hottest curries regularly. If chilli seasoning causes any lasting irritation to the mouth, stomach or bowel when eaten, it is certainly too strong.

See also: **Herbs, spices and condiments**

Chlorine and fluoride in drinking water

Fluoride is added to drinking water in certain areas to reduce the risk of tooth decay, and chlorine is also added to disinfect water. Certain chemicals, including chloroform, are produced by chemical reactions in chlorinated water. There is currently little epidemiological evidence that chemical additives in foods and drinks, when their use is properly regulated, significantly affect cancer risk. However, risks may occur when there is overuse or abuse, spillage or industrial accidents.

See also: **Industrial chemicals**

Cholesterol

Cholesterol is found only in food from animal sources. Egg yolks contain around 1 per cent cholesterol and are the major source of cholesterol in most people's diets. Smaller amounts of cholesterol are obtained from meat, shellfish, poultry, fish and dairy products.

Chemically, cholesterol is a sterol compound related to sex hormones, adrenal hormones and vitamin D. It is an important raw material for production of these substances in the body. It is also an important component of cell membranes and the acids in bile.

Diets high in cholesterol may increase the risk of lung and pancreas cancer. Diets designed to reduce the risks of heart disease commonly recommend limiting the amount of cholesterol in the diet.

See also: **Eggs**

Citrus fruits

There are many kinds of citrus fruits because the original types – orange, lemon, tangerine, lime and pomelo – have been hybridised to produce varieties such as the grapefruit, clementine, mineola, ortanique and others. Citrus fruits are a rich source of vitamin C. Within the evidence that diets high in vegetables and fruits decrease the risk of cancer at a number of sites, there is convincing evidence that diets high in citrus fruits reduce the risk of stomach cancer, and may reduce the risk of cancers of the mouth and pharynx and oesophagus.

See also: **Fruits**

Coffee

Evidence on drinking coffee is generally reassuring, suggesting no significant link to any type of cancer. Coffee contains several substances, including caffeine, that are biologically active. Caffeine, also found in tea, is a stimulant well known for its ability to increase arousal and prevent sleep.

Coffee, whether brewed, instant, or decaffeinated, is mutagenic to bacteria. Since mutation is a first crucial step in the development of cancer, a great deal of attention has focused on coffee as a possible cause of cancer. However, the scientific judgement on evidence from more than 50 studies is that regular drinking of coffee has no significant relationship with the risk of cancer at any site. The only possible exception is an increase in the risk of bladder cancer for people who drink more than five cups of coffee a day. There is convincing evidence that there is no relationship between coffee drinking and breast cancer. Further evidence suggests that there is probably no relationship between coffee drinking and stomach, pancreas and kidney cancer.

It may be that coffee has both positive and negative effects on the risk of cancer which cancel each other out. Coffee contains flavonoids and phenols which may have anti-cancer properties and experimental studies have shown that coffee induces enzymes in the body which break down potentially harmful chemicals including, perhaps, the mutagens in coffee itself. There is no significant increased risk of coronary heart disease or stroke with drinking up to six cups of instant or filter coffee daily.

See also: **Bioactive compounds, Tea**

Colourings

Colourings are added to foods and drinks for their cosmetic effect, they have no other value. The soft drinks industry is the single largest user of food colours. The most extensively used food colour is caramel, which accounts for 95 per cent by weight of all food colour consumed. It is used to colour dark beers, cola drinks, gravy browning and many other foods including ice-cream and bakery goods. Caramel is also used as a flavouring.

In the past a number of food colours have been found to be carcinogenic in animal experiments and have now been banned in most countries. Caramel, in common with other additives, is not linked to the risk of any cancer, but an excessive intake of one type of caramel (Class 3 caramel) affects the immune response by reducing white cells in the blood, making a person vulnerable to infection.

See also: **Food additives**

Condiments

Condiments are added to foods to increase or enhance flavour. Herbs, spices, salt, and certain sauces may all be classed as condiments. They are generally used in small amounts and so they do not contribute to the diet in the nutritional sense. However herbs and spices may have quasi-pharmacological effects on the body, and more research may show that some have a role in modifying cancer risk.

See also: **Herbs, spices and condiments, Salt and salting**

Contaminants and residues

Many foods and drinks (including water) contain traces of chemicals used in agriculture, food manufacture, and industry.

Synthetic fertiliser is an indispensable part of modern intensive agriculture. As a result, the nitrate content of soil and water, and thus of foods and drinking water, has steadily increased. Modern intensive farming also depends upon the regular use of pesticides, herbicides and other chemicals. Drugs are used on farm animals raised by intensive methods, to treat and prevent disease and to promote growth. Some of these same drugs are also used to prevent human disease. Traces of these drugs and chemicals, often called residues, find their way into human food.

Residues of some industrial chemicals in particular accumulate in fatty foods at various stages in the food chain, and also accumulate in fatty tissue. Some of these show female hormone activity. A large number of these chemicals are known to be toxic, and some have been determined to be mutagenic or carcinogenic in experimental conditions. The use of such chemicals is subject to evaluation and regulation by national and international bodies.

There is no substantial evidence from human studies that chemical contamination of foods and drinks, resulting from properly regulated use, significantly affects cancer risk. Nevertheless accidental contamination of food and drink with large quantities of chemicals, or environmental pollution caused by overuse, abuse, spillage or industrial accidents, may cause exceptional health problems not considered here.

See also: **Fertilisers and other agricultural chemicals, Food additives, Industrial chemicals, Microbial contamination of food, Packaging, Veterinary drugs**

Coumarins, see Bioactive compounds

Cumin

Cumin is a strongly aromatic spice used in Latin America, Spain, North Africa, the Middle East and Asia. It is commonly an ingredient of curries. There are two types: black cumin and yellow-brown (white) cumin. In common with some other spices, there is a hint of evidence that cumin might protect against some types of cancers.

See also: **Herbs, spices and condiments**

Curry

Curry, used in flavouring Indian foods, is a mixture of turmeric and other spices which may include cardamom, cinnamon, cloves, coriander, cumin, fenugreek, mustard, chilli and pepper. Different curries vary in their ingredients and their proportions.

As yet, there is not enough evidence on whether the various spices in curry are linked to the risk of cancer. However, a pragmatic look at the evidence suggests that it may be wise to avoid heavy use of chilli and the hottest curries. If chilli seasoning causes any lasting irritation to the mouth, stomach or bowel when eaten, it is certainly too strong.

See also: **Herbs, spices and condiments, Chilli peppers, Cumin, Turmeric**

Cured foods

Meat is cured by injection with, or immersion in, a solution of nitrate or nitrite, salt, and other condiments. The nitrates and nitrites act as preservatives, preventing growth of bacteria in the meat. They also colour the meat.

Nitrates and nitrites from cured meats may be converted in the body into nitrosamines which are highly carcinogenic. Cured meats and fish also contain some preformed nitrosamines which may be more significant as carcinogens than nitrite. With the more widespread use of refrigeration, fewer cured foods are eaten than in the past when curing was an important means of preservation of foods. Curing solutions now contain smaller quantities of nitrates and nitrites, and include substances such as vitamin C to prevent the formation of nitrosamines.

Diets high in cured meats possibly increase the risk of colorectal cancer.

Our recommendation is to eat cured meats only occasionally.

See also: **Nitrates, nitrites and N-nitrosamines**

Dairy products, see Milk and dairy products

Dioxin compounds, see Industrial chemicals

Dithiolthiones, see Bioactive compounds

Eggs

Eggs provide useful amounts of protein, fat, and various vitamins. The fat in eggs is 35 per cent saturated and 50 per cent unsaturated. Eggs are also a major source of cholesterol in the diet.

Diets including a lot of eggs possibly increase the risk of colorectal cancer. A large consumption of eggs will significantly increase the amount of fat and cholesterol in the diet, and high intakes of cholesterol possibly increase the risk of lung and pancreas cancer. An excessive consumption of eggs will also contribute significantly to total fat intake, which also increases the risk of several cancers.

Diets designed to reduce the risk of heart disease commonly recommend limiting the number of eggs eaten. Eating fewer eggs may be important in reducing the risk of heart disease for people who have risk factors such as smoking, overweight, diabetes, raised blood pressure or a family history of heart disease, but probably not for others. Eating only five or fewer eggs per week is probably wise. People with heart disease risk factors may be advised to eat two eggs or fewer a week.

See also: **Cholesterol**

Energy

Carbohydrate, fat and alcohol are all converted by the body into energy. Protein is broken down by digestion into its constituent amino acids, some of which are used for growth and repair, and the remainder converted into energy. Surplus energy is stored in the body as fat.

The energy yield of foods and the energy expenditure of the body are both measured in calories. Nutritionists actually make their measurements in kilocalories (kilo = 1,000) which are often referred to as calories for short and written in the form: kcal or cal. By convention, energy is measured by other scientists in joules or kilojoules which are abbreviated as J or kJ.

Fat provides more than twice the energy for a given weight than sugar or starch, or, put another way, it has twice the energy density. When water and indigestible fibre is taken into account the range of energy density in foods is even greater. Vegetables and fruits have a low energy content for a given weight whereas biscuits or cake have a high energy content for the same weight. For example, a 100 gram (3½ ounce) apple or carrot provides 35kcal of energy, whereas 100 grams of digestive biscuits provide 483kcal. Therefore a digestive biscuit has almost fourteen times the energy density of an apple or carrot – or other vegetables and fruits.

Energy is used by the body to maintain its basic metabolic activities even when a person is not physically active. Energy is needed to maintain tension in muscles at rest, to maintain circulation of the blood, respiration, nerve and brain activity, and run the chemical activities of all the body organs. The energy required for these functions is called the basal metabolic rate and can be measured from the oxygen consumption of the body at rest.

More energy is used when a person is physically active. Most people eat approximately the right amount of food to provide enough energy for their basal metabolic rate and physical activity. When a person consumes more energy in food than he or she uses, the energy is stored as fat and so body weight increases. Overweight and obesity are associated with an increased risk of cancer. Our recommendation is that overweight should be avoided and that weight gain during adulthood should be limited to less than 5 kilograms (11 pounds).

Fat

Both animal foods and plant foods contain fat; animal products generally contain more fat than foods of plant origin. The fat in beef, lamb, pork, and other meat products constitutes 40–75 per cent of their energy content. Approximately 65 per cent of the energy content of eggs comes from fat and about 50 per cent of the energy content of cow's milk comes from fat. Apart from nuts, which contain 80–90 per cent of their energy as fat, plant products have a relatively low fat content. Manufactured foods such as meat products, cakes, biscuits and baked goods are generally high in fat.

In many countries much less fat is eaten than in Europe and North America where fat supplies 35–40 per cent or more of total energy. In low and middle income Asia fat supplies about 15–22 per cent of energy, showing that a diet with much less fat is possible. Consumption of fat in Europe and North America is now falling because packaged and prepared foods contain less fat as a result of dietary advice for prevention of heart disease.

Natural oils and fats of animal or vegetable origin are mixtures of the three main types of fat: saturated fats, polyunsaturated fats, and monounsaturated fats (see page 145). Animal fats contain a high proportion of saturated fats whereas vegetable oils, with the exception of palm and coconut oils, contain relatively little saturated fat.

Fats and oils are digested in the small intestine where they mix with bile which splits up large fat droplets into smaller droplets, so making them more available to digestive enzymes. These enzymes break the fat up into glycerols and fatty acids which are taken to the liver where they are processed and returned to the bloodstream.

Certain fatty acids cannot be synthesised in the human body and so must be included in our diets. These fatty acids, called essential fatty acids, include linoleic acid and alpha-linolenic acid (an omega-3 fatty acid). Linoleic

Types of fat

All natural fats and oils are a mixture of different chemical types of fat and oil. Each molecule of fat or oil consists of a fatty acid molecule, of which there are many types, joined to a glycerol molecule.

Saturated fats are fats which, chemically, have a full complement of hydrogen atoms attached to the carbon backbone of the fatty acid molecule. Saturated fats are generally solid at room temperature. Most plant oils contain a relatively small amount of saturated fat but coconut oil and palm oil are exceptions. Coconut oil is 90 per cent saturated and semi-solid at room temperature. Palm oil is a thick oil which is 45 per cent saturated fat. Soft margarines often include some palm or coconut oil mixed with liquid oils to make the product semi-solid and contain 20–30 per cent saturated fats.

Animal fats generally contain a high proportion of saturated fats. In meat, butter, lard, and hard margarines, between 45–50 per cent of the fat is saturated. The fat in milk is about 75 per cent saturated. The fat in poultry and eggs is 30–35 per cent saturated. Fat in fish is 10–25 per cent saturated.

Saturated fats raise the levels of cholesterol in the blood and so are a risk factor for heart disease as well as certain cancers. It is generally recommended that the amount of saturated fat in the diet should be limited for this reason.

Polyunsaturated fats are liquid oils which do not have a full complement of hydrogen atoms attached to the fatty acid backbone of the molecule. Some carbon atoms in the fatty acid backbone are left with two bonds that are without their full complement of hydrogen atoms and so are said to be unsaturated.

Polyunsaturated oils are found in their most concentrated form in safflower, sunflower, wheatgerm, corn, soya and cottonseed oils which contain 50–75 per cent polyunsaturated fat, mostly linoleic acid. Margarines and shortenings made from vegetable oils, and nuts, contain between 15–45 per cent polyunsaturated fat. Meat, poultry, eggs and dairy products contain relatively little polyunsaturated fat, although the meat from wild animals contains more. Fish contain large amounts of omega-3 fatty acids, a type of polyunsaturated fat.

Polyunsaturated fats (pufa) do not raise the level of cholesterol in the blood and when included in the diet reduce the risk of heart disease.

Monounsaturated fats are liquid oils which have one chemical bond (see above) in the fatty acid backbone which lacks hydrogen. Monounsaturated fats are found in a wide variety of foods including meat, eggs, milk and butter, nuts, margarines, and oils. The most concentrated source is olive oil which contains 70–90 per cent. Rapeseed oil also contains a relatively high proportion. The fat in avocados is 60–70 per cent monounsaturated. Monounsaturated fats do not raise the level of cholesterol in the blood and when included in the diet reduce the risk of heart disease.

Hydrogenation is a process in which hard or semi-hard fats are made from liquid oils by treating them with hydrogen. The hydrogen combines chemically with free carbon bonds causing the fat to become saturated or partially saturated. Many margarines are made by hydrogenation of liquid oils but may also be made by including semi-solid oils such as coconut oil. Hydrogenated fats, like saturated animal fats, increase cholesterol in the blood and so are a risk factor for heart disease. The process of hydrogenation also produces trans-fatty acids which may be an additional risk factor for heart disease.

acid and certain other fatty acids are made in the body into prostaglandins which have an essential role in dilation of blood vessels, blood clotting and transmission of nerve impulses. Fats also have an essential role in the diet as carriers of vitamins, which are soluble in fat.

Diets high in fat possibly increase the risk of cancers of the colon, rectum, breast, prostate and lung. It has been suggested that a high-fat diet may promote breast cancer through its influence on hormone metabolism. The main effect probably occurs during childhood growth and breast development. However the risk of postmenopausal breast cancer also seems to be increased by a high-fat diet and by obesity.

A diet high in fat increases the risk of obesity because fat contains more energy for a given weight than any other dietary constituent. A relatively small overconsumption of fat in terms of weight may therefore lead to a considerable overconsumption of calories and a substantial increase in body weight. There is convincing evidence that obesity increases the risk of cancer of the womb. Obesity probably also increases the risk of breast cancer after the menopause and of cancer of the kidney.

Additional evidence suggests that saturated or animal fats may increase the risk of cancers of the lung, colon and rectum, breast, womb and prostate. On the other hand monounsaturated fats and polyunsaturated fats do not seem to increase the risk of these cancers. The logical conclusion is to reduce the amount of saturated/animal fat in the diet. A lower intake of saturated fats has been widely recommended in expert reports. Consumption of fish and fish oils (in particular omega-3 fatty acids) have been recommended for prevention of heart disease.

Our recommendation is to keep fat in the diet in the range 15–30 per cent of total energy – considerably less than we consume at present – and to use vegetable oils rather than other types of fat.

Fat substitutes

Several fat substitutes, designed to replace certain uses of fat while providing fewer calories, have been invented. One fat substitute, a sucrose polyester, remains undigested and so passes through the bowel unchanged. It does not yet have widespread approval from regulatory authorities and is generally restricted to limited use in snack foods because it may cause leakage of faeces.

Fat-soluble dietary constituents such as carotenoids are dissolved in sucrose polyester and so may be carried out of the bowel. There is thus a danger that if people consume substantial amounts of these fat substitutes their bodies may be depleted of carotenoids and other fat-soluble vitamins. Since carotenoids may possibly reduce the risk of cancer, scientists have expressed concern that long-term use of sucrose polyester or similar fat substitutes could increase the risk of cancer.

See also: **Food additives, Vitamins**

Fertilisers and other agricultural chemicals

Modern intensive farming methods developed since the 1940s depend on the regular use of a broad spectrum of agricultural chemicals. Pesticides, herbicides, and nitrate fertilisers are used widely to increase farm yields. These chemicals enter the human food chain and are found, generally in trace quantities only, in human food. Because of their potential toxicity in humans, the use of these chemicals is subject to regulation by national and international bodies.

In the past, a number of agricultural

chemicals have been withdrawn from use because in field studies or experimental studies they have shown unusual toxicity. These chemicals are not meant to be in foods, and there is a public fear that contamination of food and drink by agricultural practices is a significant cause of human cancer.

In fact, there is currently surprisingly little evidence from studies in humans to suggest that residues of pesticides and other agrochemicals in foods and drinks increase the risk of cancer. An exception is DDT (dichlorodiphenyltrichloroethane). This has been extensively studied, but the evidence for any risk to human health is equivocal. Current evidence suggests that agricultural chemicals are probably not a significant cancer risk when used according to instructions and regulations. Such chemicals can of course cause ill health to those involved in their manufacture or use if adequate precautions are not taken or if accidental spillage occurs.

There is a general lack of useful human data on cancer incidence and the contamination of food by agricultural chemicals. So there is often inadequate evidence on which to base judgements. Scientific evidence on the carcinogenicity of residues of agricultural chemicals in the food chain is clouded by controversy and is capable of various interpretations.

DDT and other organochlorine pesticides and herbicides tend to accumulate in fat-containing foods such as meat, fish, poultry and dairy products, and also in human fat tissue. In developed countries, the organochlorines are present in relatively small amounts in both home-produced and imported foods. In developing countries the problem may be more significant because inadequate processing and storage facilities may lead to overuse and misuse.

Organic foods

Organic foods are produced without the use of agricultural chemicals and by less intensive, sustainable means of agriculture. Production of organic food is rigorously regulated. Food produced in this way might have health advantages but evidence of this is not available. There are theoretical disadvantages to organic food as well as advantages. For example, food grown with pesticides is less prone to infestation by insects.

Also, the use of pesticides makes vegetables and fruits more readily available all year round, and the benefits of eating plenty of vegetables and fruits almost certainly greatly outweigh any human health hazard from pesticide residues in food.

Chlorinated pesticides have now been largely replaced by organophosphate and carbamate pesticides which are much less persistent in the environment, and the levels of residues in food are low. The use of insecticides as well as fungicides may actually reduce the risk of cancer because insecticides reduce insect damage to food which is frequently followed by fungal damage. Damage by the fungus *Aspergillus flavus*, which affects a wide range of crops, produces a substance, aflatoxin, which may cause liver cancer.

Nitrogen fertiliser (NPK) has become an indispensable part of modern agriculture. Nitrate from NPK enters ground water and is assimilated into fruit and vegetables. Under certain conditions, nitrates in plants may be converted into carcinogenic nitrosamines, however there is little evidence to suggest that these nitrates increase risk of cancer.

National and international regulatory bodies carry out assessments to determine safe levels of contaminants in foods and acceptable daily intakes. Nevertheless, in large parts of the world, these chemicals are in practice unregulated. There is little or no data from human studies on which to judge whether use of agricultural chemicals carries a risk of cancer. Experts have generally come to the view that there is no substantial evidence that the small amounts of chemicals found in food increase human cancer risk, although effects of lifetime exposure to these chemicals is not known.

See also: **Microbial contamination of food, Nitrates, nitrites and N-nitrosamines**

Fibre

Vegetables and fruits and starchy staples such as wholemeal bread, pasta, rice, beans, peas and potatoes are all good sources of fibre. Fibre, a carbohydrate consisting mostly of polysaccharides, is found in plant cell walls in the form of cellulose, hemi-cellulose, pectin and gums.

Refined and processed foods are depleted of dietary fibre. Intake of fibre is greater for those who eat more unprocessed foods including plenty of vegetables and fruits, cereals, pulses, roots and tubers. In Africa and India, where relatively few refined foods are eaten, the consumption of dietary fibre is about twice that of the UK or, say, Japan, where it is 10–13 grams (about $^1/_2$ ounce) per day.

Diets high in fibre possibly decrease the risk of cancer of the pancreas, colon and rectum, and breast. In addition to the human evidence, there is evidence from experiments with animals that diets low in fibre induce bowel cancer. On a low-fibre diet, the interval between bowel movements is greater. This allows carcinogens to accumulate in the bowel increasing the risk of bowel cancer. Conversely, a high-fibre diet produces regular bowel movements and in this way may

decrease the risk of bowel cancer.

See also: **Carbohydrate**

Fish

Fish are a good source of protein; about 20 per cent by weight. Oily fish, such as salmon, herring, mackerel, sardine, pilchard, trout, tuna and whitebait, contain about 15 per cent fat while white fish, such as cod, haddock, halibut, plaice and sole contain only 1–2 per cent fat. Fat from fish contains less saturated fat (20–25 per cent) than meat or poultry, and oily fish are a rich source of omega-3 essential fatty acids. Farmed fish contains more fat than free-range or wild equivalents.

Fish is also a rich source of B vitamins, as well as other micronutrients. Oily fish is a rich source of retinol and vitamin D. Small fish eaten whole with their bones are a good source of calcium.

Recommendations concerned to reduce cardiovascular disease in industrialised countries commonly specify substituting poultry and fish for red meat. Almost all expert reports that make any recommendations on fish in the context of heart disease and chronic diseases recommend eating more fish.

As yet there is no good evidence that fish may have a role in modifying cancer risk. As with poultry, it is not clear whether any protective effect is from fish as such or whether fish reduces risk because it is substituted for red meat. Our recommendation nonetheless is to prefer fish (and poultry) to red meat.

See also: **Meat, Vegetarian diets**

Flavonoids, see Bioactive compounds

Flavours

Between 2,000 and 4,000 individual chemical compounds are used as food flavours. Most are naturally occurring substances such as those found in the essential oils of citrus fruits, herbs and spices.

Although certain flavours of the alkenylbenzene and terpenoid chemical families have been shown to induce liver or kidney tumours in experimental animals, this is at levels around 500,000 times that of human daily intakes. One alkylbenzene flavour, safrole, is a minor component of oils of nutmeg, star anise, mace and cinnamon; another, estragole, is a major component of oils of tarragon, basil and fennel.

The citrus flavour limonene has been shown on the one hand to reduce the incidence of tumours caused by other carcinogens and also to induce kidney tumours in mice. However these kidney tumours are thought to be specific to mice and not relevant to human consumption of limonene or citrus fruits.

Because of their potency, flavours are eaten in only minute quantities and, as with other food additives, there is as yet no substantial evidence that flavours in foods increase the risk of cancers.

See also: **Food additives**

Folate (folic acid) and vitamin B$_{12}$

Folates are found in abundance in foliage, that is green leafy vegetables, as well as in wholegrain cereals, vegetables and fruits. Folates play an essential part in the synthesis of some components of DNA and RNA and in the synthesis of the amino acids glycine and methionine which are components of proteins. They are thus vital for cell growth.

Vitamin B$_{12}$ is found primarily in foods of animal origin and is also synthesised by bacteria in the human colon. Meat, eggs and dairy produce are rich sources of vitamin B$_{12}$. There are relatively few data on the intake and need for vitamin B$_{12}$, but a deficiency causes pernicious anaemia when immature red blood cells are released into the circulation.

Diets in industrialised regions and countries are typically low in folate, but people who eat five or more portions of vegetables and fruits per day and seven servings of a variety of cereals as recommended here will be consuming plenty of folate. Low maternal intake in pregnancy causes neural tube defects (spina bifida) in babies, and supplementing of flour or other foodstuffs with folate has been suggested as a means of overcoming this problem.

See also: **Lipotropes, Vitamins**

Food additives

Most manufactured foods and drinks contain chemicals that are added to enhance flavour, texture, or appearance, to improve shelf life and to protect against contamination, or for other purposes. They include colourings, flavours, antioxidants, emulsifiers, stabilisers, solvents and processing aids.

Because additives are not meant to be in foods, there is public concern that they may degrade foods in some way, and a public misconception that individual additives are particularly harmful in relation to cancer.

Some food additives have been found to cause cancer in animals, so this concern has some justification. However, assessment of the effects of additives on human health is difficult because there is little data from human studies. Regulation of additives depends on use of data from tests of additives fed to laboratory animals. National and international bodies review this data and set acceptable levels for use of additives in foods. Some additives which have been found to be mutagenic or carcinogenic in experimental studies have been withdrawn from use; examples include a number of food dyes. The use of other additives has been increasingly restricted; an example is nitrates and nitrites used in curing meats. In addition, many additives are not permitted for use in foods and drinks manufactured for babies and small children.

As a general rule, additives found to be mutagenic or carcinogenic in rats or mice are permitted for use in food only at levels far below those at which any experimental toxic effect is detected. Acceptable daily intakes (ADIs) of additives are typically fixed by regulatory agencies at 1/100th of the level that has no effect in animals.

However, toxicology is an inexact science and substances known to be toxic in laboratory animals may have no effect on humans. The reverse is also true: substances which have no toxic effects on animals may be toxic to humans. Furthermore safety evaluations may make untested assumptions. Some people, for example, consume unusually large amounts of certain foods and drinks and so may exceed recommended acceptable daily intakes (ADIs). Or, a number of additives consumed at the same time in food and drink might act together in some adverse way, although no direct evidence has been found that this does occur. The cumulative effect of consuming additives over a lifetime is also unknown.

Scientists have assessed the role of additives in the risk of cancer in a number of expert reports and have generally come to the view that additives are relatively unimportant in any contribution they might make to the risk of cancer compared with foods and drinks, dietary constituents and other aspects of food processing. Nevertheless the scientific evidence on additives must remain subject to evaluation and regulation by national and international bodies.

See also: **Colourings, Fat substitutes, Flavours, Preservatives, Sweeteners**

Fruits

Fruits are rich in fibre, vitamins, minerals and many bioactive micronutrients including antioxidants. Dried fruits are good sources of energy, sugar, fibre and iron.

Vegetables and fruits together supply less than 5 per cent of energy in most industrialised countries. By contrast, in some parts of China, the Middle East, Oceania, the Caribbean and Latin America, vegetables and fruits provide over 10 per cent of dietary energy. In traditional Mediterranean diets, vegetables and fruit supply more than 6 per cent of dietary energy, much of this is as green leafy vegetables and as fruiting vegetables such as tomatoes and aubergines. In Britain, the amount of fruit in our diets is declining (although we are drinking more fruit juices). On average we eat around 250 grams (9 ounces) of vegetables and fruits a day, compared to the recommendation of at least five servings or 400–800 grams (15–30 ounces) a day.

More than 200 human studies have investigated the relationship between eating fruits and the risk of cancer. The evidence is most convincing for cancers of the stomach, mouth and pharynx, lung and oesophagus. Diets high in fruits reduce the risk of cancer at each of these sites. Fruit probably also reduces the risk of cancer of the larynx, pancreas, breast and bladder. Citrus fruits and tomatoes are particularly beneficial.

At least 20 animal studies have looked at whether vegetables and fruit decrease the risk of artificially induced cancers and most have shown that vegetables and fruits are effective. Vegetable and fruit extracts have also been shown to reduce mutagenicity, one of the first stages in the induction of cancer, in the laboratory. Many of the vitamins and bioactive compounds in vegetables and fruits are also known to protect against cancer.

Overall, when studies of vegetables and fruits at all cancer sites are taken together, nearly 80 per cent have shown a significant decrease in risk for higher intake of at least one type of vegetable and/or fruit. Several recently published expert reviews of around 150 scientific studies agree that higher consumption of vegetables and fruits is generally associated with reduced risk of cancer at many sites. The biological pathways that may be involved are reasonably well understood.

A World Health Organization report in 1990 recommended a goal of at least 370 grams (13 ounces) of vegetables (excluding potatoes) and fruits daily, while many expert reports concerned with heart disease and other chronic diseases have recommended higher consumption of vegetables and fruits. Diets high in vegetables and fruits protect against a number of other diseases apart from cancer. Carotenoids, vitamin C and other antioxidants from vegetables and fruits protect against cataracts. They also decrease the oxidation of cholesterol in arteries and so protect against heart and blood vessel disease. Vitamin C may help maximise intestinal iron absorption and thus help prevent iron-deficiency anaemia. Fibre from vegetables and fruit helps to control diabetes, protect against heart disease, diverticular disease and other digestive disorders. Potassium may help to prevent or control hypertension and so reduce the risk of stroke and heart disease.

See also: **Bioactive compounds, Fibre,**

Vegetables, Vitamins

Garam masala, see Herbs, spices and condiments

Garlic, see Onions, garlic and related vegetables

Ginger

Ginger is a root which is used in powdered form in baking and in fresh grated form in other cooking. Crystallised ginger is also common. Ginger oil is able to induce enzymes which may protect against induction of cancer and prevent attack of DNA by carcinogens. Ginger also contains several antioxidants which prevent degradation of DNA and other cell constituents.

See also: **Herbs, spices and condiments**

Glucosinolates, see Bioactive compounds

Glutathione, see Bioactive compounds

Goitrogens, see Bioactive compounds, Iodine

Grains, see Cereals

Green leafy vegetables

'Green leafy vegetables' is rather an imprecise term which is commonly used to describe vegetables of the cabbage family, including the many common varieties of cabbage, Brussels sprouts, kale, Chinese leaves and spring greens. The term also includes vegetables such as spinach, lettuce, and endive (chicory).

Both common types of spinach, ordinary spinach and Swiss chard, are rich sources of carotene, and good sources of vitamin C and dietary fibre. Spinach is also a rich source of folate. Lettuce is not a particularly good source of nutrients, but is a good source of fibre. Endive provides some useful carotene.

Within the evidence that diets high in vegetables and fruits decrease the risk of cancer at a number of sites, there is convincing evidence that diets high in green vegetables decrease the risk of cancers of the lung and stomach, and evidence that they probably reduce the risk of cancers of the mouth and pharynx and may reduce the risk of cancers of the oesophagus, colon and breast.

See also: **Bioactive compounds, Cabbage family, Vegetables**

Herbicides, see Fertilisers and other agricultural chemicals

Herbs, spices and condiments

Herbs, spices and condiments, by their nature, normally make up only a very small part of any diet, but this is not in itself a reason to dismiss them as insignificant for health. Many herbs and spices have therapeutic qualities, and some contain potent bioactive compounds which might significantly affect human cancer risk.

However, to date, there have been few scientific investigations of herbs, spices and condiments, and no firm scientific judgements can yet be made. (Salt, generally considered to be a condiment, is considered in a section of its own.)

Since some studies suggest that certain herbs and spices may increase and others may decrease the risk of cancer, we need to take a pragmatic position on herbs and spices. Herbs and spices are not a necessary part of the diet from a nutritional point of view and so they could be dispensed with entirely. However, this would be a great culinary loss. People who like highly spiced food may be particularly concerned about possible risks of chillies and chilli pepper. It may be wise not to eat chilli and the hottest curries regularly.

The limited evidence available on other herbs and spices leads to the conclusion that some of them might actually reduce the risk of cancer, and they are certainly a better choice for flavouring foods than salt.

See also: **Chilli peppers, Cumin, Ginger, Pepper, Saffron, Salt and salting, Turmeric**

Indoles, see Bioactive compounds

Industrial chemicals

Many foods and drinks contain traces of chemicals that are by-products or waste products of industrial processes. A number of these substances, for example, persistent chlorinated biphenyls, the dioxins and related compounds, are known to be highly toxic, and have been found to cause cancer in animals. Foods may also be contaminated with traces of packaging materials and with heavy metals such as lead. In addition water supplies may contain fluoride, added to protect against tooth decay, and/or chlorine, added to protect against microbial contamination. Both these chemicals can be toxic at high doses or give rise to other toxic substances.

Fear of contaminants, particularly chemical residues, is understandable. They are not meant to be present in food. Concentrations in fish and seafood as a result of dumping in rivers and at sea can be quite high and they can accumulate in fat-containing food and in human fat tissue. Judgement on contaminants and residues is made more difficult by the strong evidence that exceptional environmental pollution caused by large-scale industrial use and disposal, or by industrial accidents, is a hazard to human health and may increase the risk of cancer. Use of these chemicals has been subject to increasingly stringent assessment and regulation by national and international bodies, on the basis of various studies showing unusual toxicity.

Regulation also involves setting and monitoring allowable levels of the residues of industrial chemicals, heavy metals and waterborne chemicals that are found in foods and drinks. Exposure of humans to any regulated contaminant is mostly at levels thought to be safe.

Evidence on whether chemical and other residues in the food chain may increase the risk of cancer is capable of various interpretations, is clouded by controversy, and is confused by evidence on environmental pollution in general. The present judgement is that there is no substantial evidence that human cancer risk is significantly increased by chemical residues when these are used according to specified regulations, guidelines, and good practice. The effects of residues in foods and drinks of chemicals that are unregulated, or used in amounts above those in the regulations are not known.

See also: **Chlorine and fluoride in drinking water, Packaging**

Iodine

Most of the iodine in our diets comes from seafoods (and seaweed, where this is eaten), although some plants take up iodine from the soil. Both too little or too much iodine in the diet may increase the risk of thyroid cancer. Iodine is necessary for the formation of thyroid hormones which regulate the metabolism of the body, and are necessary for the integrity of connective tissue. Iodine is also needed in pregnancy for development of the baby's nervous system.

Iodine deficiency is a major public health problem affecting over a billion people worldwide, and in some countries iodine is added to salt to make up for any possible deficiency.

Iron

Iron is found in the easily absorbed haem form in foods of animal origin such as meat and eggs and as the less easily absorbed non-haem form in vegetables, grains and pulses. As well as carrying oxygen in haemoglobin, iron is important in oxidative metabolism within the cell and has a central role in cell growth. But iron can also catalyse the generation of reactive oxygen that damages cell compounds including DNA (genetic material). Most iron is bound to proteins to prevent this happening.

The requirement for iron in the diet is difficult to specify because iron from animal sources is much more readily available for absorption into the body than iron from plant sources, and plant sources also vary in the availability of iron for absorption. Anaemia caused by deficiency of iron in the diet is common throughout the world, particularly in children and women of child-bearing age.

The average person needs to absorb 0.5–1.5 mg of iron per day but larger amounts are generally needed by pregnant women and by women who have heavy periods. More iron is absorbed if vitamin C (in the form of orange juice, for example) is taken at the same time as iron-containing foods.

Isothiocyanates, see Bioactive compounds

Lectins, see Bioactive compounds

Legumes, see Pulses

Limonoids, see Bioactive compounds

Lipotropes

The major lipotropes are methionine, choline, folate and vitamin B_{12}. Lipotropes are bioactive compounds involved with synthesis of DNA (genetic material), cell membrane metabolism and lipid metabolism. It is therefore possible that they have a role in protecting against cancer. Lipotropes are involved in controlling the activity of DNA by methylation – a process which in effect switches genes on and off. Abnormalities of DNA methylation are characteristic of cancer, and, hence, lipotropes might modify cancer risk.

However, human research on the role of lipotropes is at an early stage and, although what evidence there is suggests that diets rich in lipotropes may be protective, no firm judgements can yet be made.

See also: **Folate (folic acid) and vitamin B_{12}**

Meat

Our recommendation is only about red meat – that is beef, lamb and pork – not game, such as deer and rabbit, which is different in its fat content from farmed meat, as are fish and poultry, which are considered separately. Offal (liver, kidney and other organ meats) also differs in its composition from muscle meats.

Meat contains about 20 per cent of protein by weight, and is a rich source of zinc, selenium and iron. The iron is in a form which is more readily absorbed by the body than iron from non-meat sources. Meat is also a rich source of B vitamins as well as other micronutrients. Liver is rich in retinol, folate and copper. However, meat is high in fat, up to 30–40 per cent by weight in domesticated

farm animals, and up to half of the fat is saturated. Game is typically much lower in fat. When consumption of meat is high, it provides up to 50 per cent of the protein in the diet and up to 40 per cent of the fat.

Consumption of meat varies greatly from country to country, and generally increases with economic development. The highest intake of meat is in Denmark where meat and poultry contribute 24 per cent of total energy. In Australia, New Zealand, Argentina and Bermuda, meat contributes 20 per cent of total energy. Many people, in India for example, eat no meat at all. Meat is not necessary for a healthy diet. In Britain, an unnecessarily high proportion of our dietary energy comes from red meat and meat products.

Red meat was first identified as a possible cause of cancer in the mid-1970s. Diets high in red meat probably increase the risk of cancers of the colon and rectum and possibly increase risk of cancers of the pancreas, breast, prostate and kidney.

Red meat may increase risk of cancer because it contains a lot of fat. People who eat a lot of meat have an energy-dense diet which is associated with an increase in risk of cancer. Meat may also increase the production of carcinogenic nitrosamines in the large bowel. Furthermore certain methods of cooking meat may cause carcinogens to be formed. Grilling and barbecuing of meat possibly increases the risk of stomach cancer. Grilling, barbecuing and frying at high temperatures possibly increases the risk of colon and rectum cancer.

Recommendations concerned to reduce cardiovascular disease in industrialised countries commonly specify that less animal fat and fatty meat should be eaten. Our recommendation is to consume less than 80 grams (3 ounces) of cooked red meat per day.

See also: **Fish, Poultry, Vegetarian diets**

Microbial contamination of food

Moulds which grow on certain types of food, notably in Africa and Asia, may produce substances (mycotoxins) which increase the risk of primary liver cancer. Crops which are harvested or kept in damp conditions are most likely to be affected by growth of fungi. Over 300 mycotoxins are known, produced predominantly from three types of fungi: *Aspergillus, Fusarium,* and *Penicillium.* Some mycotoxins are highly carcinogenic in laboratory animals, suggesting that long-term, low-level consumption of foods contaminated with these toxins may pose a human health problem.

Mycotoxins have been found in a wide variety of crops including wheat, barley, oats, peanuts, cottonseed, tree nuts, maize, rice, dried beans and apples. They have also been found in fish, animal feeds, and various products that are allowed to ferment before eating, and in the milk of animals that have eaten contaminated feed. In 1985 the Food and Agriculture Organization estimated that approximately 25 per cent of the world's food crops were contaminated with mycotoxins.

Mycotoxins are probably not a public health problem in Britain, but peanuts contaminated with mycotoxins, for example, may be imported into Europe. No quantity of aflatoxin in food can be regarded as safe, but practical limits are imposed by a number of countries, and imported crops are strictly monitored.

Milk and dairy products

Milk, and dairy products such as butter, cream, cheese and yoghurt, are major sources of fat in the diet, and can be important sources of protein, vitamin D and calcium. Two-thirds of the fat in milk is saturated. Full-fat milk, yoghurt and cheese are also good sources of a number of vitamins and minerals. Our recommendation is that fatty foods, particularly those of animal origin, should be limited. Except for children under two, choose low-fat dairy products and prefer vegetable oils rather than butter for cooking.

In Britain, milk and dairy products provide 10 per cent of total energy, and 15–25 per cent of all the fat in our diets.

A number of studies have found that diets high in milk and dairy products may increase the risk of prostate cancer and kidney cancer. However, milk and dairy products are not strongly associated with risk of cancer at any site. This could be because these foods contain some constituents which may decrease and some which may increase the risk of cancer. Separate evidence indicates that diets high in fat and in saturated fat possibly increase the risk of cancers of the lung, colon and rectum, breast and prostate, and diets high in saturated fat may also increase the risk of endometrial cancer. Calcium and vitamin D possibly protect against the risk of colorectal cancer.

Recommendations concerned to reduce risk of heart disease in industrialised countries usually specify low-fat milk and dairy products.

Many expert reports have recommended a reduction in consumption of full-fat milk and a reduction in consumption of cheese and other dairy products in order to reduce the risk of heart disease.

Since any risks of a high consumption of milk are associated with the fat in milk it makes sense for people who drink a lot of milk to prefer semi-skimmed, skimmed, or low-fat products. However official advice is not to give low-fat milk and dairy products to children under two who need a high intake of high-calorie food. Consumption of low-fat milk and milk products will also reduce the intake of the fat-soluble vitamins A and D, but these may generally be obtained from other sources.

Minerals

Certain minerals required by the body cannot be synthesised in the body and need to be supplied in our diets. Zinc, iron, and calcium are required in relatively large quantities. Some other 'trace minerals', such as copper, chromium, iodine, manganese, molybdenum and selenium are required in much smaller amounts.

Intakes of some minerals such as zinc and iron largely reflect the intake of foods that are themselves good dietary sources. Intakes of other minerals such as selenium and iodine are largely determined by the amounts of these trace elements present in the soil where the food is grown. Diets high in selenium possibly decrease the risk of lung cancer. Deficiency of iodine probably increases the risk of thyroid cancer and excess iodine possibly increases the risk of thyroid cancer.

See also: **Calcium, Iodine, Iron, Selenium**

Monounsaturated fat, see Fat

Nitrates, nitrites and N-nitrosamines

Nitrates and nitrites are natural constituents of plant foods and used by plants to make proteins. Plants also take up nitrate from the soil in which they grow, and so the amount of nitrate in food also depends on the amount of fertiliser – which contains nitrates – used in agriculture. Nitrate may also drain into drinking water when excessive amounts of fertiliser is used on fields. Nitrites are formed from nitrates. Nitrates and nitrites are also used for curing meat products. The nitrite reacts with a protein, myoglobin, in the meat to give cured meat its characteristic pink colour. N-nitrosamines may be formed in cured meats when they are stored, and may also be present in salted foods.

In the body, nitrates may be changed into nitrites by bacterial action in the mouth, and then, in the stomach, the nitrites may be converted into nitrosamines. Extensive experimental studies have shown that although nitrates and nitrites are not themselves carcinogenic in laboratory animals, N-nitrosamines are highly carcinogenic. Nitrosamines have been found to induce tumours of the stomach, kidney, liver, oesophagus, lung and bladder in experimental animals. Because of these studies there has been concern that nitrates, nitrites and nitrosamines may be involved in stomach cancer.

Studies in humans show that the nitrates that occur naturally in vegetables probably neither decrease nor increase stomach cancer risk. Evidence relating to fertiliser residues is unclear, but these residues are generally not thought to pose a risk. Studies on nitrites are limited, but the amount of nitrite used in curing foods has been reduced in recent years, and substances such as ascorbic acid (vitamin C) are now included in the curing mix to inhibit the formation of nitrosamines.

Nitrosamines could be a factor contributing to the risk of stomach cancer and other cancers. Nitrites and amines present in food may combine together to form carcinogenic nitrosamines notably in people who have little or no acid in their stomachs, a condition known as achlorhydia which is often associated with infection of the stomach by a bacterium, *Helicobacter pylori*. Achlorhydia is commonly found in people with stomach cancer and it is possible that lack of stomach acid puts a person at greater risk of stomach cancer. About one person in 20 has achlorhydia, generally with no apparent symptoms, although it may be associated with certain types of gastritis. People who suffer from persistent gastritis might consider avoiding cured foods (and smoked foods which are also cured, see below) as a precautionary measure.

However, overall, there is not yet sufficient evidence for relating nitrosamines to an increased risk of stomach cancer.

See also: **Contaminants and residues, Cured foods, Fertilisers and other agricultural chemicals**

Nuts and seeds

Nuts and seeds do not now form a major part of most diets, although they were important before the advent of agriculture.

Nuts are the dried fruits of trees, and are often encased in a hard shell. Nuts commonly eaten include hazelnuts, almonds, walnuts, pine nuts, pistachio nuts, pecans, Brazil nuts, Macadamia nuts and cashews. (Peanuts are not true nuts but pulses.) Seeds are the fruits of plants such as sunflower, sesame, pumpkin, poppy and squash.

Nuts and seeds are important sources of protein, particularly in diets that do not contain meat. Nuts are also high in fat and energy-dense, are good sources of fibre (particularly if they are eaten with their skins) and are rich in vitamins and minerals. Although high in fat, nuts and seeds form such a small part of most diets that they contribute little to the overall fat in the diet.

To date, there have been few studies of the consumption of nuts and seeds and cancer risk, but it is biologically plausible that nuts and seeds protect against cancer because of their content of vitamins, minerals and other bioactive compounds.

Consumption of nuts and seeds has been recommended by WHO to reduce the risk of heart disease.

Onions, garlic and related vegetables

Onions, garlic, shallots, spring onions, leeks and chives belong to the allium group of vegetables.

Experiments with animals have shown that some organic chemicals in these vegetables inhibit the growth of cancer, probably because they increase the activity of certain enzymes in the liver which break down carcinogens.

Allium vegetables produce sulphur-containing compounds which account for their distinctive flavour. These allium compounds have been reported to have many medicinal effects, including antibiotic properties and action against a bacterium which commonly invades the stomach, *Helicobacter pylori*. Allium compounds may protect against cancer by inhibiting the conversion of nitrate to nitrite in the stomach, a step in the formation of carcinogenic nitrosamines, and by inducing enzymes in the liver which chemically break down and inactivate toxic substances.

Allyl sulphide compounds in garlic decrease the tendency of blood clots to form, reduce total and LDL cholesterol levels, and thereby protect against heart disease.

Within the evidence that diets high in vegetables and fruits decrease the risk of cancer at a number of sites, there is convincing evidence that diets high in allium vegetables decrease the risk of cancer of the stomach, and evidence that they may reduce the risk of cancer of the colon.

See also: **Bioactive compounds, Nitrates, nitrites and N-nitrosamines**

Organic food, see Fertilisers and other agricultural chemicals

Packaging

Many foods and drinks contain traces of chemicals used in packaging: these chemicals can get into the food during preparation, processing or food storage. The plastic materials used in packaging are a mixture of inert polymer and plasticising agents and the plasticisers can migrate into food. Some of these plasticisers have been found to cause cancer in animals, but in the absence of human data the effect on human cancer risk cannot be judged.

See also: **Contaminants and residues**

Pepper

The pepper we use as a condiment comes from the berry of a tropical vine, *Piper nigrum*. Peppercorns may be black, green or white depending on when they are picked and how they are processed.

See also: **Herbs, spices and condiments**

Phenolic compounds, see Bioactive compounds

Phytic acid, see Bioactive compounds

Phytoestrogens, see Bioactive compounds

Plant sterols, see Bioactive compounds

Pollution, see Fertilisers and other agricultural chemicals, Industrial chemicals

Polychlorinated, polybrominated biphenyls, see Industrial chemicals

Polyunsaturated fats (pufa), see Fat

Potatoes

Potatoes are a good source of starch and also supply some useful protein and various vitamins, notably vitamin C. Eaten whole, they provide a useful amount of fibre. Potatoes are a major starchy staple food for many European people.

There are reasons to believe that diets high in potatoes, or other tubers, roots or plantains, might protect against some cancers, but evidence is currently limited. Diets high in fibre possibly decrease the risk of cancers of the pancreas, colon and rectum, and breast. Diets high in starch possibly decrease the risk of colorectal cancer.

Our recommendation is to eat more potatoes and other starchy staple foods, adding up to 600-800 grams (20–30 ounces) a day of potatoes, cereals, pulses, and roots and tubers.

See also: **Roots, tubers and plantains**

Poultry

Poultry contains about 20 per cent protein by weight, and is a rich source of zinc, selenium, and haem iron which is more readily absorbed by the body than iron from non-meat sources. Poultry is also a rich source of B vitamins and other micronutrients. Chicken liver is rich in retinol, folate and copper.

Poultry contains less saturated fat and a higher proportion of polyunsaturated fats than red meat, although intensively reared poultry contain more fat than free-range poultry.

Recommendations concerned to reduce cardiovascular disease in industrialised countries commonly specify that less animal fat and meat should be eaten and that poultry and fish should be substituted for meat. To date, there have been relatively few studies on poultry and cancer risk and there is no substantial evidence suggesting that diets high in poultry increase cancer risk. Our recommendation is that poultry is to be preferred to, and can be substituted for, red meat.

See also: **Fish, Meat**

Preservatives

Preservatives are used to prevent spoilage of food by micro-organisms and to inhibit growth of bacteria which might cause illness. The commonly used preservatives are sulphur dioxide and sulphiting agents, sorbic, acetic and proprionic acids, nitrates and nitrites. Antioxidants are also used as preservatives to retard deterioration, rancidity or discolouration due to oxidation.

Nitrates and nitrites are not in themselves carcinogenic but they may give rise to N-nitroso compounds in the stomach which are potentially carcinogenic.

See also: **Antioxidants, Nitrates, nitrites and N-nitrosamines**

Protease inhibitors, see
Bioactive compounds

Protein

Protein in the diet is essential for growth and maintenance of the body. Pulses, nuts and seeds and cereals, meat, fish and eggs are all rich sources of protein. In the economically developed world protein in the diet comes mainly from animal sources, that is meat, fish, eggs and dairy products. In the economically developing world most protein comes from plant sources, particularly from cereals and pulses. Malnutrition caused by a deficiency of protein and energy in the diet is common in the developing world, but people in the developed world and urban areas of the developing world generally have adequate protein in their diets.

In Britain, protein provides about 13 per cent of the total energy of our diets, and two-thirds of the protein comes from foods of animal origin.

Proteins are made from long chains of up to several thousand amino acids. Chemically, amino acids are organic acids which contain an amino (nitrogen-containing) group. There are 21 different amino acids that commonly make up animal and plant proteins. Some amino acids can be synthesised in the body and others, called essential amino acids, cannot, and so need to be included in our diets.

Protein in the diet is broken down by the process of digestion into its constituent amino acids. Some of these are recycled and some are re-built to form other amino acids. Finally the amino acids are assembled by the body into proteins. Excess amino acids are broken down and used as a source of energy.

In the body, proteins are a necessary part of the framework of tissues and organs including skin, cartilage, bone, tendon and hair. Muscle is constructed primarily from protein. Blood is made up of numerous proteins including in particular haemoglobin and albumin. Enzymes, the biological catalysts that rule metabolism, are made from protein.

Protein from animal sources differs considerably from plant proteins in the proportions of the 21 amino acids. Proteins from grains tend to have lower levels of the amino acids lysine and tryptophan, and pulses contain lower levels of sulphur-containing amino acids. In combination these differences tend to cancel each other out, so that mixtures of pulses and grains provide a range of amino acids that allow the body to grow at a similar rate as it does when meat is the major source of protein.

There are no clear data on protein and human cancer risk.

Pulses

Pulses (beans, peas, lentils and peanuts) are the seeds of leguminous plants and so are also known as legumes. They are the most important plant sources of protein, and are also rich sources of fibre, certain vitamins, minerals and other bioactive compounds. Pulses are low in fat. They are the staple source of protein for populations who consume little or no food of animal origin.

Pulses such as fresh green peas, fresh broad beans and lima beans are eaten when the seed is still immature. Other pulses such as black-eyed peas, kidney beans, lentils, mung beans, split peas, chickpeas, broad beans and white (cannellini or navy) beans are allowed to mature and dry on the plant. They may then be stored dry and cooked when convenient.

Regular consumption of pulses is important as a means of controlling diabetes, obesity and heart disease. Soya bean foods have been shown in clinical trials to lower cholesterol and triglyceride (fat) levels in people who have raised levels. A WHO report in 1990 recommended a daily minimum consumption of 30 grams (1 ounce) of pulses, nuts and seeds.

In Europe and USA consumption of pulses is generally low and probably does not have much of an effect on health except in special groups such as vegetarians.

There are reasons for believing that diets high in pulses might protect against cancer although the evidence for particular sites is very limited. Pulses are high in fibre, which may reduce the risk of cancer of the stomach, pancreas, colon and rectum, breast and perhaps other sites. They contain folic acid which may protect against colorectal and cervical cancers. They are also rich in bioactive compounds which may reduce cancer risk.

Refrigeration

Wide use of refrigeration has only emerged in the second half of the twentieth century and is now of great importance in transport and storage of meat, fish, vegetables and fruits. Refrigeration enables storage of meat and fish without the salting or curing which are associated with increased risk of stomach cancer. Refrigerated storage of vegetables and fruits lengthens the season through which fresh vegetables and fruits are available. Year-round consumption of a variety of fresh vegetables and fruits reduces the risk of cancer.

See also: **Salt and salting**

Retinol

Retinol, preformed vitamin A, is found only in foods of animal origin such as liver, milk and dairy products, egg yolks and fish liver oils.

Retinol is soluble in fat and so intake is dependent upon fat intake as well as on intake of fruit and vegetables that contain it; it can be stored for considerable lengths of time in the body in fatty tissue.

Retinol is important in cell differentiation, in

maintaining epithelial tissues, in the immune response and in night vision.

The considerable amount of evidence on retinol and cancer risk generally shows that high intakes of retinol in the diet neither decrease nor increase the risk of cancer. The evidence is strongest for melanoma of the skin. Retinol possibly has no relationship with the risk of cancers of the lung, stomach, breast or cervix.

See also: **Carotenoids, Vitamins**

Roots, tubers and plantains

Tubers such as potato and yam, plantains such as bananas, and roots such as cassava, are the staple starchy foods in some parts of the world. Roots and tubers contain varying amounts of starch: sweet potatoes only 12 per cent, cassava up to 50 per cent by weight. Tubers, plantains and roots are generally good sources of fibre, carotenoids, vitamin C, potassium and some other vitamins.

There are theoretical reasons for believing that diets high in roots, tubers and/or plantains might protect against some cancers but evidence is currently very limited. Diets high in fibre possibly decrease the risk of cancers of the pancreas, colon and rectum, and breast and diets high in starch possibly decrease the risk of colorectal cancer. (And although diets high in refined starch possibly increase the risk of stomach cancer this is thought to be related to diets that are monotonous and deficient in essential vitamins and minerals.) Greater consumption of potatoes and other starchy staple foods is recommended, adding up to seven portions, 600–800 grams (20–30 ounces) a day of potatoes, cereals, pulses and roots.

Many expert reports concerned with chronic disease and diet have recommended a higher consumption of potatoes, other tubers,

starchy foods or complex carbohydrates.

See also: **Potatoes**

Saffron

Saffron is a strongly aromatic, bright yellow/orange spice that is obtained from the stigmas of crocus flowers. It is used as a food colour and to treat disease in Azerbaijani and Indian medicine. Laboratory experiments have shown that saffron might act against tumours, but at present there are no human studies to support this.

See also: **Herbs, spices and condiments**

Salt and salting

The remarkable fall in incidence of stomach cancer across most of the world is correlated with a decrease in intake of salt and an increase in the use of refrigeration. The industrial use of freezing and chilling has meant that salt is used much less widely to preserve foods. As well as replacing preservation by salting, refrigeration has enabled storage of vegetables and fruits for use all year round.

Natural foods are poor sources of salt. Salt is used by food manufacturers to enhance flavour and most people in developed countries consume far more salt than their bodies need. All of a person's requirement for salt is met by 500 mg per day but average intake is about 10 grams, that is 20 times the requirement. The excess sodium is passed out of the body in the urine.

Most of the salt in our diets comes from processed and preserved foods. Only a relatively small amount is added in cooking and at the table. Salt is added to a vast range of manufactured foods such as bread, biscuits, cakes and other starchy processed foods, breakfast cereals, savoury snacks such as potato crisps, pretzels and peanuts, bacon, ham and sausage.

Common salt is known chemically as sodium chloride. Sodium is necessary for regulation of body fluids and the acid-base balance, and for maintaining the electrical potential of membranes in the body. It is very rare for a person to become deficient in sodium, even in populations where intake of sodium is low. Deficiency only occurs in people who sweat profusely for long periods, or people who have diarrhoea or kidney disease.

There is very good evidence that diets high in salt and in salted foods increase the risk of stomach cancer. Stomach cancer rates are highest in those parts of the world where diets are very salty because meat, fish and vegetables preserved in salt are eaten regularly. In Portugal, where salt cod is a national dish, and other salted items are popular, deaths from stomach cancer are the highest in western Europe. Although we may think of these diets as very salty, diets high in manufactured foods may contain just as much salt. Diets high in both salt and salted foods increase the risk of stomach cancer. It is not only foods salted for the purpose of preservation that carry this risk.

Sodium is now recognised to be an important cause of high blood pressure and stroke when substantial amounts of salty or salted food are included in the diet.

Our recommendation, in line with that of other expert bodies, is for an intake of less than 6 grams of salt per day.

See also: **Cured foods, Smoked foods**

Saponins, see Bioactive compounds

Saturated fat, see Fat

Seeds, see Nuts and seeds

Selenium

Selenium, a trace element, is found in cereal foods (grains), meat and fish. The amount in plants depends on the amount of selenium in the soil. Selenium works in the body, with the enzyme glutathione peroxidase, as an antioxidant although it has no antioxidant activity of its own. It has also been shown to suppress cell proliferation, enhance immunity, and alter the metabolism of carcinogens to less toxic compounds.

A number of studies have reported a protective relationship between selenium in body tissues and lung cancer. Ecological and experimental studies have also shown a protective effect of selenium. There is also some evidence suggesting that selenium may protect against the overall risk of cancer but it is not strong and not entirely consistent. Diets high in selenium possibly protect against lung cancer.

Smoked foods

Meat and fish are smoked by exposure to smoke from wood or coal. Cured meat may also be smoked. Wood or coal smoke, like cigarette smoke, coal tar and soot, are well known to contain carcinogens in the form of polycyclic hydrocarbons. Exposure to flame or heat may also produce nitrosamines in foods.

In such countries as Iceland, Hungary and Latvia where diets include a regular intake of meat and/or fish preserved by smoking, deaths from stomach cancer are high. Evidence from the small number of studies that have looked at smoked foods alone (rather than other preserved foods) are inconsistent. However, it is likely that smoked foods contain carcinogenic nitrosamines and polycyclic hydrocarbons and so there might be a link between high consumption of smoked foods and an increased risk of stomach cancer. It is not advisable to eat these foods as a regular part of the diet.

See also: **Cured foods**

Spices, see Herbs, spices and condiments

Starch

Starch, one of the three types of carbohydrate, is made up from many sugar molecules of various types joined together to form large complex carbohydrates. Starch is found mainly in cereals, pulses, roots, tubers and plantains. In the economically developing world starch may provide as much as 70–80 per cent of the total energy in the diet, while in Europe and North America starch intakes have dropped to around 20–25 per cent of total energy. Although no specific nutritional requirements have been established for starch (or other carbohydrates), it should be one of the main staples of the diet, simply because diets high in fat and diets high in protein are undesirable. Generally, around the world, when the amount of carbohydrate in the diet is high, the amount of fat is low – and vice versa. Most of the starch-containing foods we eat are processed in some way before we eat them; starch that is processed is called refined starch.

Dietary recommendations designed to prevent heart disease, and other chronic diseases such as obesity, now always recommend diets high in starchy staple foods. First, there is quite good evidence that diets high in starchy foods are directly protective against these diseases. Second, diets high in starchy foods are relatively low in energy-dense, fatty, sugary foods, and saturated fat is agreed to be an important cause of heart disease.

In the case of cancer the evidence is not so clear-cut – not yet, anyway. Diets high in starch possibly reduce the risk of colorectal cancer; on the other hand, there is some evidence that diets very high in starch increase the risk of stomach cancer. Again, there is some evidence that diets high in wholegrain cereals protect against stomach cancer, whereas diets very high in refined cereals possibly increase the risk of oesophageal cancer.

The best explanation for this rather confused story relates not so much to starch or cereals as such, but to how refined they are. Minimally processed cereals (such as wholegrain bread) and other starchy foods help to prevent cancers of the digestive system; whereas diets very high in refined cereals (such as highly processed bread and pasta) might be a problem, either because they are poor in nourishment, or because such 'poverty diets' are poor in vegetables and fruits and other protective foods.

Minimally processed cereals and other starchy foods are rich in 'resistant starch', that is starch and fibre that resist digestion in the small intestine and are digested mainly in the colon by bacteria. Digestion in the colon produces bulky faeces which are rapidly evacuated from the bowel. Faeces produced from diets that contain mostly refined starch remain longer in the body. When the faeces are bulky, any carcinogenic chemicals that may be present in the bowel have a lower concentration and less time to cause harmful changes to cells in the bowel.

Bacteria in the colon, stimulated by the starch and fibre, produce considerable quantities of short-chain fatty acids which are a source of energy for the cells lining the colon and rectum and may have a protective effect against cancer. These fatty acids may nourish normal cells and inhibit growth of malignant cells in the bowel.

Overall, the best guidance is that diets high in relatively unrefined starch products, such as wholemeal bread, potatoes, rice and pasta, protect against cancer. Such diets certainly protect against obesity, which itself increases the risk of some cancers. This is an important recommendation because we need to know what foods should make up the bulk of our diets.

See also: **Carbohydrate**

Sugars

Much of the sugar in our food is refined sugar, added during cooking or processing, or at the table. Table sugar, whether white or brown, is extracted from sugar cane or sugar beet and is highly refined. Other 'extrinsic sugars' are corn syrup, maple syrup and honey.

Many manufactured foods such as cakes, biscuits, confectionery, and soft drinks, contain a high percentage of added sugar. In Britain and Europe refined sugar may provide up to 15 per cent of the total energy in our diets.

Sugar is digested and absorbed in the small intestine and appears in the blood as glucose, relatively quickly.

The evidence that diets high in refined sugar are associated with an increased risk of colon and rectum cancer comes from several studies of different types. Some evidence suggests that diets high in sugar carry an increased risk of adenomatous polyps, benign growths which may occur in the lining of organs including the bowel. As a result of continuing exposure to carcinogens and conditions which provoke abnormal growth, polyps may eventually become malignant. Other evidence shows that diets high in sugar possibly increase the risk of colorectal cancer itself.

Regular consumption of substantial quantities of sweet foods causes tooth decay.

There is no evidence that the intrinsic sugars in vegetables and fruits affect cancer risk.

Our recommendation to reduce the consumption of refined sugar to less than 10 per cent of total energy is similar to that of other expert reports concerned with reducing the risk of chronic diseases.

Sweeteners

Saccharin, cyclamates and aspartames are widely used as sweeteners instead of refined sugar in soft drinks and in manufactured foods and are added to drinks and foods at table. Some people use sweeteners to control diabetes, others to control obesity, although evidence for the efficacy of this is limited.

Saccharin and cyclamate sweeteners were once thought to increase the risk of bladder cancers and a large number of studies have investigated this. Evidence now shows that there is unlikely to be a relationship between high consumption of saccharins or cyclamates and bladder cancer.

However, because of the results of studies in rats, saccharin is classified as a possible human carcinogen and remains banned in a number of countries. Cyclamates, banned in the USA and some other countries in the 1970s, is now approved for use.

International regulations have set acceptable daily limits of intake for both saccharin and cyclamates.

See also: **Food additives**

Tea

After water, tea is the most widely consumed drink in the world, and in Britain we drink more tea than any other country.

Tea contains several substances, including caffeine, that are biologically active, together with insignificant quantities of vitamins and minerals. Caffeine, also contained in coffee, is a stimulant well known for its ability to increase arousal and prevent sleep.

Black tea and green tea are both made from the leaves of the same plant. Black tea is the type generally drunk in Britain. Green tea, which is widely drunk in China, is also available in UK supermarkets and popular with some people. Production of black tea involves a fermentation step before the leaves are roasted and dried. In the case of green tea the leaves are exposed to a very high temperature soon after harvesting which ends all biological activity and prevents fermentation. The green leaves are then dried.

Most evidence from human studies shows there is no relationship between drinking tea and the risk of cancer. Drinking black tea probably does not increase or decrease the risk of cancers of the stomach, kidney, or bladder, and possibly does not increase or decrease the risk of pancreas, breast and prostate cancer. There is some evidence that drinking green tea may reduce the risk of stomach cancer.

See also: **Coffee**

Terpenoids, see Bioactive compounds

Tomatoes

Tomatoes are a good source of carotene, vitamin C and fibre. Within the evidence that diets high in vegetables and fruits generally decrease the risk of cancer, there is specific convincing evidence that diets high in tomatoes decrease the risk of stomach cancer and may decrease the risk of lung cancer.

See also: **Fruits**

Turmeric

Turmeric is derived from a rhizome (underground stem) of a plant in the ginger family. The spice, which is yellow in colour, is a major ingredient of curry powders. Oleoresin, an extract of turmeric, is becoming more widely used in food processing.

Some experimental evidence on turmeric and one of its principal components, cucumin, suggest that turmeric has a protective effect, but at present there are no human studies to support this.

See also: **Herbs, spices and condiments**

Vegetarian diets

Vegetarian diets may decrease the risk of various cancers, lower the risk of heart disease and increase life expectancy. However the lifestyle of vegetarians differs in ways other than diet which may contribute to, or even account for, the reduction in risk of cancer. There are many different kinds of vegetarianism and they may be expected to vary in their efficacy in reducing the risk of cancer.

In many societies round the world meat is not eaten. People may be vegetarian through poverty or from choice – often through religious conviction. People who choose to be vegetarians tend to differ in other ways from those who eat meat as well as plant foods. They tend not to smoke and they tend to take more exercise, both important contributors to good health. Those who are vegetarian because of chronic poverty are much more vulnerable to infectious disease. These considerations need to be taken into account in interpreting the evidence on vegetarianism.

Vegetarians who simply exclude flesh foods

from their diet but continue to eat milk, eggs and other animal products are called lacto-ovo vegetarians. If they exclude eggs but not milk, as do strict Hindus, they are called lacto-vegetarians. Those who exclude all animal products are called vegans. Some lacto-ovo and lacto-vegetarian diets are very similar in their nutrient content to diets that include meat.

Macrobiotic diets are predominantly vegetarian and emphasise natural minimally processed foods. They are based on plant foods but do not proscribe meat, fish and seafood. Fruitarians typically eat only fruit, nuts, honey and oils.

An important study of British vegetarians who were followed for twelve years found that deaths from cancer were 41 per cent of cancer deaths in the general population and 61 per cent of cancer deaths in a comparison group of meat eaters, after adjustment to remove distortion that might be caused by differences in smoking, body weight and social class. When the comparison was limited to non-smokers, mortality of vegetarians over the twelve-year period was 56 per cent of that of the meat eaters. Similar results have been found for German vegetarians showing that after 20 years of vegetarian living, the risk of dying from cancer is reduced by at least half.

Seventh-day Adventists are an evangelical religious denomination with strong views on healthy living. About half follow a lacto-ovo vegetarian diet and virtually all abstain from pork. Most avoid alcohol, coffee, tea, hot spices and condiments, and do not smoke tobacco. Studies of Adventists in California, Norway, the Netherlands and Japan have found that they have a reduction of up to 50 per cent in cancer of the lung, mouth, pharynx, oesophagus and bladder – cancers which are related to smoking and alcohol. Some studies have also shown major reductions in cancers of the stomach, pancreas, colon, rectum, ovary and breast which are possibly related to their diet. However, more detailed studies comparing the diets of Adventists who eat meat and those who do not eat meat have established that risk of breast cancer is not linked to the consumption of animal products or the age at which a vegetarian diet began. On the other hand a higher consumption of soya-based products was found to be associated with a markedly lower risk of cancer of the pancreas.

In general, vegetarian diets are associated with a major reduction in risk of cancer and there are plausible biological mechanisms to explain this finding. Vegetarians and vegans generally eat a wider range of plant foods with a greater intake of certain key nutrients and bioactive compounds. They also tend to eat more fibre and plant material which is digested by bacteria in the colon. So vegetarians generally have a more active colon than do meat eaters who as a rule consume fewer vegetables and fruits. The different bowel activity of vegans and lacto-vegetarians is associated with a lower excretion of cholesterol and bile acids in the faeces. A high excretion of these substances and others derived from them have been associated with colon cancer. Vegetarians have also been found to have steady growth of cells in their colon whereas people who have a high risk of bowel cancer commonly have abnormalities in the growth of colon cells.

Women who are vegetarian have been found to have a different sex hormone profile from meat-eating women. Vegetarian women tend to have lower levels of the female hormones, oestrone, 17 beta-oestradiol and prolactin, in their blood than women who eat meat. Women normally have male as well as female hormones in their bodies, but vegetarian women have been found to have less of the male hormones, testosterone and androstenedione, in their blood than women who eat meat. Vegetarian women also have less regular menstrual periods. All these differences have been found to be generally associated with a lower risk of breast cancer.

Male vegetarians have been found to have different hormone levels from men who eat meat but the findings are confusing. One study has found lower levels of male sex hormone in older vegetarian men and another has found lower levels of active male hormone in vegetarian men. However when vegetarian black men in South Africa changed to a western diet for three weeks the level of male hormone in their blood decreased and the level of female hormone increased – this is a pattern of hormone production associated with abnormal growth of cells in the prostate gland and with cancer of the prostate.

Vegetarian diets may not protect against cancer simply because they exclude all or some foods of animal origin. The combination of low or no animal fat and a wide variety of plant foods is probably what makes these diets beneficial. Diets that include flesh and other foods of animal origin only occasionally or in small amounts are probably of equal benefit. Some vegetarian diets which include relatively large quantities of eggs, cheese and other dairy products may have no health advantage over diets that contain meat together with plenty of vegetables and fruits. Care must be taken with vegetarian diets to obtain an adequate balance of nutrients.

Vegetables

Vegetables are rich in vitamins, minerals and a wide range of bioactive compounds. They are also good sources of fibre and are low in fat. Compared to most other foods, they are low in energy for a given weight – that is, they are less energy-dense than most other foods.

Vegetables and fruits together supply less than 5 per cent of energy in industrialised countries. By contrast, in some parts of China, the Middle East, Oceania, the Caribbean and Latin America, vegetables and fruit provide over 10 per cent of dietary energy. In the traditional Mediterranean diets, vegetables and fruit supply more than 6 per cent of dietary energy. Much of this is as green leafy vegetables and as fruiting vegetables such as tomatoes and aubergines. In Britain, the amount of vegetables in our diets is declining. On average, we eat around 250 grams (9 ounces) of vegetables and fruits a day, compared to the recommendation of at least five servings or 400–800 grams (15–30 ounces) a day.

More than 200 human studies have investigated the relationship between eating vegetables and the risk of cancer. The evidence is most convincing for cancers of the stomach, mouth and pharynx, oesophagus, lung and colon and rectum. Diets high in vegetables reduce the risk of cancer at each of these sites. Diets high in vegetables also probably reduce the risk of cancer of the larynx, pancreas, breast and bladder, and possibly reduce the risk of cancers of the ovary, cervix, womb, thyroid, prostate, kidney, and liver (primary).

Various groups of vegetables which have been studied in detail have been found to be particularly beneficial in reducing the risk of cancer. There is convincing evidence that raw vegetables, allium vegetables and tomatoes reduce the risk of stomach cancer. Diets high in green vegetables reduce the risk of stomach cancer and lung cancer, and probably reduce the risk of cancer of the mouth and pharynx. Cruciferous vegetables probably reduce the risk of colorectal and thyroid cancers, and diets high in carrots probably reduce the risk of cancers of the lung, stomach and bladder.

Overall, vegetables have been found to have a more consistent effect in reducing the risk of various cancers than any other type of food. Eating five portions or more of vegetables and fruits a day could reduce the overall incidence of cancer by 20 per cent.

At least 20 animal studies have looked at whether vegetables and fruits decrease the risk of artificially induced cancers and most have shown that vegetables and fruit are effective. Vegetable and fruit extracts have also been shown to reduce mutagenicity, one of the first stages in the induction of cancer, in the laboratory. Many of the vitamins and bioactive compounds are also known to protect against cancer.

Overall, when studies of vegetables and fruits at all cancer sites are taken together, nearly 80 per cent have shown a significant decrease in risk for higher intake of at least one type of vegetable and/or fruit. Several recently published expert reviews of around 150 scientific studies agree that higher consumption of vegetables and fruits is generally associated with reduced risk of cancer at many sites. The biological pathways that may be involved are reasonably well understood.

A World Health Organization report in 1990 recommended a goal of at least 370 grams (13 ounces) of vegetables (not including potatoes) and fruits daily, while many expert reports concerned with heart disease and other chronic diseases have recommended higher consumption of vegetables and fruits. Diets high in vegetables and fruits protect against a number of other diseases apart from cancer. Carotenoids, vitamin C and other antioxidants from vegetables and fruits protect against cataracts. They also decrease the oxidation of cholesterol in arteries and so protect against heart and blood vessel disease. Vitamin C may help maximise intestinal iron absorption and thus help prevent iron-deficiency anaemia. Fibre from vegetables and fruit helps to control diabetes, protect against heart disease, diverticular disease and other digestive disorders. Potassium may help to prevent or control hypertension and so reduce the risk of stroke and heart disease.

See also: **Bioactive compounds, Fibre, Fruit, Vitamins**

Veterinary drugs

Drugs are often included in the feed of intensively reared animals, to prevent disease and to promote growth. Traces of these antibacterial drugs then enter the human food chain. Some drugs previously used in agriculture have been found to be carcinogenic in experimental animals and so a number of products have been removed from veterinary use – for example, nitrofurans, carbadox, gentian violet and chloramphenicol.

Many of the drugs currently used in farming are also common human drugs. Their use as drugs in humans is closely regulated by medical authorities in many countries and they are not known to provide any significant risk of cancer. The use of these drugs in farming and their presence in small quantities in the food chain is therefore unlikely to affect human cancer risk when they are used according to regulations, although there may be other risks such as the spread of drug-resistant bacteria.

The majority of other veterinary drugs might also be expected not to have any significant cancer risk. However, there are some antibacterial drugs which are used exclusively in veterinary medicine and the use of unapproved drugs still persists. Anabolic steroid hormones, used to promote the growth of animals, may enter the food chain but probably have no effect on the risk of human cancers. If properly used, with adequate withdrawal periods before slaughter of animals and before milk from treated animals is used, veterinary drugs should not enter the human food chain in significant amounts. Some hormones used in animal husbandry are known to be carcinogenic in humans if administered at a level high enough to have a hormonal action. But these drugs would not be expected to have any effect at the levels found in meat or milk, which is below that needed to induce hormonal activity in the human body. Nevertheless these drugs may be inappropriately or illegally used and if they found their way into food at high levels could conceivably contribute to risk of cancer.

See also: **Contaminants and residues**

Vitamin A

Vitamin A is formed in the body from carotenoids, and is taken in through the diet, preformed, as retinol. Retinol occurs only in foods of animal origin such as liver, milk and dairy products, egg yolks and fish liver oils. Retinol and carotenoids are soluble in fat and so intake is dependent upon fat intake as well as on intake of fruit and vegetables that contain them. They can be stored for considerable lengths of time in the body in fatty tissue.

Vitamin A is important in the body for normal growth and development of cells. Deficiency in vitamin A is the leading cause of blindness in developing countries, affecting some 500,000 children world-wide each year. Low levels of vitamin A status also decrease resistance to infections such as measles.

See also: **Carotenoids, Retinol, Vitamins**

Vitamin B$_{12}$, see Folate (folic acid) and vitamin B$_{12}$

Vitamin C

Vitamin C is present in vegetables, tubers, fruits and milk, including breast milk. Good sources include broccoli, cabbage and other green leafy vegetables, peppers, tomatoes, pumpkin, potatoes, cassava, yams, citrus fruit, mangoes, pawpaw, guava, banana, strawberries and melons. Vitamin C is added to a number of manufactured foods as an antioxidant preservative and for fortification.

Because vitamin C is water-soluble it is leached out of food which is cooked in a large quantity of water and can be destroyed by heat. The body has only a limited capacity to store vitamin C, so foods containing vitamin C need to be eaten regularly, all year round.

Vitamin C is an important part of the body's antioxidant defence system and protects cells against damage by reactive oxygen. It has an important part in making calcium available for the building of bones and blood vessels, and enhances the absorption of iron. Vitamin C has an important role in the formation of collagen which is an essential component of membranes in the bowel, lung, bladder and reproductive tract. Vitamin C is also involved in wound healing and the immune response.

Vitamin C may help prevent heart disease by reducing the degree of oxidation of cholesterol in the blood. The use of megadoses of vitamin C to prevent and treat the common cold in general show no clear benefit either in preventing the cold or in shortening its duration. Megadoses greater than 1,500mg may have adverse health effects including renal tract stone formation, gastrointestinal disturbances, altered vitamin B$_{12}$ metabolism, and iron overload, although such effects have been disputed.

The conclusion from almost all of the considerable evidence is that vitamin C reduces cancer risk at a number of sites. High dietary intakes of vitamin C probably reduce the risk of stomach cancer, and possibly reduce the risk of cancers of the mouth and pharynx, oesophagus, lung, pancreas, and cervix.

See also: **Antioxidants, Vitamins**

Vitamin D

Vitamin D is formed in the skin as a result of the action of ultraviolet rays in sunlight. Its role in the body is closer to that of a hormone than a vitamin. Deficiency in vitamin D, causing rickets in children or osteomalacia in adults, is generally the result of lack of exposure to sunlight. Dietary sources of vitamin D may be important in northern latitudes where exposure to sunlight is inadequate. Egg yolk, butter, fatty fish and enriched margarine are all good sources of vitamin D. Vitamin D stimulates the absorption of calcium from the intestine and controls calcium metabolism in the body.

Vitamin D and calcium reduce the growth of cells in the lining of the bowel.

See also: **Calcium, Vitamins**

Vitamin E

Vitamin E is found in vegetable oils (including safflower, sunflower, corn, cottonseed, olive, rapeseed, and soya oils) and products made from them such as margarine, shortening and mayonnaise. Other valuable sources are wholegrains, nuts, seeds and wheatgerm. Significant losses of vitamin E can occur in food during processing, storage and preparation.

Vitamin E is an antioxidant which protects the body against the destructive effects of reactive oxygen. It is necessary for the proper functioning of the immune system and the nervous system, and to prevent red blood cells from destruction.

Vitamin E may be a factor active in prevention of heart disease.

A small amount of evidence suggests that vitamin E possibly reduces the risk of cancers of the lung and cervix.

See also: **Antioxidants, Vitamins**

Vitamins

Until the 1980s vitamins were thought of mainly as nutrients that were required in the diet in small quantities to prevent certain well-known deficiency diseases. Since then it has become evident that, for optimum health, vitamins may be required at higher levels, and that the risk of cancer may be decreased for those people who have higher intakes of vitamins as part of their natural diet.

From what we know at present, the most effective way of increasing vitamin intake is to increase the intake of a range of foods that are rich in vitamins as part of a varied diet, particularly vegetables and fruits. Diets that follow the recommendations in Chapter 3 will provide plenty of vitamins, and other necessary micronutrients. Recommending that the vitamins we need should come from the foods in our diets is important – taking vitamins as supplements, in pill form, should not be necessary, and may be harmful.

Although the role of vitamins in the diet is still being studied, knowledge of relationships between vitamins and cancer, outlined here and in the entries on individual vitamins, is helpful in understanding their importance.

A general deficiency of vitamins may increase the risk of cancer. In some regions of the developing world, diets consist mostly of a single starchy staple food which is a poor source of nutrients and is deficient in B vitamins, iron, iodine, various trace elements, antioxidants and other bioactive micronutrients. Similar multiple deficiencies can occur in developed countries in old people who have very restricted diets, in people who are anorexic, people who choose fad diets, and in heavy drinkers. Deficiency of riboflavin (vitamin B_2) and zinc may cause cell proliferation which may enhance the carcinogenic effects of nitrosamines.

Most of the studies on vitamins in foods and cancer risk shows that high intakes decrease risk. The evidence on high intakes of carotenoids and vitamin C in natural food and drinks is substantial and consistent. However, the research is such that it is not possible to be absolutely certain that carotenoids or vitamin C are themselves responsible for the reductions in cancer risk: these vitamins may act as markers for some other substance or substances in vegetables and fruits that have not been identified. Although the evidence on vitamin E and retinol is not so clear-cut, none of the evidence on vitamins suggests that they increase cancer risk at any site.

See also: **Antioxidants, Carotenoids, Folate (folic acid) and vitamin B$_{12}$, Retinol, Vitamin C, Vitamin E**

Yoghurt, see Milk and dairy products

8 An anatomy of cancers

EARLIER CHAPTERS in this book have described how, by making changes in the foods we eat or in our lifestyles, we can reduce our risk of cancer. In Britain there are now more than 280,000 new cases of cancer (excluding skin cancers) every year. Many of us will know someone with a particular cancer, or have been touched by it ourselves. This chapter tells you about some of the cancers most common in Britain and what factors, including food, drink and lifestyle, play the most important roles in cancer risk.

Overall, 30–40 per cent of all cancers could be prevented by following all our recommendations and eating the right diet. This chapter shows how, for some individual cancers, the percentage that could be prevented by diets and associated lifestyles is much higher.

The cancers are presented in this chapter depending on the number of cases that occur in Britain, with the most frequent cancer – lung cancer – first.

Index of cancer sites

Lung

Lung cancer is the most common cancer in Britain; there are over 42,000 new cases and 30,000 deaths from lung cancer each year. It is also the most common cancer world-wide, and is increasing rapidly throughout the world. Lung cancer is increasing as a cause of death among women because of the increase in the number of women who smoke. When non-smokers are regularly exposed to cigarette smoke (passive smoking), their risk of lung cancer increases by 30–50 per cent. The risk of a lifetime smoker getting lung cancer is some 20–30 times that of a non-smoker, and rises with the number of cigarettes smoked.

Cigarette smoking is now universally recognised as the most important cause of lung cancer. The loss of life caused by smoking is immense.

Treatment by surgery is possible in some cases. Anti-cancer drugs and radiotherapy are used to contain the spread of a tumour.

However, less than 10 per cent of people with lung cancer are still alive five years after the disease is diagnosed.

Evidence of increased risk

The overwhelming cause of lung cancer is smoking tobacco – it accounts for about 80 per cent of all cases. Occupational exposures to asbestos, radon and some heavy metals such as nickel and chromium also cause a small number of lung cancers. Food and nutrition play a relatively small role in the disease. Many people who drink alcohol also smoke tobacco, so it is not easy to find out whether alcohol itself increases the risk of lung cancer. Evidence from studies that do make allowance for the effects of smoking show that high consumption of alcoholic drinks may increase the risk of lung cancer, but the risk is small compared with that of smoking itself.

Diets high in total fat and in saturated fat may increase the risk of lung cancer. As for alcohol, the increased risk is minor compared to the risk from tobacco smoking. The evidence on fat comes from a range of studies, and is rather inconsistent, although it shows increases in risk for both men and women eating diets high in fat. Experiments in animals

Vitamin pills may increase the risk of lung cancer

Smokers' diets often contain fewer fruits and vegetables than the diets of non-smokers, and tend to lack sufficient antioxidants such as carotenoids, vitamin C, vitamin E and selenium. We need plenty of antioxidants in our diets because they help to reduce cancer risk, and this is particularly important in smokers because tobacco smoke has an oxidative effect on the body's metabolism.

For these reasons, it has been argued that smokers could help reduce their risk of lung cancer by taking pills which contain relatively large quantities of antioxidant nutrients.

However, two large studies, known as intervention trials, gave non-smokers a vitamin pill containing beta-carotene and vitamin E or beta-carotene and vitamin A and looked for a protective effect. Instead, surprisingly, an *increased* risk of lung cancer occurred among people who had taken either of these vitamin pills. When these results became known, the trials were stopped.

The results of the trials, which lasted four and twelve years, cannot easily be explained as due to chance. The reason why supplementation with certain vitamins might promote the growth of cancer cells is not properly understood. It has been suggested that an excess of one antioxidant (beta-carotene) with respect to other antioxidants and micronutrients may cause an imbalance in a chain reaction which occurs when oxygen radicals are deactivated. High levels of beta-carotene in the body might, for example, block the absorption of another carotenoid which is needed for this process and has a very potent protective effect against lung cancer. Or, perhaps, working as an intense antioxidant, high levels of beta-carotene obtained from supplements may actually save malignant cells which would normally be weeded out and die. Other possibilities are that beta-carotene, when present in high concentrations, actually works in reverse, increasing rather than decreasing oxidative levels in the body.

It is not absolutely clear whether beta-carotene taken as a supplement is harmful, but smokers should be warned against taking supplements. Cessation of smoking is followed by a rapid reduction in the risk of lung cancer, while dietary changes reduce only a portion of the risk. The maximum benefit that may be expected from diet, obtained by eating at least 400 grams (14 ounces) of vegetables and fruits per day, would be a 50 per cent reduction in risk. Smokers who are not prepared to give up are well advised to eat plenty of vegetables and fruits.

back up these findings: rats and mice fed a high-fat diet, particularly a diet high in polyunsaturated fats, are more likely to develop tumours. The results cannot be explained by an increase in the energy intake of people who eat more fat. It seems that fat itself is the crucial factor.

Although smoking is more widespread in Korea, China and Japan, deaths among men from lung cancer are lower than in northern Europe, and the risk of lung cancer in northern Europe among smokers is greater than in southern Europe. This has led to a suggestion of an interaction between high-fat diets and smoking. Many of the harmful chemicals in tobacco smoke need to be activated in the body before they have the ability to cause cancer. Polyunsaturated fats, together with an enzyme which is present at high levels in lung tissue, may speed up this process in the body.

Cholesterol has been found to increase the risk of lung cancer, but the evidence is mixed. Experimental studies have found that cholesterol added to the diet of animals substantially increases the number of experimentally induced tumours. Diets high in cholesterol possibly increase the risk of lung cancer.

Evidence of reduced risk

Strong and consistent evidence from more than 20 studies shows that eating plenty of vegetables and fruits reduces the risk of lung cancer. The protective effect of green vegetables is particularly good. Statistical analysis of these studies has found that the risk of lung cancer decreases very considerably as consumption of vegetables increases from 150–400 grams (5–15 ounces) per day. This decrease in risk occurs for smokers as well as for non-smokers.

The protective effects of vegetables and fruits may arise from the vitamins, minerals and other substances they contain. A large number of studies show a protective effect of high intakes of carotenoids in the diet. Higher intakes of vitamin C and vitamin E in the diet have also been shown to reduce the risk of lung cancer, as has the trace element selenium. Vegetables and fruits are the major dietary source of all these micronutrients. Other rich sources of selenium are fish and shellfish, bread, red kidney beans, lentils, liver and pork. Diets containing plenty of carotenoids probably reduce the risk of lung cancer; diets containing plenty of vitamins C and E and selenium may reduce the risk of lung cancer.

The fact that these studies looked at the levels of micronutrients from foods is important in relation to other studies in which smokers were given vitamin and mineral supplements in pill form. Contrary to expectations, the risk of lung cancer did not decrease for these smokers, and the studies were stopped (see page 173).

The best evidence we have at present is that we should get the various vitamins and minerals we need from the foods we eat, and not take pills to supplement our diets.

A high level of physical activity at work or in leisure time has been found to protect against lung cancer in a number of studies. Physical activity possibly decreases the risk of lung cancer.

Diets containing plenty of vegetables and fruits may prevent 20–33 per cent of cases of lung cancer in both smokers and non-smokers.

> The most effective dietary way of preventing lung cancer is to eat plenty of vegetables and fruits. Do not smoke tobacco.

Breast

Breast cancer is the most common cancer in women in Britain and world-wide and is becoming more frequent in all western industrialised countries. Breast cancer is also the leading cause of death among middle-aged women in western industrialised countries. In the economically developing countries, rates of breast cancer are only a fifth as high as in Britain or the USA, but in almost all these areas cases of breast cancer are increasing, and in some places rapidly. In England and Wales one woman in twelve develops breast cancer and more than half, about 14,000 a year, die of the disease.

If breast cancer is diagnosed at an early stage when the tumour is a small lump in the breast, the outlook is good. It is usually treated by surgical removal of the tumour, combined with radiotherapy and/or drugs. Sometimes the surgery may be more extensive, and the breast and associated lymph glands may need to be removed. If the cancer does recur it may be controlled for some years by radiotherapy and drugs. However, only 50 per cent of all patients survive for five years after diagnosis.

Evidence of increased risk

Women who migrate from countries where the incidence of breast cancer is low to areas where it is high find that, in time, they, or their daughters, are more likely to develop breast cancer. For example, women migrating from Poland to the USA or UK, or from Italy to Australia, increase their risk. Similarly, although Japanese women migrating to the United States are not generally at greater risk of breast cancer, their children and grandchildren do have an increased risk. These changes in risk are a strong indication that diets play an important role in breast cancer.

It has been established for many years that the risk of breast cancer is higher among women whose first menstrual period is early in life and whose growth as girls was relatively rapid, and who are taller as adults. The average age at which a girl has her first period has been declining in economically developed countries since the beginning of the century, and, at the same time, rates of breast cancer have been increasing. In Britain now, in common with the USA, girls usually start their periods around the age of twelve or thirteen years, while in rural China, this is between fifteen and eighteen years or even later. Until recently, these factors were not considered part of the diet and cancer story, but they are. It is now known that a key factor determining age at menarche and rate of growth in early life is diet. The diets of babies and children which are high in fat, sugar and protein promote growth.

Women who are overweight or obese after the menopause probably have an increased risk of breast cancer, and the risk tends to increase with increasing weight. Conversely there is little evidence of an association between overweight in premenopausal women and any increase in the risk of breast cancer. However, other studies show that gaining weight as an adult also probably increases the risk of breast cancer, particularly for women who were below average weight as adolescents but who become overweight as adults.

Drinking alcohol probably increases the risk of breast cancer. Since the relationship was first suggested in the 1950s, many studies around the world have investigated the link, and the findings are some of the most consistent. When the results of nearly 40 studies are combined, they show that the risk of breast cancer increases directly with the amount of alcohol consumed, even when this is as low as one drink a day. Alcohol consumption increases the levels of oestrogens in the blood, and women who drink regularly have higher levels of female hormone in the blood. This may be one of the mechanisms involved, as oestrogens are known to enhance the growth of breast cancer cells.

Diets high in fat have long been suspected of being the principal dietary factor in increasing the risk of breast cancer. Early international studies showed a strong correlation between low fat consumption and low rates of breast cancer in various countries, but there are many other possible differences between these countries which make interpretation of the data uncertain. Generally, although there has been much controversy about the role of fat in breast cancer over the last 20 years, on recent evidence, fat is now thought to be less important.

Evidence from over 30 human studies indicates a slight to moderate increase in risk of breast cancer with an increase in total fat intake, but the results are not consistent, and differ between different types of study. Studies of experimental animals fed a high-fat diet have found that they generally have an increase in breast tumours, but some studies suggested that it is an increase in total energy intake rather than an increase in fat which is most strongly associated with an increase in breast tumours.

Dietary fat may influence the development of breast cancer through effects on the metabolism of hormones. A high-fat diet appears to alter the levels of sex hormones in the blood towards a pattern found in breast cancer patients. A high-fat diet also increases the likelihood of a woman becoming overweight or obese, an established risk factor for breast cancer after the menopause. Furthermore, eating a high-fat diet in childhood or adolescence may promote faster growth and an earlier start to menstrual periods, another established risk factor for

breast cancer. Taking all the evidence together, diets high in total fat intake possibly increase the risk of breast cancer.

Further studies which have looked at saturated fat and the risk of breast cancer are also somewhat inconsistent, but on balance, diets high in saturated fat may also increase the risk of breast cancer. By contrast, diets high in monounsaturated fat or polyunsaturated fat possibly have no relationship with breast cancer risk, independently of that of total fat.

Breast cancer is less common in Mediterranean countries than in northern Europe or North America and this has led to a suggestion that eating plenty of olive oil protects against breast cancer. A few human and animal studies have shown a reduced risk associated with a high consumption of olive oil, but the mechanism is not clear. High consumption of olive oil may possibly decrease the risk of breast cancer, perhaps by replacing other fats in the diet that increase the risk.

Evidence from a number of studies of women shows that eating larger quantities of red meat (beef, lamb and pork) may increase the risk of breast cancer, although the evidence is somewhat inconsistent. The risk is thought not to be related to the amount of fat or protein in meat, but possibly to the carcinogens formed when meat is cooked in direct flame, for example when it is fried or grilled.

There are also a number of established non-dietary risk factors for breast cancer. Most of these relate to a woman's reproductive life. The risk of breast cancer is increased by late first pregnancy (after age 30) or having no children. It is also increased with early menarche (first period) and late menopause. The risk is decreased by breast-feeding. All these findings can be explained by the single observation that an increase in the length of the reproductive lifetime, with longer exposure to oestrogens (female hormones), increases the risk of breast cancer, and pregnancy and breast-feeding, which alter the balance of hormones circulating in the body, reduce the risk of breast cancer.

If one woman in a family has had breast cancer the risk that another woman in the family will develop the disease is doubled. This risk is further increased if more than one woman in the family has had breast cancer or if a family member has had breast cancer at a young age. About 5 per cent of all breast cancer is caused by inherited gene mutations of three genes, BRCA-1, BRCA-2 and ATM.

Evidence of reduced risk

Diets rich in vegetables and fruits probably reduce the risk of breast cancer. More than 20 studies have looked at the relationship between eating vegetables and fruits and breast cancer, and the majority show a reduction in the risk of breast cancer with increased consumption. The evidence is stronger for vegetables than for fruits. Diets rich in carotenoids may also decrease the risk of breast cancer, although the effect is not great.

Diets high in fibre may play some role in reducing the risk of breast cancer, although there have been relatively few studies. Several studies in western countries have found a small reduction of risk in women who have more fibre in the diet. However, intake of dietary fibre in western countries is quite low (5–20 grams per day) compared with, for example, rural China (70–80 grams per day). This low level may make it difficult to detect a benefit from fibre in studies in western countries. Present best evidence indicates that dietary fibre possibly decreases the risk of breast cancer.

A role for fibre in breast cancer risk is plausible. Fibre may absorb oestrogens (female hormones) in the bowel, preventing them from being reabsorbed, and so reduce the level of oestrogen in the body. Fibre may also reduce obesity and sensitivity to insulin – two other factors that are associated with an increased risk of breast cancer.

Physically active girls and women are at a lower risk of breast cancer, because activity affects their body weight and the time of the first period. Girls who play a lot of active sports have their first period later than average, and women who are more physically active have less risk of developing breast cancer. Being physically active may slow the development of breast cancer by lowering the levels of oestrogen in the body

The range of incidence of breast cancer world-wide suggests that a very high proportion of all cases could be prevented, and mortality rates significantly reduced by practicable dietary means. Alcohol may account for about 13 per cent of all cases, and 11–30 per cent of cases may be attributable to obesity. The best present estimate is that plant-based diets and avoiding alcohol, together with maintaining the right body weight and taking regular physical activity could prevent 33–50 per cent of cases of breast cancer. These diets and related lifestyle factors should be established before puberty and maintained throughout life. The potential for prevention starting in adult life may be only 10–20 per cent.

> The most effective dietary ways of preventing breast cancer are to eat diets high in vegetables and fruits, to avoid alcohol, and to maintain body weight within recommended levels throughout life.

Colon and rectum

The colon and rectum together form the large intestine, the final part of the gastrointestinal tract. Their function is the final digestion of the foods we eat. Cancers of the colon and rectum are very similar and so are discussed together here. Cancers of the colon and rectum are often called colorectal or bowel cancer.

Colorectal cancer is the third most common cancer in Britain; there are about 32,000 new cases each year. Cancers of the colon and rectum account for about 20 per cent of all cancer deaths in the UK. World-wide, rates of colorectal cancer are higher in economically developed countries, and are increasing in those countries as well as increasing rapidly in the urban areas of economically developing countries.

Colorectal cancer is usually treatable. Surgery to remove a portion of bowel has a greater chance of success when the tumour is caught at an early stage. At least 50 per cent of patients survive more than five years following an operation for cancer of the colon. Drug treatments and/or radiotherapy are sometimes given in addition to surgery, or when surgery is not possible.

Evidence of increased risk

The main factors affecting the risk of colorectal cancer are associated with diets. Evidence of increased risk is strongest for alcohol and red meat.

A large number of studies show that people who consume large quantities of alcoholic drinks probably have an increased risk of getting colorectal cancer, and the risk is increased whatever the type of alcoholic drink: beer, wine or spirits. Some people who drink a lot may have diets which are deficient in a range of nutrients because they do not eat properly; this may be a contributing factor.

More than two dozen studies from around the world show that eating large amounts of red meat (beef, pork, or lamb) probably increases the risk of colorectal cancer. Meat from domesticated animals is often high in fat, particularly saturated fat. Separate studies show that diets with high levels of both fat and saturated fat may increase risk. Other types of meat such as game and poultry generally have lower levels of fat and what studies have been done, for example on poultry, don't show that eating these meats increases the risk.

Eating processed or cured meats such as bacon, ham, sausages and salamis may increase the risk of colorectal cancer.

Most meat is cooked in some way before it is eaten, and the way it is cooked affects colorectal cancer risk. When meat is cooked at high temperatures, as in frying, grilling or barbecuing, the meat may burn or char, and so may the meat juices. Burning or charring creates some chemicals that are known to be carcinogenic. Eating large amounts of fried or well-done meat may increase risk.

People who eat larger numbers of eggs may also have an increased risk of colorectal cancer. Eggs are the major contributor of cholesterol to the diet and the observed increase in risk may be the effect of more cholesterol in the diet.

Diets high in refined sugars may increase the risk of colorectal cancer. Refined sugar (sugar from sugar cane or sugar beet) is added to a wide range of processed and manufactured foods, and added to meals at table.

In addition to studies that found people who eat larger amounts of foods containing refined sugar have a higher risk of colorectal cancer, two studies also revealed that such diets increase the risk of adenomatous polyps, which are probably the first stage in colorectal cancer. People who eat more sugary and sweet foods also tend to eat less vegetables, fruits and cereals. As a result, they take in less of certain vitamins, such as folate, carotenoids and antioxidants. The increased risk of colorectal cancer from a diet high in sugar might therefore, at least in part, be caused by a deficiency in these protective foods.

Being overweight may increase the risk of colon cancer, but the data are not entirely consistent. People most at risk are those who are physically inactive and have a high energy intake, while those who are overweight but are also physically active do not have a higher risk of colorectal cancer. Tall men and women have an increased risk of colorectal cancer, but the reasons for this are unclear.

There are also some established non-dietary causes of colorectal cancer. Some people have an inherited tendency to develop colorectal cancer. Two genes are responsible and people who inherit these variant genes are unable to repair genetic damage to cells as easily as people who inherit normal versions of the genes. People who suffer from ulcerative colitis are also at higher risk of colorectal cancer. Smoking tobacco increases risk.

Evidence of reduced risk

Strong and consistent evidence shows that eating plenty of vegetables reduces the risk of colorectal cancer. Raw vegetables, and vegetables of the cabbage family (cruciferous vegetables) particularly, have been found to reduce the risk of colon cancer.

Perhaps surprisingly, given the evidence that fruits decrease the risk of many other cancers, the evidence on fruits and colorectal cancer is inconsistent.

The beneficial effects of vegetables in reducing the risk of colorectal cancer may be due to some of the many vitamins, minerals and other substances present. Diets containing plenty of vegetables rich in one of these vitamins, beta-carotene, may reduce the risk of colorectal cancer.

While the evidence from studies of starch intake and colorectal cancer are inconsistent, other studies show that people who eat more starch are less likely to get adenomas of the colon or rectum. This finding is important because these benign tumours are often the first stage in development of cancer. The inconsistency of the cancer evidence may arise because of the different types of starch in the diet. Most dietary starch comes from cereals and other starchy staple foods such as potatoes. Where these foods are less refined, that is, where few of the nutrients have been removed during processing, they are likely to help in reducing cancer risk.

Some studies also suggest that resistant starch may be important in reducing the risk of colorectal cancer. 'Resistant starch' was first identified in the mid-1980s. It escapes digestion in the small intestine but can be broken down in the colon by bacteria. How much starch is present in various foods, and exactly what role it plays in the cancer process is still being investigated. Resistant starch may be important, but scientific understanding of it is still at an early stage.

Diets high in fibre (which is plentiful in vegetables, fruits and cereals) may also protect against colorectal cancer. The importance of dietary fibre in protecting against colon cancer was first suggested by Denis Burkitt after he observed that colon cancer was rare in Africans whose diet was high in unrefined foods. However, a belief in the benefits of dietary fibre goes back to at least the sixteenth century. More than a dozen studies have now shown that the risk of colorectal cancer is less when people eat more fibre. People who eat more fibre from vegetables and cereals have also been found to have a lower risk of adenomas which may develop into cancer at a later stage. The scientific evidence is not entirely clear because different ways of measuring fibre have been used in different studies and different types of fibre may have different effects. For example, soluble fibre such as pectin from fruit may be less helpful in preventing colorectal cancer than insoluble fibre such as wheat bran.

Consistent evidence shows that people who are more physically active, whether as part of their job or during their leisure time, have a lower risk of colon cancer, but evidence for an effect of physical activity in preventing rectal cancer is less convincing. People at highest risk from colon cancer are those who are both overweight and have a high energy intake as well as taking little exercise. It is regular physical activity throughout life that reduces the risk of colon cancer.

Because the principal causes of colorectal cancer are dietary, a high proportion of cases could be prevented if people make changes to their diets and associated lifestyles. In the early 1980s Doll and Peto estimated that up to 90 per cent of all deaths from colorectal cancer in the USA could be prevented by dietary means. More recent estimates suggest that diets high in vegetables and fruits could reduce colorectal cancer by 30–50 per cent.

The current best estimate is that by taking regular physical activity, by eating plenty of vegetables (and hence fibre) and only small amounts of meat, and by avoiding alcohol, 66–75 per cent of all cases of colorectal cancer could be prevented.

The most effective ways of preventing colorectal cancer are to eat diets high in vegetables, to take regular physical activity and to reduce consumption of red and processed meat and alcohol. Possible additional ways of preventing this cancer are to keep your weight within recommended levels throughout life and to eat diets high in fibre, starch and carotenoids, and low in sugar, fat and eggs.

Prostate

The prostate gland surrounds the urethra at the point where it joins the bladder. The prostate's function is to produce the secretions that form part of the seminal fluid during ejaculation. The ejaculatory ducts pass through the prostate and enter the urethra.

Prostate cancer is the fourth most common cancer in Britain: over 17,000 cases of prostate cancer are diagnosed each year, mostly in elderly men. It is the second most common cancer in men. The incidence of prostate cancer has been increasing in recent years in many parts of the world, and screening means that more cases are now diagnosed. Prostate cancer is much more common in the developed world, with the highest rates in Europe, North America (particularly among African-American men) and Australia. Postmortem examinations of old men often find undiagnosed latent prostate cancer. The incidence of the tumours seen post mortem is more or less the same in different parts of the world. This suggests that the factors that cause prostate cancer to grow and develop may be different in different places.

Prostate cancer grows very slowly and sometimes no treatment is recommended. This policy, known as watchful waiting, is generally favoured in the UK whereas in the United States a more aggressive treatment policy is generally adopted, even in the elderly. In younger men the tumour is either removed surgically or treated with radiotherapy. Even when the tumour has spread it can generally be controlled by reducing the level of testosterone in the body either by removal of the testes or by administration of oestrogen, or anti-androgen drugs (drugs that block the effects of testosterone). Survival rates are good; 70–90 per cent of all patients are still alive five years after diagnosis.

Evidence of increased risk

The chief causes of prostate cancer may be dietary: no other significant causes have been identified, and the geographical variations and the changes in incidence in migrants can most easily be explained by diet.

A number of studies have found that the risk of prostate cancer increases substantially with higher consumption of red meat. They include a study of 15,000 doctors in the United States, a study of 52,000 other professional men in the United States, and a study of 20,000 men in Hawaii backed up by a study in northern Italy and a study in South Africa. In all these countries the overall amount of meat in the diet is high. Diets high in meat possibly increase the risk of prostate cancer.

Diets high in milk and dairy products may also increase the risk of prostate cancer, although the evidence is inconsistent.

The amount of fat in the diet in various countries round the world correlates with the incidence of prostate cancer in those countries, and links between diets high in fat or in saturated fat show an increase in risk. However, few studies have distinguished properly between total fat intake and total energy intake. As fat contributes substantially to total energy it is important to distinguish the effect of fat from energy when drawing conclusions. For this reason, it is possible to judge only that diets high in fat and saturated fat may increase the risk of prostate cancer.

Although evidence of non-dietary causes of prostate cancer is limited, there may be an inherited susceptibility to the disease. Fathers and brothers of prostate cancer patients are at increased risk of the disease.

Evidence of reduced risk

In contrast to the evidence for most other cancer sites, data on the role of vegetables and fruits in protecting against prostate cancer are unclear. It appears that eating plenty of vegetables may decrease the risk of prostate cancer, but the evidence for the role of fruit is inconsistent.

The best present evidence is that 10–20 per cent of all cases of prostate cancer could be prevented by diets with only low levels of meat and other fatty foods of animal origin.

> The most effective dietary ways of preventing prostate cancer are to eat diets with plenty of vegetables and fruits and low in red meat, milk and dairy products, and in fat and saturated fat.

Bladder

About 12,000 new cases of bladder cancer occur each year in Britain; it is the fifth most common cancer. Incidence in men is three times greater than in women. Around the world, the highest rates of bladder cancer are in North America and western Europe, the lowest rates in South-east Asian countries. Rates are increasing in most European countries and the United States, more sharply in men than in women.

Treatment of bladder cancer is by surgical removal or diathermy (destruction by heat). Tumours frequently recur and require further treatment. Prospects of successful treatment are excellent if the tumour is discovered at an early stage. If the tumour has spread beyond the bladder wall, treatment is more difficult and long-term survival poor.

Evidence of increased risk

Food and nutrition probably have only a limited role in causing bladder cancer.

The major cause of bladder cancer is now regarded as smoking tobacco – this accounts for at least 40–50 per cent of all cases. Occupational exposure to certain industrial chemicals used in the dye and rubber industries is another known cause, responsible for maybe 20 per cent of cases of bladder cancer in men, and about 5 per cent in women. In some tropical and sub-tropical areas infestation with the parasitic fluke, *Schistosoma haematobium,* which is acquired by bathing in infested water, is the main cause of bladder cancer.

Since a study early in the 1970s reported an increased risk of bladder cancer with coffee drinking, a multitude of other studies have looked at the relationship. Results from more than 40 studies show a very slight increase in risk for people drinking a lot of coffee. However, people who smoke tend to drink more coffee than others, and the results may include some effect due to smoking. An increased risk possibly exists only for people who drink more than five cups of coffee a day.

In recent years there has also been interest in the relationship between drinking alcohol and bladder cancer and using artificial sweeteners and bladder cancer. The conclusion from more than 20 studies is that alcohol consumption is not linked with any risk of bladder cancer.

Controversy has surrounded the use of artificial sweeteners such as saccharin and cyclamate because an experiment in the late 1980s showed that rats fed large amounts of saccharin developed bladder tumours. More than 30 studies of bladder cancer in people using artificial sweeteners now show that, in the amounts normal in our diets, there is probably no relationship between saccharin and the risk of bladder cancer and possibly no relationship with cyclamate.

Evidence of reduced risk
A diet rich in vegetables and fruits probably decreases the risk of bladder cancer. Fruit, green vegetables and carrots most consistently show a protective effect.

Eating plenty of vegetables and fruits could prevent 10–20 per cent of all cases of bladder cancer.

> The most effective dietary way of preventing bladder cancer is to eat plenty of vegetables and fruits. And do not smoke tobacco.

Stomach

Stomach cancer is the sixth most common cancer in Britain; there are over 11,000 new cases and 8,000 deaths each year. Worldwide, stomach cancer is the second most frequent cancer, accounting for 10 per cent of all new cancer cases. Nearly two-thirds of all cases occur in the developing world: the highest rates are found in Japan, Central and South America and eastern Asia. Australia, Canada and the United States have the lowest rates. Stomach cancer rates are declining in nearly all countries, largely reflecting the introduction of refrigeration and the move away from eating so much cured and salted food.

Stomach cancer can be treated by surgery, if the cancer is quite localised. More widespread tumours are treated by radiotherapy and drugs. If stomach cancer is diagnosed and treated early, about 60 per cent of patients survive for five years after diagnosis. However, because the symptoms are not specific, most cases are well advanced before they are diagnosed and survival is poor. Less than 20 per cent of patients survive longer than five years.

Evidence of increased risk
The main factors affecting the risk of stomach cancer are associated with diets.

Diets high in salt and in salted foods probably increase the risk of stomach cancer. In countries where intake of salted food is high, the incidence of stomach cancer is high. An international study in 24 countries, the Intersalt study, also showed that where diets are high in salt, the risk of stomach cancer is higher.

People in China, Korea and Japan, and in parts of South America and Portugal, eat a lot of salted foods, salted fish and salted vegetables in particular, and we tend to think of these diets as being particularly salty. However, there may be as much, if not more, salt in diets with a lot of manufactured foods. About 70–80 per cent of the salt in our diets is in the ready-processed foods we eat; we add the rest in cooking or at the table. Generally, we consume much more salt each day than we need – about 15–20 times more.

Experiments on animals support the evidence from human studies: rats fed high-salt diets develop stomach tumours. The way in which salt causes stomach cancer is well explored. Although salt isn't carcinogenic in itself, it damages the lining of the stomach. The lining becomes inflamed, and the numbers of cells produced in the lining increases. This damage makes it easier for carcinogens to enter cells, and less likely that changes in the cell's genetic material, the first stage in development of cancer, will be repaired.

Infection with *Helicobacter pylori* has recently been established as a non-dietary cause of stomach cancer, but it is unlikely that the infection acts alone, because high levels of the bacteria are often found in populations with a low risk of stomach cancer. It has been suggested that *H. pylori* and salt may act together to increase the risk.

Monotonous diets high in starch, as eaten in impoverished parts of the world, may increase the risk of stomach cancer, but the effect is more likely to be related to the lack of nutrients in these diets, rather than to the starch itself.

The way in which food is cooked may also affect the risk of stomach cancer. A few recent studies show an increased risk of stomach cancer when diets have a lot of barbecued or grilled meat and fish, or well-done red meat. High-temperature cooking in direct flame is known to produce cancer-causing chemicals.

Evidence of reduced risk

Over 30 studies of vegetables and fruits have looked at the risk of stomach cancer. The evidence is strong and consistent that diets with plenty of vegetables and fruits, both separately and collectively, decrease the risk of stomach cancer. Raw vegetables, allium vegetables (onions, garlic, leeks, chives, spring onions and related vegetables) and citrus fruits are particularly beneficial.

Vegetables and fruits may reduce the risk of stomach cancer because of their high content of vitamin C and carotenoids. Evidence from more than 20 studies shows that high intakes of vitamin C probably, and high intakes of carotenoids possibly, reduce the risk of stomach cancer.

The allium vegetables all contain a group of chemicals, allium compounds, which have also been shown to decrease the risk of stomach tumours in studies on experimental animals. Allium compounds also stop or slow down the formation of certain mutagenic substances (nitrosamines) and have anti-bacterial properties which may reduce the growth of *Helicobacter* in the stomach.

Diets high in wholegrain cereals and products such as wholegrain bread, brown bread and wholegrain pasta may reduce the risk of stomach cancer. This suggests that the factor in starch that affects risk is the degree of refinement.

As the use of refrigeration, both industrially and in the home, has increased world-wide, the number of cases of stomach cancer has decreased. For individuals with a refrigerator at home, there is convincing evidence that the risk of stomach cancer decreases. The critical factor may be the length of use; it may take 30–40 years for an effect to be seen. Refrigeration reduces the need for salt to preserve food and, as the use of refrigeration spreads, less food that has been preserved by salting, smoking and curing is eaten. Refrigeration also allows vegetables and fruits to be stored, transported and kept fresher longer, so more vegetables and fruits are eaten. Both these changes reduce the risk of cancer.

Stomach cancer is, with colorectal cancer, the cancer most closely linked to diets. Some estimates suggest that a high proportion of all cases of stomach cancer could be prevented by eating the right diets, the great majority just by eating more vegetables and fruits. The best present estimate is that 66–75 per cent of all cases could be prevented by diets high in a variety of vegetables and fruits and low in salt, as well as by using refrigeration to preserve perishable food.

> The most effective dietary ways to reduce the risk of stomach cancer are to eat diets high in vegetables and fruits and low in salt, and to use refrigeration for perishable foods.

Pancreas

The pancreas is a gland that lies behind the stomach. It has two distinct parts, with different functions. One produces a group of digestive enzymes; digestive juices from the pancreas flow into the upper part of the intestine. The other part produces the hormones that regulate blood sugar.

About 7,000 cases of pancreatic cancer are diagnosed each year in Britain, making it the seventh most common cancer here. The highest rates of cancer of the pancreas occur in the United States, particularly among black people, and in other industrialised countries. The lowest rates are found in Africa and Asia. In Europe the highest mortality rates occur in northern Europe, including Britain; mortality tends to be lower in southern Europe.

Pancreatic cancer is one of the most rapidly fatal cancers. It is not generally diagnosed until it is well advanced and less than 20 per cent of people with pancreas cancer are still alive one year after diagnosis and virtually none five years after diagnosis. There are no effective means of screening or early diagnosis.

Evidence of increased risk

Smoking tobacco is a major cause of pancreatic cancer, with dietary factors playing a secondary role. Unlike other parts of the digestive tract the pancreas is not exposed either directly or indirectly to food. The effects of diet on the pancreas must therefore be the result of general metabolism or exposure to agents in the blood such as carcinogens.

The relatively large quantities of meat eaten in western diets may increase the risk of pancreas cancer. Many studies have found a greater risk of pancreas cancer in people who eat more red meat (beef, pork, lamb). As the increase in risk does not seem to be associated with higher levels of fat or saturated fat consumption, or with total protein consumption, some other factor related to meat consumption is likely to be responsible. One possibility is cholesterol: a number of studies show an increased risk of pancreatic cancer with higher cholesterol consumption. Other studies have linked eggs, the major source of cholesterol in the diet, with pancreas cancer. Cholesterol possibly increases the risk of pancreas cancer.

Another cause of pancreatic cancer may be

the carcinogenic compounds formed in meat as a result of high-temperature cooking and/or processes such as smoking and curing, but to date the evidence is sparse. However, the evidence linking smoking of tobacco with pancreas cancer suggests that these compounds may be a key to understanding the dietary studies on pancreas cancer. Tobacco smoke also contains the carcinogenic compounds heterocyclic amines which are absorbed into the body and circulate in the blood to organs, including the pancreas, where they may cause the cell damage that leads to cancer.

Diets high in energy may increase the risk of pancreatic cancer. A large international study found the risk of pancreatic cancer increased with increases in the total energy in the diet (largely due to the amount of carbohydrate). The effect is not related to people being overweight or obese, so these people were probably physically active. The increased energy consumption probably increases the body's metabolic rate and the growth rate of cells with a consequent increase in risk.

Evidence of reduced risk

Diets high in vegetables and fruits probably decrease the risk of pancreatic cancer. However, no vegetables or fruits stand out as having a particularly protective effect. As for other cancers, it is not yet possible to identify the particular constituents of vegetables and fruits that are protective. For pancreatic cancer, both fibre and vitamin C may play a role in reducing the risk, but it is not clear whether they exert an effect in themselves or represent the effect of fruits and vegetables.

Estimates of the preventability of pancreatic cancer are that a majority of all cases could be prevented by not smoking tobacco and by eating diets with plenty of vegetables and fruits, fewer calories and low in cholesterol. Just by eating diets with plenty of vegetables and fruits between 33 and 50 per cent of all cases could be prevented.

> The most effective dietary ways of preventing pancreatic cancer are to eat diets high in vegetables and fruits with, possibly, only occasional consumption of red meat. And do not smoke tobacco.

Mouth and pharynx, larynx and oesophagus

The mouth, pharynx, larynx and oesophagus are all part of the upper aerodigestive tract. Because the dietary and non-dietary factors that affect the risk of cancer at these sites are very similar, they are discussed together.

Everything we eat and drink goes into our mouths and the first stages of digestion happen in the mouth, before the food and drink passes through the pharynx (the cavity behind the mouth) and then into the oesophagus. The larynx, which is part of the respiratory system, is very close to the back of the mouth and the oesophagus, and is affected not only by what we eat, but also by anything we breathe – for example, tobacco smoke.

Cancer of the mouth and the pharynx is the fifth most common cancer in the world, but is uncommon in Britain: about 1 per cent of all new cases of cancer each year. These cancers are much more common in the developing world, largely because of the habits of chewing tobacco (as well as smoking it) and of chewing the nuts of the betel tree.

Less than 1 per cent of all new cases of cancer in Britain each year are of the larynx –

about the same as in the rest of the world. More than four out of every five cases are in men.

Cancer of the oesophagus is more common: over 6,000 new cases in Britain each year, the ninth most common cancer here. The highest rates of oesophageal cancer are in the economically developing world, particularly China, and it is more common in men than in women. A common factor everywhere is that those on lower incomes, and particularly people living in poverty and on poor diets, have a higher risk of oesophageal cancer.

Treatment of cancer of the mouth or pharynx is by surgical removal of the malignant tissue, by radiotherapy or with drugs. Elaborate reconstructive surgery is sometimes necessary to repair parts of the face that have to be removed. Between 70 and 80 per cent of people who have this cancer diagnosed and treated are still alive five years later.

Small laryngeal tumours can be destroyed with radiotherapy or laser treatment with great success. For larger tumours surgery is necessary and the voicebox is generally removed. The patient must then develop new methods of speech.

The usual treatment of oesophageal cancer is surgical removal of the oesophagus or radiotherapy plus anti-cancer drugs. A new oesophagus can be created out of a piece of colon. Survival of patients with oesophageal cancer is poor – 75 per cent die within a year of diagnosis. Relatively few patients, 5–10 per cent, are still alive five years after diagnosis and treatment.

Evidence of increased risk

Smoking tobacco is by far the most important factor in increasing the risk of cancers of the mouth and pharynx, larynx and oesophagus, and drinking alcohol is the most important dietary influence.

There is convincing evidence from about 50 studies that drinking large quantities of alcohol increases the risk of cancers of the mouth and pharynx, larynx and oesophagus.

A study in the United States in the late 1950s found the risk of mouth and pharynx cancer and laryngeal cancer to be highest in whisky drinkers, but we now know that all types of alcoholic drink are likely to increase these cancers. The risk also increases with the amount of alcohol drunk – the more alcohol consumed, the higher the risk. In France, people who drink a lot of Calvados, a spirit made from apples, have an increased risk of oesophageal cancer, and this is likely to apply to those who drink a lot of other abrasive spirits.

By contrast, Seventh-day Adventists, who do not drink or smoke, have a much lower incidence of these cancers than other people, but this may be due to other differences in the Seventh-day Adventists' lifestyles.

People who smoke tobacco as well as drinking alcohol substantially increase their risk of cancers of the mouth and pharynx, larynx and oesophagus.

A number of studies from different parts of the world have found that people who eat grain-based diets (containing large amounts of maize, wheat and millet) have an increased risk of oesophageal cancer. Studies on rats suggest that these diets are probably deficient in the B vitamins and in minerals such as zinc, selenium, magnesium and molybdenum. Grains stored in warm moist conditions often become infected with fungi which may produce toxins that cause cancer. So the evidence that diets high in cereal may increase the risk of oesophageal cancer is probably not to do with the cereals themselves, but results from the effects of lack of nutrients and the possible contamination of such monotonous diets.

People who take tea, coffee, or other drinks very hot have a higher risk of oesophageal cancer, because hot drinks may damage the membranes of the oesophagus, making them more vulnerable to carcinogens. Drinking drinks very hot regularly may increase the risk of oesophageal cancer.

Nitrosamines in food including preserved meats possibly increase the risk of oesophageal cancer. Most of the evidence comes from studies in China where, in an area well-known for a particularly high risk of oesophageal cancer, cornbread containing large amounts of nitrosamines is often eaten in a mouldy condition.

Evidence of reduced risk

Eating plenty of vegetables and fruits reduces the risk of cancers of the mouth and pharynx and the oesophagus, and probably to reduce the risk of cancer of the larynx. Eating plenty of carrots, citrus fruits and green vegetables is particularly effective in reducing risk of cancer of the mouth and pharynx. Tomatoes and citrus fruits in particular protect against oesophageal cancer.

Independently, some studies have shown that diets high in vitamin C may reduce the risk of cancers of the mouth and pharynx and oesophagus, and diets containing plenty of carotenoids may decrease the risk of cancer of the oesophagus.

Smoking tobacco and drinking alcohol are, together, thought to cause most cancers of the mouth and pharynx, larynx and oesophagus. By eating plenty of vegetables and fruits, and not drinking alcohol, 33–50 per cent of all cases could be prevented.

> The most effective dietary ways of preventing cancers of the mouth and pharynx, larynx and oesophagus are to eat diets high in vegetables and fruits, and not to drink alcohol. Do not smoke or use tobacco.

Ovary

Ovarian cancer is the fourth most common cancer in women in the UK, accounting for about 4 per cent of all cancers – about 6,000 cases each year. World-wide, ovarian cancer is the seventh most common in women, and rates are higher in Europe and North America than in Africa or Asia.

Cancer of the ovary can occur at any age but is most common after the menopause. Treatment usually involves surgical removal of the ovaries, fallopian tubes and womb, together with radiotherapy and drugs. When the tumour is limited to the ovaries, 60–70 per cent of patients survive five years; when the tumour is more widespread fewer patients survive so long.

Evidence of increased risk

The most important established causes of ovarian cancer are related to the hormonal and reproductive events in a woman's life. Women with no or few children, and those with a family history of the disease, are at greater risk.

Japanese women who migrate to the United States have an increased risk of ovarian cancer compared with Japanese women living in Japan. This led to speculation that ovarian cancer may be caused by a high-fat diet or by some other dietary factor or behaviour associated with western industrialised societies. However, evidence is limited and somewhat inconsistent and there is as yet no substantial evidence that any dietary factors increases the risk of ovarian cancer.

Evidence of reduced risk

Pregnancy and extended use of the oral contraceptive pill reduce the risk of ovarian cancer, probably related to lower levels of female hormones circulating in the body for long periods of time.

The only evidence for dietary factors reducing risk comes from a small number of studies which show that eating plenty of vegetables and fruits may protect against ovarian cancer.

The factors affecting the risk of ovarian cancer may be similar to those involved in other hormone-related cancers in women. By eating diets high in vegetables and fruits, and low in meat and other fatty animal foods, about 10–20 per cent of all cases of ovarian cancer could be prevented.

> The most effective dietary way of preventing ovarian cancer is, possibly, eating diets high in vegetables and fruits.

Endometrium

Cancer of the endometrium (the lining of the womb) is more common in the developed than the developing world. In Britain, it is the seventh most common cancer in women; there are over 4,000 new cases each year. World-wide the number of cases is declining.

Treatment of cancer of the endometrium usually involves a hysterectomy, together with radiotherapy. Survival rates are good.

Evidence of increased risk
The most important cause of endometrial cancer is diet-related: obesity. Many studies over the last 30 years have shown that women who are overweight have a two to ten times higher risk: the evidence that high body weight increases the risk of womb cancer is convincing. Risk is increased for women both before and after the menopause, but obesity seems to be particularly important when women are older. Putting on a lot of weight when older also increases the risk.

Some studies suggest that a higher intake of saturated fat may increase the risk of endometrial cancer, independently of the effects of obesity or of high calorie intake.

An established non-dietary risk factor is that relatively high or long-sustained exposure to oestrogens (female hormones) increases the risk of endometrial cancer. So women who start their periods at an early age or begin their menopause late have an increased risk of womb cancer, as do women who have few or no children. The risk of endometrial cancer also increases for women who have used oestrogen-only hormone replacement therapy for several years. This risk is reduced but not eliminated if progesterone is added to the oestrogen replacement.

The role of oestrogen in increasing the risk of endometrial cancer may also help explain why obesity increases the risk. Oestrogen and other female hormones are produced in fat tissue – and so fat women are likely to have more female hormone circulating in their bodies. The additional oestrogen increases the growth of cancer cells in the womb.

Evidence of reduced risk
The only significant evidence for foods decreasing the risk of endometrial cancer comes from a few studies of vegetables and fruits. Diets high in vegetables and fruits may decrease the risk of womb cancer.

Maintaining the recommended body weight could prevent from 25–50 per cent of all cases of endometrial cancer.

> The most effective dietary way of preventing endometrial cancer is to maintain the recommended body weight throughout life.

Cervix

The cervix lies at the neck of the womb, at the end of the vagina.

Cervical cancer is the seventh most common cancer in women in Britain. There are about 4,000 cases each year; about 3 per cent of all cancers in Britain. Europe and North America have the lowest rates of cervical cancer and in the developed world generally cervical cancer is decreasing, largely as a result of screening programmes. However, in spite of the general decline, rates are increasing in younger women. Highest rates of cervical cancer occur in South-east Asia, Latin America and Sub-Saharan Africa – worldwide, cervical cancer is the second most common cancer in women.

Treatment of cervical cancer depends on the extent of the cancer. If it is restricted to the cervix itself, a tumour may be destroyed by laser or other treatment. If it has spread to the cervical canal, a cone biopsy is performed. For more extensive tumours a hysterectomy may be needed, or radical pelvic surgery accompanied by radiotherapy. Detection by screening in the early stages, followed by treatment, is associated with a very good survival rate. If the cancer has spread, only about 60 per cent of patients survive for five years after treatment.

Evidence of increased risk

Food and nutrition play only a small role in cervical cancer.

The most important established cause of cervical cancer is sexually transmitted infection with Human Papillomavirus (HPV). Risk increases with the number of sexual partners and the number of partners' sexual partners, and with a woman starting her sexual life early. Smoking tobacco also increases the risk of cervical cancer, and there may be some interaction between tobacco smoke and HPV infection that increases risk. There is no substantial evidence that dietary factors increase the risk of cervical cancer.

Evidence of reduced risk

Evidence for dietary factors reducing the risk of cervical cancer comes from studies showing that eating plenty of vegetables and fruits may protect against cervical cancer. Diets high in vegetables and fruits may also reduce the risk of the early changes in the cells of the cervix that precede the cancer itself.

The protective effects of vegetables and fruits may come from the vitamins, minerals and other substances they contain. Quite a number of studies have been done, based either on how much vitamin C, vitamin E or carotenoids women have in their diets, or on the amounts of these vitamins in the bloodstream. For each of these vitamins, the evidence shows that high intakes in the diet possibly reduce the risk of cervical cancer.

The very variable rates of cervical cancer around the world suggest that the great majority of all cases may be preventable. Protection against sexually transmitted HPVs and ceasing to smoke tobacco would achieve major reductions. Eating diets high in vegetables and fruits could reduce the number of cases of cervical cancer by 10–20 per cent.

The most effective dietary way of preventing cervical cancer is to eat diets high in vegetables and fruits and the associated vitamins C and E and carotenoids. Do not smoke tobacco.

Other Cancers

Gallbladder

The gallbladder, which lies on the underside of the liver, stores bile, the digestive fluid which is produced by the liver. Cancer of the gallbladder is uncommon, accounting for less than 1 per cent of all cases world-wide.

Gallstones, which may form in the bile when the ratio of cholesterol to acid is high, are an established risk factor for gallbladder cancer. However, even people who have gallstones have only a low risk of developing the disease.

Obesity has been associated with an increased risk of gallstones, and a couple of studies have found a direct association between gallbladder cancer and obesity. This combination of rather weak direct and indirect evidence suggests that obesity may increase the risk of gallbladder cancer.

Kidney

Cancer of the kidney is relatively rare, accounting for less than 2 per cent of all cases world-wide. It is about ten times more common in Europe and North America than in Asia, Africa and South America. Men are twice as likely to get kidney cancer as women.

Treatment involves surgical removal of the kidney, and survival depends on the tumour being diagnosed at an early stage.

Only a limited number of studies have investigated dietary factors and kidney cancer, and obesity has been identified as probably increasing risk. This is particularly evident in women, and may be related to hormonal changes and changes in the metabolism of fat. Eating large amounts of red meat and of dairy products may both increase the risk.

Smoking tobacco also increases the risk of kidney cancer.

Current evidence, although not entirely consistent, suggests that a high consumption of vegetables possibly reduces the risk of kidney cancer. Evidence on fruits, however, is limited and no overall judgement can be made.

Liver

Primary cancer of the liver is common in many economically developing countries but uncommon in Britain and other developed countries. The predominant cause of primary liver cancer is infection with the hepatitis B virus: some 80 per cent of cases of liver cancer world-wide are believed to be caused by the infection.

There are no effective treatments for liver cancer; it is almost always fatal.

Compared to infection with the hepatitis B virus, food and nutrition play only a limited role in liver cancer. However, both high consumption of alcohol and eating fungally contaminated food increase risk.

Dozens of studies in many countries have repeatedly found that heavy and persistent drinking of alcohol increases the risk of primary liver cancer. Alcoholic liver disease passes through three progressively severe stages: fatty liver, alcoholic hepatitis and cirrhosis, ultimately leading to liver cancer. However only 10–30 per cent of people with cirrhosis of the liver develop liver cancer.

In tropical and sub-tropical areas, where the climate is warm and damp, crops that are stored for a long time may become contaminated with the highly toxic by-products, aflatoxins, of some common moulds, *Aspergillus flavus* and *Aspergillus parasiticus*. The Food and Agriculture Organization has estimated that up to a quarter of the world's crops may be contaminated each year. Many studies have examined the effects of eating food contaminated with aflatoxins and have found that this is linked with liver cancer. Aflatoxins seem to be the agent responsible for inducing the cancer. In Britain, crops imported from regions of the world where aflatoxin contamination may be high are subject to inspection and regulation, and any suspect produce rejected.

Smoking tobacco is also a non-dietary cause of liver cancer.

Eating plenty of vegetables may reduce the risk of liver cancer, but the evidence is weaker than for some other cancer sites, and there is not enough data on the relationship between fruits and liver cancer to come to any conclusions.

Secondary cancer of the liver, that is a cancer which has begun in some other part of the body, is much more common in the UK than primary liver cancer. Most of these secondary liver cancers originate from cancers in the stomach, pancreas or large intestine. The primary cancer in these other sites may remain small and cause no symptoms, only being found after the secondary cancer in the liver becomes evident.

Dietary causes of primary liver cancer are thought possibly to interact with infection from hepatitis B or C. It has therefore been estimated that 33–66 per cent of all cases of liver cancer could be prevented by eliminating aflatoxin contamination of food and by reducing consumption of alcoholic drinks.

Thyroid

Cancer of the thyroid is rare: only about 1 per cent of cancers in Britain and similar levels world-wide. It is two to three times more common in women than in men, which suggests that hormones may affect its development.

Thyroid cancer may be successfully treated by surgery followed by injections of radioactive iodine.

The only well-established risk factor for thyroid cancer is non-dietary – exposure to ionising radiation. Japanese atomic bomb survivors and people exposed to fallout from the Chernobyl accident have increased risk of thyroid cancer. Using X-rays to treat disease, particularly in children, also carries an increased risk: wherever possible such treatment is now avoided.

The role of diet in thyroid cancer is not well understood, but both an excess of iodine in the diet and iodine deficiency are associated with increased risk. A mechanism involving the hormones produced in the thyroid may be involved. Lack of iodine in the diet can be corrected by using iodised salt.

Eating plenty of vegetables and fruits may reduce the risk of thyroid cancer, but the evidence is weaker than for other cancers.

INDEX OF RECIPES

Pasta and noodle dishes

Cracked wheat and chapatis

Rice dishes

Potato dishes

Pulse dishes

Meat dishes

Chicken dishes

Fish dishes

Fruit desserts

Fresh fruit desserts

Non-fruit desserts

INDEX